Ethics

AND COLLEGE STUDENT LIFE

A CASE STUDY APPROACH

SECOND EDITION

Kenneth A. Strike

UNIVERSITY OF MARYLAND

Pamela A. Moss, Ph.D.

CORNELL UNIVERSITY

Prentice
Hall

Upper Saddle River, New Jersey
Columbus, Ohio

Library of Congress Cataloging-in-Publication Data

Strike, Kenneth A.
    Ethics and college student life : a case study approach / Kenneth A. Strike, Pamela A. Moss.
        p. cm.
    Includes bibliographical references.
    ISBN 0-13-093101-2
    1. College students—United States—Conduct of life.   2. Ethics—United States.   3. Moral
    education—United States.   I. Moss, Pamela A.   II. Title.

LA229 .S665 2003
378.1'98—dc21   2002017691

Vice President and Publisher: Jeffery W. Johnston
Senior Acquisitions Editor: Sande Johnson
Assistant Editor: Cecilia Johnson
Production Editor: Holcomb Hathaway
Design Coordinator: Diane C. Lorenzo
Cover Designer: Jeff Vanik
Cover Art: Super Stock
Production Manager: Pamela D. Bennett
Director of Marketing: Ann Castel Davis
Director of Advertising: Kevin Flanagan
Marketing Manager: Christina Quadhamer

*For Daniel and Janet,
who survived college
and became fine people
without the benefit of this book.*

*And for Madeleine and Cora,
who will be spared the
necessity of doing so.*

This book was set in Janson by Aerocraft Charter Art Service. It was printed
and bound by Hamilton Printing. The cover was printed by Phoenix Color Corp.

Pearson Education Ltd., *London*
Pearson Education Australia Pty. Limited, *Sydney*
Pearson Education Singapore Pte. Ltd.
Pearson Education North Asia Ltd., *Hong Kong*
Pearson Education Canada, Ltd., *Toronto*
Pearson Educación de Mexico, S.A. de C.V.
Pearson Education–Japan, *Tokyo*
Pearson Education Malaysia Pte. Ltd.
Pearson Education, *Upper Saddle River, New Jersey*

10 9 8 7 6 5 4 3 2 1
ISBN 0-13-093101-2

CONTENTS

1

INTRODUCTION

CAN WE THINK ABOUT ETHICS?

This book asks you to use case studies to reflect on the ethical aspects of being a college student. The very suggestion that you can think about ethics might raise some big questions: "Aren't moral questions about values, and aren't values private things? Are you going to try to impose your values on us?" And, "Aren't ethics connected to religion? Can you really discuss ethics apart from religion, and can you get anywhere discussing ethics in religiously diverse situations?" Perhaps you might even ask, "Why should I be ethical? There may be times when I'm better off if I'm not. For example, I can get a better grade if I cheat cautiously on tests. If I can get away with it, why shouldn't I?"

We are going to say a few things about these questions later. We think, however, that our suggestions will make more sense if we first explain how using case studies can help you learn to think through moral dilemmas, and then demonstrate what productive "thinking about ethics" might look like.

USING CASE STUDIES TO THINK ABOUT ETHICS

Using the case studies in this book can help you learn to think clearly and powerfully about ethical issues and moral dilemmas, especially those that come up in your life as a college student.

A case study tells the story of a real-life situation, focusing on the moral complexities involved. It gives you an opportunity to test your moral intuitions—those "gut feelings" you have about what's right and wrong, and why. It also provides an opportunity to practice moral reasoning, using the ethical principles that you will be learning, in order to expand on your moral intuition and help you develop a solution to the problem posed in the case.

The case studies in this book can help you make sense of the complex issues and situations you face in college. In fact, after reading some of our cases, you may want to write a case study of your own, based on a dilemma from your own experience.

Discussing these case studies with your fellow students has another benefit: it can help you develop meaningful dialogue about the important issues in your life.

By "dialogue," we mean a special kind of discussion or conversation that involves mutual understanding and, when possible, moral consensus. It is an argumentative process that requires an open mind. To participate, you have to be willing both to argue for your own views and to listen to the arguments of others with an open mind—even when you sharply disagree with them. You must also be willing to consult your conscience, and to reason from your intuitive sense of right and wrong. Finally, in a dialogue everyone must be equal. No authority figure should dominate the conversation, because a dialogue is more like a conversation between friends than a lecture or a sermon. Everyone has a right to be heard and taken seriously.

This kind of conversation is essential in a moral community. People in a moral community don't always agree, but they believe ethical discussions matter, and they try to achieve some shared understanding of what's right and wrong. We want to encourage you to think of your college or university as a moral community, and we hope this book can help you make it one.

Each chapter in this book will open with a somewhat complex case study that is relevant to the topic of that chapter. After this main case there will be questions, and then a discussion. But before you read our discussion of the main case, we urge you to *develop your own reactions first*—make a few notes about your initial reaction and your answers to the questions. The moral intuitions in your initial reaction are valuable! *Then read the discussion.* The discussion will analyze the issues involved in the case and suggest approaches you might use to construct a solution, but it won't give you "the right answer." (There is rarely one right answer to moral dilemma.)

It will be your job to decide which of the ethical principles described below might best apply to the case, and then to use the principles you've chosen to judge the actions of the people in the case and to argue for what they should do, and why. (Each chapter also contains a number of related "Additional Cases" you can use to practice identifying issues and applying ethical principles.)

What do we mean by "issues" in the case studies and the "ethical principles" you can use to develop solutions to them? *Issues* are the morally controversial topics involved in the case, such as "cheating—is it sometimes OK?" or "diversity—a desirable goal?" or "alcohol use—the pros and cons." Cases often will involve several related issues.

Ethical principles are ethical ideas or ideals that people have found useful in reflecting about morally complicated situations. (Because this term is sometimes used in a special, technical way by philosophers, we want to note that we have nothing technical in mind.) There are many ethical principles you could use; in this book, we will concentrate on five particularly useful ones. They come from different moral traditions.

SOME ETHICAL PRINCIPLES

1. The greatest good. This principle judges actions by looking at their consequences. It says that the best actions are those that have the best outcomes for the greatest number of people. So if we want to compare action A to action B, we need to know the consequences of A and B, whether these consequences are good or bad, and whether A or B has the best overall consequences for everyone affected. The principle of the greatest good requires that we always seek the greatest good for the greatest number (a philosophy sometimes referred to as *utilitarianism)*.

2. Equal respect and the Golden Rule. The principle of *equal respect* assumes that every person is an object of intrinsic worth; that is, each one of us is someone of value and importance just because we are a human being. Therefore, each one of us deserves to be treated with dignity and respect. Another way of saying this is that because people have intrinsic worth, they cannot be treated as though they are merely the means to someone else's ends. It is not right, according to this principle, to use people to get what we want. Everyone is of equal worth, so we must treat everyone fairly.

One way to decide whether we are showing equal respect for people is to apply the Golden Rule ("Do unto others as you would have them do unto you"). The Golden Rule instructs us to treat others as we would like to be treated by them. It thus asks us to judge our actions by their consistency. Would we approve of a given action if we were in the other person's shoes? If not, then very likely we are not treating that person with equal respect.

3. Relationship. This principle judges actions by their effect on the relationships of the people involved. It affirms that the relationships we form with other people add value and meaning to our lives; they are important. This doesn't mean that our relationships are valuable only if they are useful in advancing our careers or in helping get people to do things for us. Instead relationships such as friendship, companionship, caring, love, and affection are intrinsically worthwhile. These relationships help make life worth living. Sports events, concerts, and trips are more enjoyable when we have someone to share them with. A good conversation may be thought-provoking or comforting. Loving and being loved in turn can provide some of our greatest joys.

But it is difficult to maintain such positive relationships while also treating people unfairly. No meaningful relationship can be built on a foundation of deceit and exploitation. This principle thus asks us to examine actions for their potential to build or to hinder meaningful relationships.

4. Community. This principle evaluates actions based on how they might affect the community involved. Activities that disrupt people's sense of community are regarded as unethical. The idea of "community" has two aspects, and actions can affect each aspect in various ways.

First, a community is a network of relationships. In healthy communities, people can form non-exploitative and mutually beneficial relationships. In damaged communities, past actions have destroyed some of the personal relationships on which the community depends. Without strong relationships, the community will dissolve; therefore, actions that damage relationships between community members violate the principle of community.

Communities are also structured groups that allow people to pursue shared values and common goals: participants in a religious community desire to worship God together; members of a tennis club want to further their sport and play it with each other; the brothers of a fraternity seek friendship and camaraderie in their House. This principle condemns any action that is inconsistent with the values a community serves, for such actions weaken members' feeling of shared beliefs and common goals.

For example, if a member of a tennis club constantly called shots "out" when they were in, this would violate both aspects of community. First, it is unlikely that a consistent cheater could retain many friends in the club. Who wants to play with someone who wins by cheating? Such cheating would thus disrupt the club's network of relationships. Second, since fair scoring is essential to the game, cheating destroys the fairness of the competition and the fun of playing together. By undermining fair play, cheating thus hurts the tennis club community's sense of shared values.

5. Character growth. Finally, one of the consequences of our actions is to contribute to making us into a certain sort of person. People who behave dishonestly become dishonest people. People who exploit others become exploitative "users."

We can therefore judge our actions according to our image of the kind of person we would like to be, depending on whether our actions make us more or less like this ideal person. This principle asserts that behaving unethically is likely to harm you eventually, one way or another. Perhaps its ultimate harm is to turn you into the sort of person who no longer cares about being ethical. And if that happens, you are morally lost.

We might also use this principle to think about whether people have a duty to engage in moral leadership. If you observe some unethical behavior and stand by mutely without trying to stop it, might this damage your character? Could ignoring evil (or merely unpleasantness) make you more evil (or unpleasant) yourself?

A SAMPLE CASE STUDY ANALYSIS

Now, let's explore a sample case study of ethically dubious behavior, and show you what thinking about ethics can look like in this case.

The File CASE 1.1

The Co-op was a cooperative residence unit at Memorial College. Memorial was a commuter school. Most of its students were local and lived either with their families or in their own apartments. The Co-op had started as a way for students to save a few dollars on rent and food. A large, somewhat decrepit old house near campus, it was owned and operated by its twenty-five current residents. It provided a social life for students who would otherwise have been disconnected; members often studied together and hung out together. New members were admitted only with the consent of a governing board, and many students wanted to join, not so much because they needed housing, but because they needed friends. Unfortunately, Co-op members were not known to be models of industry or studiousness. They were only occasionally successful athletes. While they usually managed to avoid failing outright in their academic work, some made it a matter of pride to get by with minimal effort. Few Co-op members permitted intellectual activity to interfere with the real work of having fun and making friends.

John wasn't entirely certain that he wanted to join the Co-op. He had been a reasonably serious student in high school, and he felt that academic work was important to his future. Nevertheless, his college experience so far had been lonely and joyless. He lived alone. He didn't have any place to belong, and he had only a few friends. Thus, when one of those few friends decided to seek admission to the Co-op, John did, too. He was a little surprised that he was admitted, but he was pleased that his social life seemed secured.

Somewhere near the end of his first semester of membership, John began to get a new picture of his role in the Co-op. Carl, the Co-op's vice-president, introduced him to The File. The File contained A papers that members of the Co-op had collected from a wide range of large courses. The role of The File was to provide a database of successful papers that Co-op members could use in developing their own papers for various courses. What "developing" seemed to mean was that members were under strict instructions to modify any paper that they turned in sufficiently so that the plagiarism would not be obvious. The File even contained a meticulous record of when each paper had been used and to whom it had been submitted. Each paper was on disk so that adaptation was easy.

Carl explained to John that because he seemed academically talented, it was expected that he would be more of a provider than a user. Apparently each year the Co-op carefully selected a few providers to assist their less fortunate members. They would contribute their better papers to The File. Indeed, they were occasionally advised as to which courses needed additional contributions, and were expected to "seriously consider" enrolling for such courses. The providers, Carl assured John, were especially valued members of the Co-op, except for those selfish few who put their own interests ahead of the interests of the group. They often seemed to move out after a year or so because they just didn't fit in. Carl knew that John would fit in.

ISSUES

Consider some of the things we might ask about the ethical issues in this case. First, is anything wrong with the Co-op's maintaining The File? It seems intended to assist members in cheating or plagiarism. Why might cheating or plagiarism be wrong? Might The File have legitimate uses? Is it wrong for a student to get a grade that the student hasn't earned?

Is John being exploited? Carl seems to be offering John a trade of friendship for work. Is there anything wrong with such a trade? If so, what? Aren't many human relationships based on such exchanges? How does a trade of friendship for work differ from a trade of a salary for work? Is John being coerced?

What are the effects of The File on the college community? Is the community being harmed? Does the college community have purposes that are undermined by The File? Does the Co-op have any responsibility for the welfare of the college community? Are the students of this college even members of a community, or are they just customers paying a fee for a service?

APPLYING ETHICAL PRINCIPLES TO THE CASE

Let's see how each of the moral principles discussed above can be used to think about why the behavior in "The File" is unethical. Each principle can be the basis for a different argument about the case. You may want to consider whether you agree with the arguments we make using each principle, and if there might be other applications of these principles besides those developed below.

1. The greatest good. We can apply the principle of "the greatest good" to the case by thinking about the consequences of using The File to plagiarize or cheat. Does cheating benefit a greater number of people than not cheating? Well, there are some benefits to cheating, especially for those who are not caught. But it seems likely that there are also many negative consequences, for the cheaters themselves as well as for others. First, when students cheat, they do not learn, and so they deny themselves the benefit of learning. Second, when some students cheat and others do not, cheating distorts the value of the cheater's grade in comparison to the grades of those who don't cheat. Honest students are denied the benefit of their work, and so they are harmed by cheating. (Indeed, if cheating were so commonplace that all students' grades became suspect, everyone would be harmed; no one would believe college transcripts or grade point averages. See Chapter 2.)

Using this principle, it seems that cheating cannot provide the greatest good for the greatest number, and thus The File is unethical.

2. Equal respect and the Golden Rule. This principle supports an argument that Carl is exploiting John. Carl does not seem to care about John. He treats John as if he is worth being nice to only insofar as he is useful. Thus he treats John as a means to his, Carl's, ends, not as someone who is worthy of dignity and respect in himself.

If we apply the Golden Rule here, we might ask: "Would Carl approve of The File, and of recruiting some bright but friendless person to provide for it, if Carl himself were the person being exploited?" Quite likely Carl would not be willing to be used in such a way. If so, then Carl is being inconsistent and not treating John with equal respect. Because his behavior violates this principle, it is unethical.

3. Relationship. It seems likely that Carl couldn't have recruited John to the Co-op if he had been honest about the role he expected John to perform. Because Carl means to exploit John, he must also deceive him; and deceit and exploitation are no basis for friendship. John is outside the circle of friends in the Co-op. As long as its members do not care for John's welfare, they cannot be his friends, no matter what they pretend; their relationships with him will be false and insincere. This principle thus condemns Carl's behavior as unethical because of its effects on his (and other Co-op members') relationships with John.

4. Community. College is a kind of moral community. A college or university is organized around shared values such as the pursuit of truth and the dissemination of knowledge. Dishonesty disrupts such a community, because when some people are intellectually dishonest, learning cannot thrive, and friendships cannot form around the collective pursuit of shared values. So according to this principle, maintaining The File is unethical because it would seem to disrupt the college community.

5. Character growth. This principle asks us to think about how Carl's actions could be affecting his character. What kind of a person is he becoming? His behavior with John seems deceitful and exploitative, but he might not want to think of himself as a deceitful, exploitative person. How can he avoid it?

Carl might justify his conduct by rationalizing, saying to himself that he's not really hurting John. He might even claim to be helping him in some way. Or he might tell himself that John deserves this treatment, by attaching a disparaging name to John like "nerd" or "dork," and persuading himself that somehow it's all right to exploit someone with such unfavorable traits. If John is a member of a different race, religion, or ethnic group, Carl might use this as a justification.

Such reasoning would suggest that Carl's moral damage to himself is even greater than we had supposed. Not only is he becoming deceitful and exploitative, but in order to keep thinking of himself as a good person, he must engage in rationalization and self-delusion. To feel good about his behavior, he must lie to himself—both about himself and about John. He thus increases the harm done to both of them.

This principle also suggests that students who use The File to cheat may hurt their character development in the long run. Not only do they fail to learn when they plagiarize papers, but by passing off someone else's work as their own, they must knowingly lie. This lack of integrity can lead them to be distrusted by others, and may eventually become a source of pain to themselves.

Are other principles involved in this case? Of course. In fact, in developing these we have hinted at others, such as honesty, privacy, and trust. Our reasons for selecting these principles are that we believe that they are broad enough to allow you to reflect seriously about most ethical problems, and that using them to discuss issues will eventually lead you to other important ethical concepts. It is also significant that many thinkers throughout the history of philosophy have viewed these concepts as among those most central to ethical reflection.

As you analyze the case studies that follow in this book, we'd like you to keep in mind three ideas that will help you come to workable—and ethical—solutions to the problems they pose.

First, remember that people have thought about these issues before, even if not in exactly this form. Your dialogues and solutions will be much better if you learn all you can about what previous thinkers in religion, law, philosophy, art, and culture have said about ethics in their fields. Be respectful of these traditions of moral reflection, but not subservient—you may see something they didn't.

Second, keep in mind that you have a conscience as well as a mind. Dialogues and analyses of case studies must appeal to your conscience as well as to your judgment. Whatever decisions you reach, they should be both reasonable and conscientious; they should not only make sense, but also feel fair. And assume that other people have a conscience too—at the end of the day, everyone is responsible for his own actions and decisions.

And last, the fact that you are ultimately responsible for your own choices does not mean you should ignore the views of others, nor become a moral isolationist. In life, many times what "we" decide counts more than what "I" want. There will be occasions when you will need to act and decide as a member of a group. Engaging in moral dialogue with your group can help you learn a lot; and what's more, it can produce better solutions to the cases.

In the chapters that follow, we are going to provide you with a set of cases that seem to us to represent a reasonable range of ethical issues that are especially important to students. We are not going to attempt any deep or detailed analysis of these cases. We will, however, follow each case with some questions that will point to possible applications of some of the principles sketched above. When we have finished, we will return to some of the questions asked in the first paragraph of this introduction.

FOR FURTHER INQUIRY

Where do the five different principles we've discussed come from? Do some of them conflict with others? Are some merely applications of other, more important principles? And how do you know which ones to apply to which issues?

Reading the ideas of some of the thinkers who helped to develop these principles can help you answer such questions. Here are a few of the original sources for each ethical principle we've described:

The greatest good. Utilitarianism, the idea that the best or most just society is the one that produces the greatest good for the greatest number, is represented in two works by the English philosopher John Stuart Mill (1806–73). In *Utilitarianism*, Mill lays out the basic principles of utilitarianism; *On Liberty* provides a utilitarian argument for individuality (freedom of lifestyle) and freedom of opinion. Mill's arguments are, perhaps, the best source for understanding the commitments required for a free society.

Equal respect and the Golden Rule. In the modern era, the main philosophical competitor to utilitarianism has been the ethics of German thinker Immanuel Kant (1721–1804). Kant resisted the view that actions should be judged primarily by the desirability of their consequences, and argued instead that actions should be evaluated according to whether or not they show consistency and respect for persons. These views are developed in Kant's central ethical works, *Critique of Practical Reason* and *Groundwork of the Metaphysics of Morals*.

Mill's and Kant's Enlightenment philosophies have had a profound impact not only on how we understand our own ethical choices, but also on how we evaluate the morality of liberal democratic institutions. For a contemporary classic that takes a Kantian rather than a utilitarian approach to political philosophy, see American philosopher John Rawls' *A Theory of Justice*. Rawls argues that utilitarianism is defective, in part, because it permits some to benefit at the expense of others so long as the average welfare is increased. He insists that justice consists not in the greatest good for the greatest number, but in a scheme of social cooperation that all can accept under conditions of equality and impartiality.

Community, relationship, and character growth. Some contemporary philosophers have argued that both of these Enlightenment philosophies fail to take into account the centrality of community in human life. One important source of this argument is Scottish philosopher Alaisdair MacIntyre. In his book *After Virtue*, MacIntyre argues that our sense of self and our moral beliefs are necessarily shaped by our family backgrounds and the communities that form us. Thus our ethical choices are not purely rational, as Mill or Kant believe, but deeply influenced by our personal and cultural histories, which we must try to understand.

Many communitarians consider themselves influenced by the works of Greek philosopher and scientist Aristotle (384–322 B.C.), who tries to show how community, relationships, and character growth are linked. Aristotle argues that human beings are social and political animals who live best only in well-ordered communities that sustain the virtues, such as honesty, justice, courage, and moderation, necessary for both good lives and good communities. Aristotle also argues a point that we will frequently echo: in judging conduct it is important to remember that moral virtues or habits are formed by engaging in moral acts. Aristotle's major works include *Politics*, which contains his philosophical theory of the state, a detailed study of the forms and methods of government, and a vision of the ideal state; and *Nicomachean Ethics*, which summarizes his ethical views at the end of his life.

Some contemporary religious ethicists have also argued for the centrality of community. An illustrative work is *A Community of Character: Toward a Constructive Christian Social Ethic* by Stanley Hauerwas.

Some feminist philosophers have recently developed an ethic that emphasizes relationships and character growth in opposition to the more abstract concerns involved in ethics emphasizing justice. Two examples are *Caring: A Feminine Approach to Ethics and Moral Education* by American philosopher Nel Noddings and *In a Different Voice* by American Carol Gilligan. Noddings sets out "an ethic of caring" in which caring for others and being cared for by them, rather than principles or rules, form the basis of our moral responses; ethical judgments should be particular to each situation, rather than universally applicable. Gilligan's work contrasts women's moral reasoning, in which relationships are central, to the more typically male emphasis on justice, described in Lawrence Kohlberg's developmental theory of moral reasoning.

Finally, two works specifically discuss the character of university communities: *The Idea of a University* by John Henry Cardinal Newman (1801–1890) and *The Ideal of the University* by contemporary thinker Robert Paul Wolff.

REFERENCES

1. Aristotle. *Nicomachean Ethics.* Translated from the Greek and with an introduction by David Ross; revised by J. L. Ackrill and J. O. Urmson. New York: Oxford University Press, 1980.

2. ———. *Politics.* Translated from the Greek and with an introduction, notes, and glossary by Carnes Lord. Chicago: University of Chicago Press, 1984.

3. Gilligan, Carol. *In a Different Voice: Psychological Theory and Women's Development.* Cambridge, MA: Harvard University Press, 1982.

4. Hauerwas, Stanley. *A Community of Character: Toward a Constructive Christian Social Ethic.* Notre Dame, IN: University of Notre Dame Press, 1981.

5. Kant, Immanuel. *Critique of Practical Reason.* 1790. Translated from the German and with an introduction by Lewis White Beck. Indianapolis, IN: Bobbs-Merril, 1986.

6. ———. *The Moral Law; or, Kant's Groundwork of the Metaphysics of Morals.* 1794. A translation from the German with analysis and notes by H. J. Paton. London: Hutchinson University Library, 1961.

7. MacIntyre, Alaisdair. *After Virtue: A Study in Moral Theory.* Notre Dame, IN: University of Notre Dame Press, 1984.

8. Mill, John Stuart. *On Liberty.* 1859. Edited and with an introduction by Gertrude Himmelfarb. New York: Viking Penguin Inc., 1987.

9. ———. *Utilitarianism.* 1863. Indianapolis, IN: Hackett Publishing Co., 1979.

10. Newman, John Henry. *The Idea of a University Defined and Illustrated: I. In Nine Discourses Delivered to the Catholics of Dublin. II. In Occasional Lectures and Essays Addressed to the Members of Catholic University.* Edited and with an introduction and notes by I. T. Ker. Oxford: Clarendon Press, 1976.

11. Noddings, Nel. *Caring: A Feminine Approach to Ethics and Moral Education.* Berkeley, CA: University of California Press, 1984.

12. Rawls, John. *A Theory of Justice.* Cambridge, MA: Belknap Press of Harvard University Press, 1971.

13. Wolff, Robert Paul. *The Ideal of the University.* Boston: Beacon Press, 1969.

2

ACADEMIC INTEGRITY, GRADING, AND CHEATING

CASE 2.1 *Cheating*

Sarah Benson was a senior in the engineering program of Andersonville College. She had been a marginal student since she entered Andersonville. She had been on probation twice, and had had to take one semester off. She was still in danger of not finishing. In addition to her marginal grade point average, she still had two required courses to complete in her major. She was currently enrolled in one of these, Physics for Engineers, which was offered only during the fall semester. She was not doing well.

Not only that, but she had been accused of cheating on the midterm exam. There seemed little doubt that she was guilty. The responses on her answer sheet, even the wrong answers, exactly matched those of the person who was seated directly in front of her. The probability that two students could produce an identical set of incorrect answers on ten different items was close to zero. Moreover, given their positions in the room, it was virtually impossible that the other student could have copied from Sarah.

Professor Hsu, the instructor, prided herself on her firm sense of academic honesty. She thus decided to charge Sarah with violating the college's academic integrity code, although she wasn't required to do so. Because Sarah wasn't exactly a model student, it also seemed important to Professor Hsu to protect the engineering profession from someone who wouldn't bring credit to it.

Andersonville College had a committee on academic integrity. A student accused of cheating had to be charged before that committee by the instructor of the course in which the alleged cheating took place. The committee would then consider the evidence, make a judgment, and, if the student was found guilty, decide on a penalty. This semester, the academic integrity committee was chaired by Professor Bloom, who had a reputation for fairness unburdened by mercy.

Professor Hsu made a persuasive case against Sarah. Sarah admitted her guilt and excused herself by saying that she had panicked because she was afraid that if she failed the exam she wouldn't be able to complete the program. She still hoped to enter the Master of Engineering program at Andersonville. She was afraid that failing Hsu's course would doom her admission. The committee then sent her out of the room while they discussed their verdict.

The verdict was that Sarah was to be suspended for the rest of the academic year, after which she could reapply for admission. In announcing the verdict, Professor Bloom delivered a sermon on the importance of intellectual honesty to the academic community. He explained that the college's central values included the pursuit of truth and excellence in one's work, and that absolute honesty was required by these goals. He concluded, "Thus you have violated the central moral principle of an academic community, intellectual integrity, and we have no choice but to protect the college against such behavior. However, we have also decided that after you have undergone your punishment and learned your lesson, you may have another chance to complete the program."

Sarah didn't say much, and that seemed to be the end of it. She left, and the committee members started to leave, too. However, some of Sarah's friends had waited for her outside the hearing room; they were commiserating with her when the committee was leaving. Unhappily, Professor Bloom overheard Sarah say, "I wish the old fart would apply those standards about 'community integrity' to his colleagues. Maybe then I wouldn't have had to cheat."

Professor Bloom was irate. He called the committee back into the room and demanded an explanation and an apology from Sarah. He got neither. Instead, through angry tears, Sarah gave an indictment of the education she had received. It went something like this:

"You talk about the integrity of the academic community. There has never been a community here for me! When I came here you made me take 'screening' classes that felt more like boot camp than education. My faculty 'advisor' has never even learned my name. When I tried to get involved in research, I was told that research opportunities were only for students who could 'really contribute.' Professor Hsu barely prepares for her class, and that seems the norm here, not the exception. So far as I can see, you people stole the tuition money I paid, refused to teach me, refused to treat me as a member of any community, and used my money to pursue your own consulting careers. If I cheated, I did nothing but copy your example. The only moral principle teachers at this college seem to follow is 'do whatever is necessary to further your career.' *That's* one thing you taught me well!"

QUESTIONS

1. Professor Bloom says that intellectual honesty is the central value sustaining a college community. Why might this be? What are some other values that might be similarly important?

2. If Sarah's description of her education is accurate, has the engineering faculty of Andersonville also failed to show professional integrity? Do you think this is how students are treated in your college or university? What could be done to create a stronger sense of community?

3. Some institutions have an honor code in which students promise not to cheat and also promise not to tolerate cheating in others. Would such a code work at your school? Why or why not? Is it possible to create an academic moral climate that would make students not want to cheat? How? What values would be essential?

4. Many students often sympathize with those who cheat. Even if they don't exactly approve of cheating, students rarely turn in or even criticize those who cheat. Should they? In many situations, loyalty to friends or solidarity with members of one's group are important virtues. Are they in cases of cheating? How do you see your responsibilities here?

5. Sarah's last reaction to Professor Bloom seems common in real-life ethical discussion. She accused him of inconsistency because he and his colleagues seem to violate the same values they blame her for violating. Is Sarah's claim that she just copied the faculty's example plausible? If it is, does it justify her cheating? Is "and you're another" or "everybody does it" ever a reasonable defense of unethical conduct?

6. Another common defense for some kinds of unethical behavior is that it doesn't really hurt anyone. Does cheating harm anyone? If so, whom, and how?

7. If teachers' salaries are substantially paid by students' tuition, do teachers have a stronger obligation to perform conscientiously than they would if their money came from somewhere else, such as an endowment? Is their failure to teach students the same as theft? Might it be a breach of an implied contract?

ISSUES

Why shouldn't Sarah Benson cheat? Suppose we say that cheating is a kind of victimless crime because no one is hurt. Had Sarah succeeded, she would have gotten a passing grade. Professor Hsu wouldn't have been damaged by this. Neither would the other students. Their grades would have been the same. If nobody is hurt, can cheating be wrong? When we say that some action is wrong, don't we mean in part that it harms someone?

APPLYING ETHICAL PRINCIPLES TO THE CASE

There are a number of approaches you might take to this problem. We'll first note some that you might consider, but that we won't explore here:

One approach appeals to the idea of *character growth*. If Sarah cheats now, maybe she'll find it easier to cheat the next time. She might develop a habit of dishonesty. Does this argument seem believable? If it does, how might cheating on this test affect Sarah's life? How is integrity or trustworthiness valuable?

Another possibility is to look at Sarah's actions in light of the principle of the *Golden Rule*. How might Sarah feel if her role and Professor Hsu's role were reversed? Would she be willing to allow cheating?

A third argument might claim that Sarah erodes her *relationships* with other students by cheating. After all, they worked hard for their grades. How would they feel about someone who got a good grade by cheating when they had to study hard for theirs?

You might want to see whether you can develop some arguments about cheating along some of these lines. We'll show you what we mean by "develop some arguments" as we explore two different approaches in more detail. First, we'll use the principle of the greatest good to think about whether, in fact, someone is hurt by Sarah's cheating. Second, we'll ask about how intellectual integrity might be required to make an academic community work.

The *greatest good* suggests that we should prefer practices that make a society more efficient in its use of human resources. A society that hires the people who are best able to do a particular job is more efficient than one that does not. Similarly, a society that provides educational opportunities and career training to those who are most able to profit from such training can make better use of its resources than one that does not. If a society is to be efficient in these ways, it needs to measure ability to perform a job and ability to profit from an education. One measure of these capacities is grades. Moreover, if grades are used to award jobs or further education, students who want these positions will compete for grades. Cheating might then have the following consequences: it would make it harder to award positions on the basis of merit, and it would give cheaters an unfair advantage over those who don't cheat.

Who is hurt? One answer is that people who confer benefits on the basis of grades are hurt. An employer who hires Sarah, believing that she is a capable engineer, might be hurt because she isn't competent. A university that admits Sarah to graduate school might be injured because it would believe, erroneously, that it was investing its limited resources in a competent student. Had Sarah not been caught cheating, these people would have been lied to and injured.

Other possible victims of cheating are other students. In many cases, students compete with one another for jobs or for admission to further education. If Sarah succeeds in cheating, she would appear more qualified in relation to other students than she really is, and thus unfairly improve her competitive advantage with them. Her position would be similar to that of someone who had bought something with counterfeit money.

Surely it's in everyone's best interest for employers and universities to hire or admit the best qualified people. Better qualified employees are likely to do better work. Their employers will benefit, and so will those who buy the employers' product or service. Similarly, if universities admit the most qualified students, these students can be expected to do better work. This means that eventually we all benefit from having better trained people. Thus, everyone in society is hurt by cheating.

The arguments presented demonstrate the use of the greatest good principle: in short, cheating ultimately undermines society's ability to use human resources efficiently. When that happens, everyone is worse off. Can you think of other examples in which everyone suffers when some people cheat? Are there any cases in which cheating is genuinely victimless?

Applying the principle of the greatest good usually requires that we make some assumptions about the consequences of our actions. These assumptions may be arguable. In this case, our argument assumes that grades are a reasonable measure of the ability to perform on a job or to profit from further education. Are they? If these assumptions are incorrect, is cheating acceptable?

Another assumption in these arguments is that what is learned is a kind of commodity—something that has economic value and that can be exchanged or used to get other valued things. Is this how you think of your education? Are you a student primarily because you believe that education has economic benefits? What other reasons might there be for getting an education? (See Chapter 8.) In these other views of the purpose of learning, is cheating still harmful? For whom?

Suppose that the course in which Sarah cheated was unrelated to her engineering major and her intended profession, such as a literature course. Could Sarah argue that it was acceptable for her to cheat in this course because her knowledge of literature has nothing to do with her professional credentials?

Using the *community* principle is another way to examine why cheating is wrong. Colleges and universities are not simply employment agencies; they are places where ideas are important, and where, ideally, new knowledge is sought and ideas are debated and evaluated. Honesty is absolutely central to this pursuit. Any form of intellectual dishonesty is thus damaging to an academic community. Professor Bloom believes that cheating violates the academic community's central commitment to intellectual honesty. Is he right?

What would life be like in a college or university that couldn't count on the intellectual honesty of its members? For example, consider professors' research. If scholars were not routinely honest in reporting data and in making arguments, we couldn't rely on the results of their research; immense effort would have to be put into policing and checking everything they did. Under these conditions, the academic community couldn't accomplish its purpose of seeking and communicating results that are as fair and accurate as researchers can make them.

A similar argument might be made about teaching. Suppose you couldn't rely on the honesty of your professors in teaching their subjects. Suppose they were willing to misrepresent their own fields to advance their careers or to defend their pet theories. Suppose that instead of relying on arguments and persuasion in class, they relied on lying, misrepresentation, or even coercion to win arguments. What would your education be like? Would its value for you change?

We think that Professor Bloom's view that intellectual integrity is essential to academic communities is clearly right, but we're less sure that it applies clearly to Sarah's case. To examine why, let's consider some distinctions among three ways of judging students' work:

1. *Criticism* emphasizes discussing the merits of an argument or problem-solving approach, the quality of students' writing or calculations, and so on. It is feedback, usually provided in comments on papers or tests. Criticism is crucial to learning because it helps us see how to improve.

2. *Grading* involves putting a performance or an object into a category. It may involve a judgment of quality, such as when a paper is judged as good, bad, or average. Colleges and universities often grade because they want to know whether students have achieved minimum competence in a subject, or whether they have passed enough courses to earn a degree. However, grading need not involve such quality judgments. We don't judge the worth of eggs, for example, when we grade them into size or color groups.

3. *Ranking* involves a comparative judgment. We rank when we order a series of examples according to our judgment of how good each is compared to the others.[1]

What we call "grading" in most educational settings may involve all of these. If colleges were interested only in the pursuit of truth and in making students into scholars, they would probably use only criticism. Instead, they use grading or ranking so that they can award credit and grant degrees, and because they view grades as commodities. Grading and ranking have little to do with evaluating arguments or with scholarship. They have much to do with an attempt to communicate students' comparative levels of success to other colleges and employers.

[1] Our description of these three ways to judge students' work follows Wolff, *The Ideal of the University*, p. 59.

What does this have to do with Sarah? We think it suggests that the argument that Sarah has implicitly lied to future employers or schools is stronger than the argument that she has violated the essential intellectual honesty of an academic community.

First, we suspect that the kind of test on which Sarah cheated was intended to grade or rank students more than to criticize them. We suspect that this is often, if not always, the case with tests and that it is especially true of tests on which it is possible to cheat by copying the right answer from another student, as Sarah did. Such a test has not been designed to allow students to present arguments or evaluate claims, both of which would be hard to copy and perhaps reveal more of what students understand. However, professors give multiple-choice and fill-in-the-blank tests because they are asked to grade and rank their students.

Second, Sarah has not been accused of falsifying data or misrepresenting a bad argument as a good one. She has not plagiarized ideas, or "cooked" data. She has copied test answers. Our point isn't that Sarah's cheating is acceptable or even that it is less bad than these types of dishonesty. However, we suggest that Sarah hasn't violated the central value of an academic community, because intellectual honesty isn't really involved here. Tests of the sort that Professor Hsu gives don't ask students to engage in any intellectual process other than showing that they have learned required material. The primary purpose of such tests is to grade and rank students, not critique them. Sarah's dishonesty is thus more like a case of theft—in this case, of credentials or ranking—than like a case of misleading others about her ideas or research. It is more like stealing than lying.

However, Sarah's cheating still may have serious consequences for Andersonville. In cheating, Sarah may have helped to create a climate at Andersonville in which other students will find it easier to cheat. At some point, if students come to believe that a lot of cheating is going on, they may feel pressure to cheat in order to keep up. Or they may rationalize cheating by telling themselves that everyone is doing it. What are some of the things that influence how you feel about cheating?

In summary, our two arguments about cheating assume two different pictures of higher education. With the principle of the *greatest good*, knowledge is viewed as a commodity. Scholars produce it and provide it to various consumers, such as governments, industries, and students who, in turn, can exchange it for jobs and income. In this image, cheating seems most like a form of theft because the cheater gets an undeserved benefit and deprives others of this benefit. The other view, expressed by Professor Bloom, sees a college or university as an intellectual *community* engaged in a shared project of inquiry. In this picture, cheating undermines the assumption of intellectual integrity that is essential to serious inquiry. It's more like lying. These pictures are different. Are they incompatible? How do you see your own education? Does the answer to these questions affect the way you view cheating? In either case, cheating can undermine the climate in which colleges and universities attempt to accomplish their purposes. Does your college have a climate that encourages honesty or cheating? How do you think this affects the quality of your education?

EXAMPLES OF COLLEGE AND UNIVERSITY CODES ON ACADEMIC DISHONESTY

I. Excerpt from the *Code of Academic Integrity* of the University of Maryland[2]

Introduction

The University is an academic community. Its fundamental purpose is the pursuit of knowledge. Like all other communities, the University can function properly only if its members adhere to clearly established goals and values. Essential to the fundamental purpose of the University is the commitment to the principles of truth and academic honesty. Accordingly, the *Code of Academic Integrity* is designed to ensure that the principle of academic honesty is upheld. While all members of the University share this responsibility, the *Code of Academic Integrity* is designed so that special responsibility for upholding the principle of academic responsibility lies with the students.

Definitions

ACADEMIC DISHONESTY: any of the following acts, when committed by a student, shall constitute academic dishonesty:

a. CHEATING: intentionally using or attempting to use unauthorized materials, information, or study aids in any academic exercise.

b. FABRICATION: intentional or unauthorized falsification or invention of any information or citation in an academic exercise.

c. FACILITATING ACADEMIC DISHONESTY: intentionally or knowingly helping or attempting to help another violate any provisions of this *Code*.

d. PLAGIARISM: intentionally or knowingly representing the words or ideas of another as one's own in any academic exercise.

Responsibility to Report Academic Dishonesty

Academic dishonesty is a corrosive force in the academic life of a university. It jeopardizes the quality of education and depreciates the genuine achievements of others. It is, without reservation, a responsibility of all members of the campus community to actively deter it. Apathy or acqui-

---

[2] *Code of Academic Integrity*, University of Maryland at College Park (Gary Pavela, Director of Judicial Programs).

escence in the presence of academic dishonesty is not a neutral act. Histories of institutions demonstrate that a laissez-faire response will reinforce, perpetuate, and enlarge the scope of such misconduct. Institutional reputations for academic dishonesty are regrettable aspects of modern education. These reputations become self-fulfilling and grow, unless vigorously challenged by students and faculty alike.

All members of the University community—students, faculty, and staff—share the responsibility and authority to challenge and make known acts of apparent academic dishonesty.

2. Excerpt from *The Honor Code* of Stanford University[3]

A. The Honor Code is an undertaking of the students, individually and collectively:

    (1) that they will not give or receive aid in examinations; that they will not give or receive unpermitted aid in class work, in the preparation of reports, or in any other work that is to be used by the instructor as a basis for grading;

    (2) that they will do their share and take an active part in seeing to it that others as well as themselves uphold the spirit and the letter of the Honor Code.

B. The Faculty on its part manifests its confidence in the honor of its students by refraining from proctoring examinations and from taking unusual and unreasonable precautions to prevent the forms of dishonesty mentioned above. The faculty will also avoid, as far as practicable, academic procedures that create temptations to violate the Honor Code.

C. While the faculty alone has the right and obligation to set academic requirements, the students and faculty will work together to establish optimal conditions for honorable academic work.

3. Excerpt from the student handbook of Tompkins Cortland Community College[4]

A. Plagiarism

Plagiarism is the dishonest use of the work of others.

[. . .] Plagiarism means presenting, as one's own, the words, the work, or the opinions of someone else. It is dishonest, since the plagiarist offers, as his or her own, for credit, the language, or information, or thought for which he or she deserved no credit. It is unproductive, since it defeats the

---

[3] *The Honor Code*, Stanford University (Student Legislative Council, 1977).

[4] "Statement of Academic Integrity" in *The 1992–93 Student Handbook*, Tompkins Cortland Community College (Dryden, NY), pp. 40–41.

purpose of the course—improvement of the student's own powers of thinking and communication. It is also dangerous, since the penalties for plagiarism are severe. [. . .]

Examples of plagiarism as it might occur in term papers, research papers, laboratory reports, and other written assignments are listed below:

- Failure to use quotation marks: All work which is quoted from a source should be enclosed in quotation marks and followed by a proper reference giving the exact page or pages from which the quote is taken. Failure to use the quotation marks, even if a footnote source is provided, is plagiarism.

- Failure to document ideas: When a student uses one or more ideas from and/or paraphrases a source, he or she must give the exact page or pages from which the ideas or paraphrasing were taken. [. . .]

- False documentation: Falsifying or inventing sources or page references is plagiarism. [. . .]

- Ideas which are part of the general fund of human knowledge (e.g., George Washington was the first President of the United States, Albert Einstein developed the Theory of Relativity, etc.) need not be documented in papers.

ADDITIONAL CASES

The Tutor   CASE 2.2

David was having a lot of trouble writing the paper for his English 200 course, and he was beginning to panic—there was only one week left until it was due. Then one evening he noticed an ad on the library bulletin board: "English grad student, experienced editor, offers tutoring and paper-writing assistance." He called the listed number and found that for a not unreasonable fee, the tutor would work intensively with him in the upcoming week and help him write "a good paper." He ended up spending many hours with the tutor in the next few days, going over ideas and drafts. He was happy to spend a lot of time on the paper because this was an important course for him, and it didn't hurt that the tutor turned out to be a friendly, attractive young woman named Maria.

At last the paper was done—just in the nick of time. David was quite proud of it. He recognized that Maria had helped him tremendously: she explained the assignment more clearly than the professor had and helped him clarify his paper topic, she talked through his ideas (adding many good ones of her own), she edited and rewrote the two drafts he prepared for her, and she showed him how he could reorganize his argument to make it much clearer and more forceful. David was happy to pay Maria's fee. In fact, he gratefully realized that this paper was far better than anything he could write on his own, and he'd learned a lot from working with her. When the paper got an A– instead of the C– he'd gotten on his first paper, David was elated. "Too bad I can't afford to pay you to tutor me in all my classes!" he said wistfully.

QUESTIONS

1. Maria seems to have done a substantial amount of David's work, and he knows he couldn't have done as well by himself. When does "help" become "cheating," or getting credit for someone else's work?
2. Is there a problem with relying heavily on someone else to do your work if you are also learning a lot at the same time?
3. Is the outside tutoring David got fair to other students in the class? What if David had gotten all this extra help from the professor?
4. Would your reactions to this case differ if Maria had been David's girlfriend rather than a paid tutor? In other words, does it matter whether the helper is paid in cash or in something less tangible, such as friendship or sexual favors? (See Case 1.1 in Chapter 1.)

CASE 2.3   *Time Crunch*

Micaela has been working extra hours at her part-time job in a clothing store. The store needs her help because the holiday rush is starting, and she needs the money to pay next semester's tuition and to fix her car so that she can drive home for the holidays. The coming holiday season also means the end of the semester and, unfortunately, final exams. Micaela simply doesn't have time to study for all of her exams and also work the extra hours she needs.

Something has to give, and she decides to fake being sick on the day of her Biology exam so that she can take the make-up exam the next week and have more time to study. She knows that it won't be hard to get a note from the busy school health clinic saying that she's too sick to take the exam; her friend Debbie works there and can "borrow" a page of their letterhead stationery. "Even if I have to lie, it's fair that I get extra time to study," Micaela tells herself, "because I have to work, and I can't study all the time like students who get mommy and daddy to pay for everything."

QUESTIONS

1. Micaela seems to see her lie as a simple case of manipulating an unfair system. Is there anything wrong with manipulating the system? Is her strategy fair to the other students in her Biology class?
2. She seems to justify her behavior with a vague idea that "unfair" differences between people that have nothing to do with effort or intelligence, such as wealth, should not be reflected in their grades.

What do you think about her claim that she deserves more time to study than other students because they don't have to earn money?

Take Note: Help or Hindrance? CASE 2.4

Many introductory and low-level courses at Cornell University have a service offered by a private company called TakeNote. For $45 per course, students can purchase a complete set of class notes, taken at every lecture by a graduate student in that field. In fact sometimes the notes are taken by one of the T.A.s for the class. The detailed notes are printed on red paper so that they can't be photocopied by students unwilling or unable to buy the service. Graduate students are happy to earn extra money by taking notes, and TakeNote's customers are happy to have class notes that are usually more complete and accurate than those they take on their own. TakeNote's satisfied customer comments include "having TakeNote lets me just concentrate on listening to the professor!" "Now if I have to miss a class I don't get so anxious!" "With TakeNote, I know that when I study for the exams, I have all the material and didn't miss any important points!"

The only people unhappy with the service seem to be some students who can't pay for it and some of the professors of the courses for which it's offered. These teachers feel that buying class notes encourages students to skip class and keeps them from learning to take their own good notes. (One teacher said, "Learning to take notes is an important skill; when you take notes, you're processing and organizing information, and connecting it to things you already know, in a way that you can't do with someone else's notes. Taking good notes really helps you learn.") Of course, professors can refuse to allow TakeNote in their classes, but there is considerable pressure from students to have the service. Instructors also have no choice about who takes the notes, and some feel that poor note takers have misled students ("I know who's buying TakeNote when I get the same wrong answer on 40 percent of the exams").

QUESTIONS

1. Do you think that paying someone else for class notes keeps students from learning how to take good notes, or encourages them to skip class?
2. Do TakeNote customers have an unfair advantage over students who can't or won't pay for the service?
3. Could TakeNote be considered a form of cheating? If so, who is being cheated?
4. What are the implications of Cornell University's implicit, if not official, sanctioning of TakeNote? Should TakeNote customers have any (legal?) redress against note-takers who supply them with wrong or misleading information?

5. Would there be any problem with such class notes if they were given out by the professor to all students? Many professors now put their lecture notes, outlines, and even class announcements on the Web, or they use a list-serve to distribute study and summary questions to everyone in the class. Does having all this information on their computers mean there's little reason for students to attend class?

CASE 2.5 *A Question of Plagiarism*

Shirpad sighed as he examined the student's paper, and then he looked back to the neatly typed title page: The Rise of the Modern Nation-State, by Steven Zanko. "I'm sorry, Steven, whoever you are," he thought to himself, "but not only are you going to fail this paper, I'm also going to report you for plagiarism to the Honor Board. This is just too blatant." Shirpad recognized the source on which Steven had, to put it politely, modelled his paper; and Steven did not credit this work even once. In fact, Steven seemed oblivious to the need for footnotes and a bibliography in a research paper. Not only did the argument of Steven's paper closely follow a single source, but many of the ideas also came from this work, and numerous phrases in the paper were lifted directly from it. The copied phrases were mostly in quotation marks, it was true; however, no references were given, and Steven had been careless about including end-quote marks. Quite a few were missing, so that one had to guess exactly where the quotation ended and Steven's words (or those of some other source) began. With a sigh, Shirpad wrote a big red "F—See Me!" on the title page.

Steven did go to see Shirpad right after the papers were handed back. He turned out to be a tall, beefy young man, who was red with anger and close to tears. Shirpad carefully explained why the paper was unacceptable and said that he would have to report Steven for plagiarism. Steven sullenly claimed that he hadn't realized his paper plagiarized anything; he hadn't had many chances to write papers before, and he thought this was the way to do it. He added heatedly that it wasn't fair to punish him for not knowing how to do something he hadn't been taught; he certainly wasn't a liar, but wasn't that what Shirpad was calling him?

QUESTIONS

1. Consider the fact that because of his large class size, Shirpad did not even know who Steven was when he was reading his paper. Do Shirpad, other instructors at the college, or the college administration bear responsibility for Steven's ignorance about how to write an acceptable research paper? Is it plagiarism if a student does not intentionally cheat but apparently doesn't know how to write an acceptable paper? Would the problem be resolved if Steven added appropriate footnotes to the paper?

2. Steven's paper did seem to contain a few ideas of his own. Is plagiarism involved if *all* of the ideas in a paper are someone else's, but credit is given? In other words, is there a moral and intellectual difference between misrepresenting someone else's work, and complete reliance on someone else's work?

3. Because much academic work involves learning from others' arguments and ideas, exactly what is wrong with plagiarism?

4. Do colleges have a responsibility to notify students about what they will count as plagiarism? Can they enforce rules against plagiarism if they do not clearly define what it is?

There Isn't Enough to Go Around   CASE 2.6

Bruce's parents have been going over his financial aid application very carefully. In fact they have had him rewrite some sections to hide their true assets. Bruce feels a little funny about this, but his parents have explained several facts to him. First, without at least some financial aid in addition to Bruce's student loans, they cannot pay for four years of college for both him and his two siblings. Second, they feel that colleges reward middle-class people who don't save money by giving them financial aid, rather than rewarding people who've saved all they can. His mother gives him a long speech on the subject:

"We've scrimped and saved for years, putting all of our savings in a college fund for you kids since you were infants. But that money will just barely cover your educations because tuition costs have gotten way out of line! And it just kills me when I hear that our neighbors the Joneses got financial aid for Samantha. I happen to know that their income is very similar to ours, but they've never saved anything. They've always lived high off the hog, taking fancy vacations and living the good life. So of course they have no liquid assets at all now, which is exactly why Samantha qualifies for financial aid. You should get financial aid, too; if anything, we deserve it more than the Joneses because we've been planning for the future and saving as much as we could, while they spent everything."

Bruce's father adds that given the excessive cost of tuition today and shrinking government support for students, large numbers of middle-class students are unable to finish college, or they go into enormous debt to get their degrees. "When I was in school, we had the G.I. Bill to help us pay for college. It was our country's way of investing in the future. But no more! Now each individual is fighting against all the others for the limited money out there. You've got to do whatever you can to get ahead because a college degree is more important than ever today. It's all the fault of the current political climate, and those crazy Republicans. They—"

"OK, Dad, I get your point," Bruce hastily interrupts. He hates it when his father gets into one of his long-winded political tirades. And anyway, his parents have convinced him that it's fine to fudge a bit on his financial aid application.

QUESTIONS

1. Are you convinced by Bruce's parents' arguments that lying on his financial aid application is acceptable? If not, why not?

2. What ethical principles might apply to this case? How could you use them to argue for or against the morality of cheating or lying in this way?

3. Is there something unethical about the basis on which colleges award financial aid? If so, how might they assign financial aid more fairly?

4. Are there other ways that financing a college education (through loans, grants, aid, or savings) might have moral implications?

BACKGROUND READING

• For information about how the Internet has made plagiarism easy and more widespread than ever before, see "Cybercheats: Term-Paper Shopping Online: Colleges Helpless Against Internet-Aided Plagiarism," by John N. Hickman, *The New Republic*, 23 March 1998, vol. 218, no. 12, p. 14(2); "High-Tech Cheating Hits the Campus: Computers Make It Easy for College Students to Break Rules," by Victoria Benning, *The Washington Post*, 4 October 1998, p. A01; and "Students Get A+ for Easy Cheating," by Stephen Goode, *Insight on the News*, 20 September 1999, vol. 15, i. 35, p. 18. These articles describe the ease with which students today can download ready-made term papers on a huge variety of topics from more than 72 sites (up from 28 in 1997, according to Anthony Krier, a research librarian at Franklin Pierce College in New Hampshire who maintains a database of term-paper Web sites). Several of these sites claim more than a million hits, and although hits are not sales, most sell thousands of papers a year. There are also at least 38 sites where students generously make their own papers available to others for free.

Concern over Internet plagiarism has led colleges and professors to try everything from sting operations against these on-line paper mills, to installing software that scans the text of student papers and recognizes word-for-word similarities to plagiarized work as short as 32 characters long.

High-tech cheating is not limited to term papers. Students also use information from the Internet without proper attribution in their papers, get their math problems solved at special sites, post requests for homework answers on on-line message boards, and share answers and course work with others in their classes via e-mail or diskette. The computer has made cheaters out of students who otherwise would never have considered such trickery, some educators say.

• Several newspaper stories have looked at cheating on campus: Rudy Abramson, "A Matter of Honor," in *The Los Angeles Times*, 3 April 1994, sec. E, p. 1, col. 2, talks about the movement (often initiated by students) to make honor codes a fixture on more campuses. Jeff Prugh, "Extent of Cheating Isn't Easily Measured" in *The Los Angeles Times*, 3 April 1994, sec. E, p. 2, col. 2, discusses the difficulty of measuring cheating on campus and various ways in which schools are trying to deal with the problem. And Reagan Walker, "Tech Students, Faculty Consider New Honor Code to Cut Cheating," in *The Atlanta Journal and Atlanta Constitution*, 15 November 1994, sec. E, p. 2, col. 1, describes the apparently increasing frequency of cheating at colleges and the methods that one school (Georgia Tech) is considering to combat it.

• For a different perspective on cheating, see "Abigail Witherspoon" (a pseudonym), "This Pen for Hire: On Grinding Out Papers for College Students," in *Harper's Magazine*, June 1995, vol. 290, no. 1741, pp. 49–57. This slightly humorous, slightly bitter piece describes the life and moral dilemmas of a woman who writes college students' "term papers, book reports, senior theses, take-home exams" for a living.

ADDITIONAL MATERIALS

1. For articles that discuss grading practices, see "At Stanford, a Rebellion on Grades," in *The New York Times*, 31 May 1994, sec. A, p. 14, col. 6; David Margolick, "Stanford U. Decides to Make Courses Harder to Drop But Easier to Fail," in *The New York Times*, 4 June 1994, sec. A, p. 7, col. 1; Donald Kennedy, "What Grade Inflation?," in *The New York Times*, 13 June 1994, sec. A, p. 15, col. 2; and "Editorial: Making the Grade," in *The New York Times*, 5 June 1994, sec. 4, p. 16, col. 1.

Recently, Stanford University reinstated the grade of F. For about two decades, Stanford students could not fail a course. They merely did not get credit. Moreover, if they did not pass, the fact that they were enrolled in the course was not noted on their transcripts. Additionally, most students got A's and B's in their courses. Do such grading practices erode the information available in a student's transcript? Are they a form of lying by professors? Similarly, in some institutions it is rare for a professor to write a negative recommendation. What consequences might this have for the value of recommendations? Is it a form of lying?

For more information on grade inflation generally, see Carol Jouzaitis, "Easy College 'A's Become Rampant," in *The Chicago Tribune*, 4 May 1994, sec. 1, p. 1, col. 1; Anthony Flint, "Grade Inflation Losing Air at Some Colleges," in *The Boston Globe*, 4 June 1994, p. 1, col. 2; Laurel Shaper Walters, "Attention College Students: The Easy 'A' May Disappear," in *The Christian Science Monitor*, 18 October 1994, p. 1, col. 3; Gary M. Galles,

"Math-Ignorant Americans Play Games with Numbers in Order to Distort Reality," in *The Atlanta Journal*, 17 November 1994, sec. A, p. 19, col. 1; and Toby Jackson, "In the War Against Grade Inflation, Dartmouth Scores a Hit," in *The Wall Street Journal*, 8 September 1994, sec. A, p. 18, col. 3.

2. Do we even need to grade? *Punished by Rewards: The Trouble with Gold Stars, Incentive Plans, A's, Praise, and Other Bribes* by Alfie Kohn (New York: Houghton Mifflin Co., 1993) makes the provocative argument that our whole system of grading inevitably destroys interest in learning for its own sake and removes students' sense of responsibility for their own education. In short: all grading inhibits learning.

Kohn points out that most educational critics focus only on how to improve grading—compensating for grade inflation, making the grading process less arbitrary, using grading to "motivate" students—but miss what he sees as the underlying problem: all rationales for why grades are needed are "fundamentally flawed." Here are some typical ways that grades are justified:[5]

a. They make students perform better for fear of receiving a bad grade or in the hopes of getting a good one.
b. They sort students on the basis of their performance, which is useful for college and graduate school admission and job placement.
c. They provide feedback to students about how good a job they are doing and where they need improvement.

Kohn attacks each of these justifications. For number one, the "carrot and stick" rationale, he cites considerable research showing that this strategy simply doesn't work. Far from motivating students, grades "are powerful demotivators" that kill any intrinsic interest students once had in their studies and thus undermine excellence.

Rationale number two, that we need grades to sort students into what Kohn sarcastically calls "PRIME, CHOICE, SELECT, or STANDARD" categories, he refutes two ways. First, he marshals studies indicating that grades do not give businesses, colleges, and graduate schools much useful information about potential workers or students. Grades only *appear* to offer precision; in fact they are quite arbitrary, a fact that employers and universities largely recognize. Second, he cites other studies to show that using grades pits students unnecessarily against each other, discourages cooperation and teamwork, and undercuts efforts to educate.

As for the third rationale, "grading as feedback," Kohn points out that while informative feedback is important to education, "reducing someone's work to a letter or number is unnecessary and not terribly helpful." There are better ways to help students know where they stand, such as giving them

---

[5] *Punished by Rewards*, pp. 201–203.

detailed comments on papers or other exercises. What's more, the process of grading fixes students' attention on performance rather than learning, which, ironically enough, lessens performance according to many studies cited by Kohn.

3. Is cheating epidemic on campus? Professor Donald L. McCabe, Associate Provost for Campus Development and Professor of Management at Rutgers University, surveyed 1,800 students at nine medium-to-large state universities in 1993. He says that a phenomenal 87 percent of these students admitted to cheating on written work; 70 percent cheated on a test at least once (38 percent cheated on *three or more occasions*), 49 percent collaborated with others on an assignment without permission, 52 percent copied from someone, and 26 percent have plagiarized papers. More current studies confirm these findings: a 1998 survey of nearly 21,000 California students by the Josepheson Institute of Ethics in Marina del Rey found that three-quarters of all high-school and college students admit to cheating on tests and papers (and 54 percent of middle-school students do).

It hasn't always been that way. Surveys of college students in the 1940s showed that only 20 percent admitted to having cheated in high school, according to Stephen Davis, psychology professor at Emporia State University in Kansas. The steep increase in cheating in high schools and colleges didn't happen until the late 1960s and early 1970s, when it fluctuated between 75 percent and 98 percent of college students. And rates haven't fallen since.

Some things have changed, though. In the past, it was the less academically talented students who were most likely to cheat, the ones for whom book learning did not come easily. Now the best students are doing the cheating: those most likely to go to college, and consequently eager to line up A's and B's on their report cards. A poll of 3,123 students on the 1998 list of *Who's Who Among American High School Students*—the "best" of the nation's 16- to 18-year-olds—found that a whopping 80 percent of them admitted to cheating in some form to get to the top of their class. Of those who cheated, 95 percent said they'd never been caught, and a majority declared that they were untroubled by their behavior.

Also changed is the gender of cheaters. Thirty years ago, the vast majority of students who admitted to cheating were male. In most contemporary studies, little or no difference exists between the numbers of dishonest males and females.

Students justify cheating in numerous ways, among them that cheating in high school is to get the grades needed for college, while cheating in college is to help a career. Many students excuse themselves by pointing to well-known figures in government, sports, and other facets of life whose ethics are questionable.

Some people feel that current high rates of cheating are also the result of the timid way schools have been dealing with cheaters. Despite written policies and official rhetoric, many schools are now less willing to ferret out and punish cheaters. "Schools are not anxious to expend the effort required, and they don't want to expose themselves to lawsuits," says McCabe. Furthermore, professors often believe that "if they challenge a student for academic dishonesty, they themselves will wind up being the ones on trial," McCabe notes, referring to a 1992 survey of 800 faculty members at 16 institutions. Glenn M. Ricketts, a spokesman for the National Association of Scholars, adds that cheating is "difficult to prove, and the administration places such heavy emphasis on retention. Enrollments are low and administrators don't want to alienate people or upset other students." Jerry L. Martin, president of the American Council of Trustees and Alumni (formerly the National Alumni Forum), adds, "Professors are more intimidated now by students than ever before. They're worried about offending them, worried about making them unhappy."

Do these figures and attitudes about cheating seem consistent with what you know of your school? It has been found that the major predictor for the amount of cheating on a campus is the school's "cheating culture," that is, how common and acceptable cheating seems to be among the students there. How would you characterize your own campus's "cheating culture"?

Many ideas have been proposed for reducing cheating, ranging from an ad campaign sponsored by the Educational Testing Service (designer of SAT, PSAT, and GRE tests) to a teacher's requirement that students either sign a pledge saying, "On my honor I've read/not read this whole book" or be docked points off their grades. Whose responsibility should it be to discourage or punish cheating—college administrators'? Students'? Professors'? Honor boards'? Some other group's? Who benefits from reduced cheating? What steps might students and faculty take to reduce cheating at your school?

Sources: "Students Are Pulling Off the Big Cheat: College Cheating Rising," by Carol Innerst, *Insight on the News*, 9 March 1998, vol. 14, no. 9, p. 41(1); "Students Get A+ for Easy Cheating," by Stephen Goode, *Insight on the News*, 20 September 1999, vol. 15, i. 35, p. 18; and "Letter to All Faculty Members," by Kuan Wong and Gary Pavela, Office of Judicial Programs, University of Maryland at College Park, 1 December 1994.

3

TOLERANCE, DIVERSITY, AND HATE SPEECH

Hate Speech   CASE 3.1

Jake was a white male sophomore at Pinecrest College. He was viewed by his friends as a nice guy when he was sober, which was most of the time. However, when he got drunk he often embarrassed his friends, and some of them simply refused to go out drinking with him. He was not a violent drunk, but alcohol certainly weakened his normal verbal inhibitions. After a few beers he often became belligerent and offensive to friends and strangers alike.

Saturday night Jake went out drinking with a few friends after a basketball game. Pinecrest had won, which was a rare occasion this year, and a celebration seemed in order. The celebration lasted for several hours, and Jake lost count of the number of beers he had consumed. The mood was light until Jake and his friends headed back to their dorm. On the way there, they passed a group of African American students walking in the other direction.

Jake, rather unsteady on his feet, didn't seem to notice the other students until they passed by. But as their conversation faded behind Jake and his friends, he started off on a tirade against blacks that grew gradually louder and more offensive; it culminated in a stream of racial insults shouted at no one in particular. Jake's friends tried to quiet him down, without much success. Finally they steered him to his room and left him there.

Jake didn't stay. He seemed to need an audience for his drunken harangue. After stewing for a few minutes, he went out to find one. Unfortunately, he succeeded.

The police report read as follows:

"At approximately 2 A.M. Sunday, I received a call that there was someone standing outside the African-American Study Center, screaming racial abuse. When I arrived, I found Jake Miller, 18, standing in the center of a small crowd, arguing with several minority students. Apparently these students were still at the center studying for a Monday exam. A number of other students, on their way home from Saturday night partying, had stopped to watch. Miller was clearly drunk and was yelling obscenities and racial epithets in a very loud voice. His main target seemed to be the minority students who had been in the center, but he had also made loud and vulgar remarks about gays and several other groups. While no violence had occurred, it was clear that the situation was volatile. Some students were responding to Miller in kind, and others were urging him on. I arrested Miller for disturbing the peace. Once I had him in custody, the other students quieted down and left, so I saw no reason for further action."

The arresting officer was a patrolman on the municipal police force of the town surrounding Pinecrest College. Jake had been charged by the town with disturbing the peace. It seemed likely that he would plead guilty and receive a suspended sentence. However, Jake had also been charged by the college with hate speech, which could carry a much stiffer penalty.

Pinecrest College's official Code of Conduct contains the following statement:

Pinecrest College attempts to create an educational environment that is open to the widest possible range of ideas. However, it believes that speech that serves primarily to denigrate the dignity or worth of other members of the community serves no intellectual purpose, functions to silence the voices of minority groups, and undermines the climate of civility, openness, and respect that is required for free discussion and the pursuit of truth. Therefore, speech that denigrates members of the Pinecrest community on account of their race, religion, ethnicity, gender, national origin, or sexual orientation is forbidden. Members of the community who engage in such speech may be punished by community service, suspension, probation, or expulsion.

Later in the week, an African American student wrote home:

Dear Mom and Dad,

When I come home for break, I want to talk with you about transferring to another school. I don't think I can stand to be at this place another semester. The racism is just overwhelming.

Earlier this week, while I was studying at the center, some white drunk started yelling racial insults in the courtyard. Some of my friends went out and yelled back. I'm glad they did. Somebody needed to respond, but I couldn't. Fighting back just takes too much energy. I can't live where I have to be angry all of the time.

This is the third incident I know about this year. Earlier someone spray-painted some stuff on the wall of the center, and one of my friends had a note that said "Kill the Niggers" tacked to her dorm door.

What makes it worse is the reaction of the whites. My white friends usually tell me that I shouldn't care what a few jerks say and insist that most white people aren't racists. Maybe, but I wonder how they'd feel if someone threatened to kill them because of their race? The university seems to think that this is an issue about free speech. All they want to talk about is "how the First Amendment protects even offensive speech." They don't want to talk about racism. The prof in my government class is the worst. He made this incident a discussion topic in class. I don't remember exactly what he said. He was his usual confusing self. What I do remember is how white people were "US" and black people were "THEM" and how everything was about how "WE" should treat "THEM." The prof singled me out after class (there's only one other black kid in the class) to ask why I was so quiet. "Don't you have some thoughts on the topic?" he wanted to know. Well, I do have more than a few. But I didn't feel like either telling him or representing "THEM" to all the whites in the class. If anyone's free speech here needs protecting, I think it's mine. How can I talk in the climate of racism here, and why should I have to be the voice of "THEM"?

Mom and Dad, I'm tired of being "THEM." Everything that happens here makes me feel as though I don't belong. I need to consider going someplace where I can be "US" for a while.

Love,
Nelson

Questions

1. There is a child's saying: "Sticks and stones may break my bones, but names will never hurt me." It is almost certainly false. How do names hurt?

2. Words not only can hurt, they can exclude. How does hate speech exclude?

3. What issues of free speech are raised by regulations prohibiting hate speech? Does hate speech act to deny a voice to those it targets?

4. How can "US versus THEM" assumptions be avoided in classroom discussions? Should they always be avoided?

5. Are there positive steps Pinecrest could take to promote racial understanding and to diminish hate speech that do not involve bans against certain forms of speech? What might they be?

ISSUES

We hope that most of our readers believe there is something unethical about Jake Miller's conduct. Perhaps, however, it is less clear what this something is. The statement about hate speech in Pinecrest's Code of Conduct offers two suggestions.

One is that hate speech is immoral because it denies the dignity and worth of the people it targets; it thus violates the principle of *equal respect*. (This argument also applies more generally to racism, homophobia, sexism, and any other form of intolerance.)

The second objection to hate speech is that it aims to exclude the people it is directed at from participating in the *community*. It does this by making them outcasts and denying them an authentic voice in the community's conversations. Nelson's letter to his parents expresses these feelings.

Our society has been very reluctant to regulate speech of any sort. It has tended to think that the benefits of free speech are great enough to outweigh the occasional harm that can result from unlimited free speech. This is especially true of academic communities, which are inclined to believe that truth is best discovered in free and open debate. Colleges and universities have thus been very reluctant to limit the expression of unpopular views.

John Stuart Mill described the idea that the pursuit of truth requires free and open discussion in a classic statement:

> We have now recognized the necessity to the mental well-being of mankind (on which all their other well-being depends) of freedom of opinion, and freedom of expression of opinion, on four distinct grounds, which we will now briefly recapitulate:
>
> First, if any opinion is compelled to silence, that opinion may, for aught we can certainly know, be true. To deny this is to assume our own infallibility.
>
> Second, though the silenced opinion be an error, it may, and very commonly does, contain a portion of truth; and since the general or prevailing opinion on any subject is rarely or never the whole truth, it is only by the collision of adverse opinions that the remainder of the truth has any chance of being supplied.
>
> Thirdly, even if the received opinion be not only true, but the whole truth; unless it is suffered to be, and actually is, vigorously and earnestly contested, it will, by most of those who receive it, be held in the manner of a prejudice, with little comprehension or feeling of its rational grounds. And not only this, but, fourthly, the meaning of the doctrine itself will be in danger of being lost or enfeebled, and deprived of its vital effect on the character and conduct: the dogma becoming a mere formal profession, inefficacious for good, but cumbering the ground and preventing the growth of any real and heartfelt conviction from reason or personal experience. (Mill, *On Liberty*, p. 64)

Like Mill, Pinecrest College values free and open debate. But unlike Mill, the college seems to believe that it is necessary to limit some kinds of speech. Pinecrest assumes that since hate speech hinders real debate (it shuts people out of the conversation, and it damages the civil atmosphere needed for a fruitful exchange of ideas), it is necessary to ban such speech. In effect, the Pinecrest Code of Conduct hate speech regulations say that if we want free and open debate, we have to exclude some voices from the debate so that other voices will not be intimidated from participating.

Do you agree with this reasoning? Does "free speech" mean completely unregulated speech—anyone can say anything they please—or does it mean regulating speech so that more people feel free to participate? Are there other alternatives?

We should also consider what we mean by "hate speech." Here are a few examples of controversial views that have been argued in recent years:

- People of European descent are "ice people." They are morally and intellectually inferior to darker-skinned "sun people" because of a deficiency of melanin.
- Catholics cannot be good Americans because they owe allegiance to a foreign ruler, the Pope.
- Homosexuality is a sin and a perversion, not a lifestyle choice or an innate orientation.
- Poor blacks are not poor because of white racism. They are poor because of their high rate of illegitimacy.
- All Muslims and people of Arabic descent support terrorism.

Would you classify any of these statements as examples of hate speech? Might they be under some circumstances? Would any of them be punishable under Pinecrest College's policy? Should they be?

Note that there may be a significant difference between these views and Jake Miller's diatribe. Jake's harangue has an "in your face" character that the views expressed above do not have. That is, Jake is not merely expressing views that might be viewed as intolerant and racist; he is shouting racial slurs at particular individuals whom his insults are meant to hurt. His harangue thus goes beyond intolerant speech into "harassment" or "fighting words." Is the distinction between views that might be considered "racist" or "intolerant," and "harassment" or "fighting words," important? Could a college or university write a prohibition against hate speech based on this distinction?

APPLYING ETHICAL PRINCIPLES TO THE CASE

Pinecrest's Code of Conduct seems to rely on the principle of *equal respect* when it says that hate speech "denigrates the dignity and worth" of its victims. If we all have intrinsic worth, no matter what our race, sex, religion, or sexual orientation is, then speech that denies equal respect to anyone because of these personal characteristics must be unethical.

Is speech that denigrates people because of personal characteristics such as race, religion, ethnicity, gender, national origin, or sexual orientation more harmful than other kinds of hurtful speech? After all, many other personal characteristics could be used in insults: obesity, baldness, intelligence, height, wealth, and so on. Is it less offensive to insult someone because of her weight than because of her race? Why or why not? And consider the fact that some types of hate speech are true—people who are attacked because of their weight generally *are* obese. Can asserting the truth count as hate speech? Does it violate the idea of equal respect? Just how do words harm people?

Pinecrest's Code of Conduct also suggests that hate speech violates the principle of *community*, by "undermining the climate of civility, openness, and respect . . . required for free discussion and the pursuit of truth" that is essential in a college community. The college community is also damaged, the Code of Conduct implies, because hate speech tends to silence the voices of its targets and exclude them from the community's discussions. Intolerance can exclude people from such discussions in subtle, as well as obvious, ways. Would you be willing to participate in a group that seemed to devalue you or what you said? Are there other ways people can be hindered from contributing their views?

The feeling of community among a group can also be disrupted by other kinds of speech than hate speech, such as by "us" versus "them" talk, or by arguments that someone is wrong about something, or by criticisms of certain kinds of behavior associated with some particular subgroup. Would a hate speech prohibition forbid these kinds of speech? Should it?

We all like feeling part of a community of "us." Is it wrong to feel closer to people who are like ourselves (however we define this)? When does identification with people like "us" become intolerance? In his letter to his parents, Nelson claims that his white government teacher's speech patterns and behavior define Nelson and other black students as "the Other" and exclude them from the college community. In other words, Nelson believes his teacher is—perhaps unconsciously—racist. Do you think Nelson is right? Is talk of "us" versus "them" always intolerant? Can you think of some teaching practices that might tend to exclude a group of (potential) students? What kinds of teaching practices might be more inclusive?

In an academic community, might there be occasions when it is appropriate to associate with people who share your race, religion, ethnicity, or sex, and other occasions when doing so would violate the shared goals of the college or university community? If so, how do we decide which is which? (See Additional Cases 3.3 and 3.4 in this chapter.)

WORKING OUT SOLUTIONS

We can probably all agree that hate speech is immoral. But we may well disagree about whether it should be regulated, and how. (The fact that something is immoral may not be a reason to make it illegal. Can you think of some examples?) Let's consider an argument against regulating hate speech:

The problem with penalizing hate speech is that it attaches penalties to the content of speech. This is a bad idea in a free society that wants to protect free speech, and an especially bad idea in an academic community that values the pursuit of truth. A college can't say that it is important to protect people's right to make unpopular arguments, while also saying that some kinds of speech are just too hateful to be tolerated. The boundaries between an unpopular opinion and hate speech are just too vague. If what is forbidden isn't clear, then all controversial speech will be in jeopardy. So if we want colleges to be places where people can freely and openly debate ideas, we must also tolerate hate speech. This is the price of intellectual freedom.

This argument, following Mill, defends what may be the conventional view about how to maintain the climate of openness necessary for truly free speech. Can you state the assumptions it makes? If we agree with this argument, it follows that Jake should not be punished for his behavior.

But if we follow the Pinecrest College Code of Conduct's definition of hate speech, it seems pretty clear that Jake must be punished for his actions, with "community service, suspension, probation, or expulsion." Which punishment do you think would be appropriate in this case? Are there other ways that Pinecrest can deal with hate speech? Are there educational solutions to hate speech? Some religious communities deal with members whom they see as having engaged in sinful behavior by shunning them. Should Jake be shunned and ignored by everyone on campus? Do you think such treatment would be more, or less, effective and appropriate than the ones mentioned above? Can you think of some alternative to punishment that would be better? Explain what you prefer, and why, by appealing to some of the ethical principles described in the introduction of this book.

Some colleges have tried to ban hate speech by writing regulations that assume that what is important is not *what* is said (the content of speech), but the *manner* in which it's said. What are the pros and cons of this approach? Look at the following examples of college codes regarding hate speech, and see how they differ. Do any of them succeed in resolving the tension between banning hate speech and protecting free speech? How do they each reflect the principles of *community* and *equal respect?*

EXAMPLES OF COLLEGE AND UNIVERSITY CODES REGARDING HATE SPEECH

1. Excerpt from the Code of Student Conduct of The University of Pennsylvania[1]

I. Preamble

The University of Pennsylvania is a community in which intellectual growth, learning from others, mutual tolerance, and respect for freedom of thought and expression are principles of paramount importance. In an environment that promotes the free exchange of ideas, cultural and intellectual diversity, and a wealth of social opportunities, Penn students take advantage of the academic and non-academic opportunities available to them. [. . .]

II. Rights of Student Citizenship

Membership in the University of Pennsylvania community affords every student certain rights that are essential to the University's educational mission and its character as a community:

[. . .]

(b) The right to freedom of expression.

(c) The right to be free of discrimination on the basis of race, color, gender, sexual orientation, religion, national or ethnic origin, age, disability, or status as a disabled or Vietnam Era veteran. [. . .]

III. Responsibilities of Student Citizenship

Students are expected to exhibit responsible behavior regardless of time or place. Failure to do so may result in disciplinary action by the University. Responsible behavior is a standard of conduct which reflects higher expectations than may be prevalent outside the University community. Responsible behavior includes but is not limited to the following obligations:

[. . .]

(c) To respect the right of fellow students to participate in university organizations and in relationships with other students without fear, threat, or act of hazing.

(d) To refrain from conduct towards other students that infringes upon the Rights of Student Citizenship. The University condemns hate speech, epithets, and racial, ethnic, sexual and religious slurs. However, the content of student speech or expression is not by itself a basis for disciplinary action. Student speech may be subject to discipline when it violates applicable laws or University regulations or policies.

---

[1] *The PennBook 1994–95; Policies and Procedures Handbook*, University of Pennsylvania (Office of the President, 1994), p. 16.

(A National Public Radio broadcast on 18 Nov. 1994 focused on reactions to this controversial policy. A transcript [\$10] or tape [\$12] of the program is available from National Public Radio Tapes and Transcripts, Washington DC 20036, or (202) 822-2323. See also the npr.com Web site.)

2. Excerpt from the UNH policy on nonsexist language of the University of New Hampshire[2]

The University of New Hampshire, as an equal opportunity educational institution, is committed both to academic freedom and the fair treatment of all individuals. It therefore discourages the use of language and illustrations that reinforce inappropriate and demeaning attitudes, assumptions, and stereotypes about sex roles. Accordingly; all official University communications, whether delivered orally or in writing, shall be free of sexist language.

3. Excerpt from Howard University's Student Code of Conduct[3]

Howard University affirms that the central purpose of a university is the pursuit of truth, the discovery of new knowledge through scholarly research, the teaching and overall development of students, and the transmission of knowledge and learning to the world at large. The establishment and maintenance of a community where there is freedom to teach and learn, however, is dependent on maintaining an appropriate sense of order that allows for the pursuit of these objectives in an environment that is both safe and free of invidious disruption.

[. . .] It is expected that student conduct will be in concert with and supportive of the University's central purpose and core values.

[. . .] The following is an illustration of the types of conduct that are prohibited by this Code. It includes not only actual conduct, but also attempts to engage in such conduct. [. . .]

3. Discrimination

Engaging in verbal or physical behavior directed at an individual or group that, according to a person of reasonable sensibilities, is likely to create an intimidating or demeaning environment that impedes the access of other students, faculty and staff to the educational benefits available from or through the University.

---

[2] "Administrative Policies and Regulation" from the *2000–2001 University of New Hampshire Student Rights, Rules and Responsibilities* (Division of Student Affairs), p. 36.

[3] *2000–01 Howard University Student Handbook & Planner.* Office of Student Activities, Howard University, pp. 93, 105, 125. Howard University is a historically black university in Washington, DC.

4. Harassment

Engaging in verbal, electronic, visual, written, or physical behavior directed at an individual or group that, according to a person of reasonable sensibilities, is likely to provoke or otherwise result in negative or injurious response or reaction. This behavior may include:

A. Making an expressed or implied threat affecting another person's academic pursuits, University employment, or participation in activities sponsored by the University or organizations or groups related to the University, or;

B. Engaging in unwarranted retribution or interference with respect to such pursuits, employment, or participation, or;

C. Creating an intimidating or demeaning situation or environment or inflicting psychological or emotional harm, or undue stress.

Academic Freedom

It is the policy of the University to afford faculty with a fair opportunity to teach and conduct research and to provide services to the community in a setting that provides the academic freedom necessary to cultivate a wide expanse of ideas and teaching methods. It is not the intent of this Policy to inhibit the expression of such ideas or the use of such methods, provided that they are expressed or used in a manner that is consistent with the legitimate rights of students.

ADDITIONAL CASES

CASE 3.2   *The Canon*

Columbia College has long required all freshmen to take a Great Books course that has a reading list made up of canonical western writers. Recently, critics have noted that the required readings are, without exception, from "dead white males," and they are arguing for a more inclusive list that would include works by white women and male and female writers of color. In the Tuesday morning section of the Great Books course, Professor Schueller (a not-quite-dead, middle-aged white male) is arguing with Simone (an articulate and outspoken female African American student) about the choice of books in the course. The atmosphere is charged, and the other students are listening intently.

Simone heatedly asks, "What about *my* people while all this was going on? We were here in America, too, but you'd never know it from what we've been reading!" Professor Schueller responds that "they *were* here, and they played a big role in actually building the country and in creating its folk culture, popular speech, humor, and music. But they just didn't influence major

American political, legal, and economic institutions. That's what this course is about: studying the major works in the western tradition that influenced our national institutions."

Simone, however, refuses to back down in the face of Professor Schueller's calm explanation. "I know there have been important black writers, such as W. E. B. Dubois, who did influence things. How come we just ignore them? I feel that this course is trying to say that black people, including me, just don't count."

A white student sitting near Simone adds, "The same thing is true about women in general! How are we supposed to feel good about ourselves if everything we read suggests that women have made no contributions?"

QUESTIONS

1. Professor Schueller argues for sticking to the (white male) classics on the basis of their supposed historical influence, while his students argue against them because of the damage they supposedly do to non-represented students' self-esteem. Are minority and women students "oppressed" by being made to read works that don't "represent" them?

2. Does this logic discourage them from reading the same masterpieces that their parents and grandparents had no chance to read because overt racism and sexism kept them from higher education?

3. Should teaching primarily build students' self-esteem or impart "facts"?

4. Would reading works by women and people of color mainly benefit students with the same backgrounds, or would it benefit all students, including white males? Why or why not?

Self-Segregation   CASE 3.3

Like many college campuses across the country, North Carolina State has had a Black Cultural Center since the early 1970s. N.C. State's decision to move the center from a suite in the Student Annex to a new, freestanding building sparked debate among students and faculty. Seniors Kevin and Tony each wrote editorials to the student newspaper, arguing opposite sides of the issue. Their comments are excerpted here.[4]

Kevin's Piece:

On the surface, the Black Cultural Center (BCC) sounds like a good idea. Why shouldn't our Black students have a place to fraternize and study, and our African American program have a place to hold classes? [. . . .] Dig a little deeper, however, and you will find that not only is it a bad idea, it goes against the beliefs of those who fought for civil rights. Furthermore, such a center would tear at the seams of cultural unity.

[4] Excerpted from Kevin Ryan and Tony Williamson, "A Difference of Opinion," in *The Cornell Political Forum*, December 1993, vol. VIII, no. 2, pp. 25–26.

Why should North Carolina's students be separated on the basis of race? Martin Luther King, Andrew Young, and others who fought in the South wanted to insure that this generation would not be segregated. [. . . .] The debate is reminiscent of the separate but equal status of Blacks in the 1950s and '60s, but now it is Blacks arguing for segregation, not whites. [. . . .]

[. . .] I understand that the BCC will serve as an educational resource for the campus at large. But will the BCC actually strive for equality and education or will it further segregation? [. . . .]

[. . .] [A]ny person who opposes the building of the new Center is labeled a racist. In a time when students have to deal with crowded dining halls, cancelled classes and journals, and the loss of good professors to more affluent institutions, why should we pay for a duplication of services? In other words, we do not need a second student center when there are already libraries, auditoriums, and office space on campus.

Tony's piece:

Before we can all "get along," we have to know and appreciate each other's differences. The Black Cultural Center is a place where everyone can learn about the rich African American heritage. [. . . .]

[. . .] Thus, the Center provides a foundation for something that is sorely missing not only on college campuses, but in society as a whole—racial harmony.

African Americans, who have to face the daily pressures of being a minority and the frustrations of being excluded from the history and culture of America, need an outlet for self-identity and assurance. A cultural center provides such an outlet [. . . .] Since it has been proven that high self-confidence contributes to a student's academic success, the Black Cultural Center also enhances academic performance. [. . . .]

[. . .] People who are ignorant of cultural centers' functions within universities believe that they are merely havens of segregation and racism. These people fail to understand African Americans' severe need for self-identity. After all, no other race in American history has had to suffer through slavery. Some of the results of slavery (deprivation of self-knowledge, separation of family, self-hatred) still affect the African American community. The cultural center is a place where African Americans can redefine themselves through self-knowledge and expression. In essence, the Black Cultural Center is a reflection of African Americans' struggle for equality. It has nothing to do with racism. The presence of a cultural center on campus contributes to social equality. [. . . .]

[. . .] There should be a Black Cultural Center at every school in the United States; not because America owes something to African Americans, but because it has an obligation to provide all students with the chance to learn about and appreciate other cultures. [. . . .]

QUESTIONS

1. Evaluate Kevin's and Tony's arguments on the basis of the ethical principles discussed in Chapter 1. Do the two students' arguments appeal to different principles?

2. Does racial segregation on campus protect minority identity, build self-worth, raise achievement levels, and give students the support they need in a hostile world (as proponents of separate student centers or dorms, like Tony, argue)? Or does it destroy minority students' self-worth, lower their achievement levels, make their entry into mainstream society difficult, and cause them to feel like pariahs, as the Supreme Court's 1954 arguments against educational segregation in *Brown v. Board of Education* insisted?

3. How might self-segregation differ from imposed segregation? Does white students' self-segregation differ in its causes or effects from self-segregation practiced by minority students? How?

4. Historically black and female colleges were expected to disappear in the 1970s and '80s. Instead many seem to have gained new support and vigor (for example, see "Black Colleges in Demand as Never Before" in *The New York Times*, 2 January 1993, p. 1). At the same time, historically all-white and all-male colleges seem to have desegregated or gone co-ed. How might you explain these different results of the civil rights and women's movements? Do minorities and women somehow have more "right" (or more need) to self-segregate than white males?

5. Under court order to desegregate, many historically black colleges have tried to attract more white students while still maintaining their programs and cultural orientation focused on the African American experience. Is this a coherent project? If it's legitimate for a college to emphasize the African American experience, why should it have to desegregate? And if historically black colleges should desegregate, then what's the point of emphasizing the African American experience?

6. Is self-segregation by gender (such as same-sex dorms, women's centers, or women's colleges) different from racial or cultural self-segregation? If yes, how?

7. Construct your own case about a separate dorm for gay students. Would your analysis of this case differ from your analysis of the African American students' "self-segregation" case above?

Cafeteria Friendships CASE 3.4

Mary King, Director of Student Affairs at Jefferson County Community College, has noticed something that disturbs her every time she eats in the student dining hall. Unlike most of her fellow staff members (who avoid the student cafeteria), Mary enjoys mingling socially with students and trying to get to know them outside of office hours, and she thinks this is part of her job. When she takes her tray from the serving line and looks for students to join for lunch, she tries to scan the entire cafeteria first, to see who might need a friend or want to talk to her.

Over the loud clatter of silverware and even louder babble of talking, she sees a striking pattern: every table seems to be made up of students from the same racial group, and usually the same age group as well. Whites and blacks, Asians and Hispanics, older students and younger students—each group has its own table or tables, which might as well have "reserved for young Hispanics" or "reserved for older white students" on them. All of the students seem to sit consistently with people just like themselves. The groups even seem to dress similarly, such as the table of young white slackers to her left, and the conservatively dressed immigrant students at the table to her right.

Mary feels that segregated seating and segregated friendships are almost as harmful to students' personal growth and the promotion of a sense of unity and harmony on campus as official segregation would be. She explains her observations to the dean: "The cafeteria is only the most obvious place to see this segregation. If you look at students walking around campus or at sport events, the groups are just as separate. I'm told they even tend to sit in different parts of the same classroom! Just because no one's officially *keeping* students apart doesn't mean that racism and mutual distrust aren't being promoted by this pervasive unofficial segregation. If Jefferson really wants to promote tolerance and equal opportunity for all, the way we say we do, we have to do something about this situation."

QUESTIONS

1. Is de facto ("in fact" or unofficial) segregation similar in its harmful effects to de jure ("by law" or legalized) segregation?

2. Should institutions such as Jefferson County Community College intervene in what seem to be students' natural friendship patterns? If they should, what could Jefferson College (or Mary) do? When, if ever, do private choices like whom to sit next to, or date, become the business of the college community?

3. When does feeling closer to people like yourself become racism?

4. If Jefferson College, and the county itself, have a history of serious racial and ethnic tension, would mixing student groups and trying to promote intergroup friendships be more necessary (as well as more difficult)?

CASE 3.5 *Long-Lost Friend*

Megan and Greg hadn't seen each other since eighth grade, when they went to different schools. Megan still remembered Greg vividly, though. He was her best buddy from ages nine to thirteen, the person who made her laugh the hardest and think the deepest. They told each other secrets that they had never told anyone else. And Greg's family always seemed warmer and more open than her own. She used to wonder whether all black families were like his, and all white families like hers; secretly she thought it would be nicer to be black. When Greg went out of her life, Megan had gone through a big change—whether because of not having him around anymore or because of just growing up, she wasn't sure. At any rate, she stopped climbing trees, fishing in the creek, and playing one-on-one basketball and started hanging out at the mall. It was funny, but Megan had also never had a close black friend again. However, she still thought of those years with Greg as the happiest and most carefree of her life.

Why hadn't they kept in touch, she wondered? They had lived in the same suburb all those years between eighth grade and now. She was feeling nostalgic after her first year away from home, and she suddenly thought, "I should just write and tell him to come visit me here at college!"

Now she was waiting at the bus station. Greg's bus was due any minute, and Megan found herself surprisingly nervous. Maybe she hadn't visited Greg or his family all those years because she'd started to realize that white girls weren't supposed to be best friends with black boys. Maybe she'd unconsciously started to feel that as she got closer to dating age, she should stick to her own kind. Maybe she and Greg wouldn't even recognize each other—what if he'd turned into some kind of scary dude who resented her and her white privileges? And what would her (all white) friends think of him? It might be so awkward! On the other hand, what if he were still Greg and they could take up where they left off? Maybe he could help her deal with her guilty feelings about race and lost innocence. Or maybe he would think it was racist of her to want to talk to him about race . . . With Megan's thoughts in this confused muddle, Greg's bus finally arrived.

QUESTIONS

1. Megan seems to blame herself for the fact that she and Greg have drifted apart; however, despite years of official desegregation, most Americans draw most of their friends from their own racial group. What kinds of external pressures might have pushed Greg and Megan apart?

2. Do individuals of good will have a duty to try to establish or maintain friendships across racial lines? Is it racist to value a friendship (largely, or in part) *because* it is with a person of another race?

3. Is it appropriate for Megan to try to sort out her "white guilt" with Greg because he's a person of color, or is it her job to do this work on her own (or with a therapist, minister, rabbi, or close friend)?

CASE 3.6   *Consciousness-Raising*

Because of past tensions on campus, Northlake University recently instituted a required week-long orientation program for all prospective dorm students. The program featured a variety of activities, from noncompetitive games and evening dances to workshops on racism, sexism, and homophobia, and presentations about multiculturalism. The university designed the program "to promote tolerance and acceptance of difference among the diverse population of students who share dorm life," but it did not seem to be having this effect with some students. In fact, midway through the week, a sensitivity-training workshop brought on a heated argument between two students.

Jerry, who sensed that his conservative religious views were not shared by many other students, saw the whole program as indoctrination into bizarre left–liberal views, amounting to reverse discrimination against religious white males like himself. "It seems to me that the main point of all this 'consciousness-raising' is to make white guys feel as humiliated and oppressed as minorities and gays and women say they are," he said angrily. "It's not *my* fault they've had a hard time. I feel as though I'm supposed to apologize for being male, heterosexual, and white, if I want to live in the dorms!"

Isabella, a Latina psychology major, saw the workshops as personally empowering and valuable for building up empathy and esprit de corps among diverse dorm students. "You seem to feel threatened by people different from yourself," she replied in her best therapeutic manner. "If you want to get along in the dorm you have to accept the truth about your privileged position in society, and work to be less racist, homophobic, and sexist, and more empathetic."

Jerry blew up at what he saw as her condescension and insults. "Oh, right! Being persecuted is supposed to make me more empathetic. I don't *want* to get along with people who call me racist and sexist when they don't even know me! You and your politically correct friends can keep the dorms. I'm going to live off campus!" And with that, he stalked out of the room.

After a moment of shocked silence among the remaining students, Isabella said, "Well, it's too bad he can't handle it, but he probably couldn't handle living with diverse people in the dorm either."

QUESTIONS

1. Is there anything Northlake University can do to improve the orientation program so that it really does "promote tolerance and acceptance of difference" of all students? Or is Isabella right that some straight white males will inevitably feel threatened when previously disenfranchised groups assert their right to equal participation?

2. Consider the situation if Jerry's religious beliefs require that he not tolerate some other students. For example, if Jerry believes the Bible teaches that homosexuality is sinful and homosexuals should be

shunned, is the university unlawfully discriminating against his religion if it requires that he accept gay students as the price of living in the dorms?

3. What if his antigay (or antiblack, or antiwoman) beliefs were based on personal feelings and fears instead of on religion—would the school have more, or less, reason to try to change them?

4. Are students entitled to hold racist, sexist, homophobic, or otherwise offensive beliefs, so long as they don't seem to be hurting anyone? Or might these attitudes cause pain and division even if they are not expressed in hate speech or violence? Does an educational institution have a duty to try to uproot intolerance and to promote mutual understanding in an increasingly diverse society? (See Chapter 9.)

5. Northlake insists that Jerry (and all students) respect the rights of homosexual members of the University community. Is this the same as insisting that Jerry accept gay men or women as friends or approve of gay lifestyles? Can Northlake insist that the rights of gays and lesbians be respected without seeking broader acceptance for them? Should Northlake show any kind of respect for Jerry's religious views?

The Christmas Party   CASE 3.7

Nicole thought she was the only student living in Rockwell Hall who felt excluded by the dorm's upcoming annual Christmas party. Brightly printed fliers had been up for weeks advertising the fun: "Christmas caroling, Santa Claus, tree trimming, hot chocolate and cookies, and other holiday cheer." She had tried to explain to her roommate that she didn't feel comfortable going but also was sorry to miss out on the dorm's biggest party of the year. "Well, why don't you come then?" her roommate had asked. "It doesn't matter if you don't know any carols—I'm sure everyone will be glad to teach them to you. It'll be fun!"

Nicole didn't know how to explain to her well-meaning roommate that that wasn't the problem. She'd certainly heard carols before, but it felt wrong for her as a Jew (even a quite unobservant one) to sing about "Jesus the Son of God." She felt uneasy listening to everyone else sing praises to "Christ the Lord," too. And the presence of someone dressed as Santa Claus would be an unhappy reminder of the pained looks on her parents' faces when, as a child, she'd come home from school crying and asked why they couldn't be Christians so that Santa would visit them too.

Now Nicole discovered someone else who felt upset by Rockwell's Christmas party plans. Fatima, a Muslim student on the second floor, agreed that the dorm's holiday festivities inadvertently made non-Christians feel slighted and left out. "My friends have told me that there won't be anything especially Christian about the party—no crosses or nativity scenes or anything. They just don't get it. There's no way a Christmas party won't be Christian, and uncomfortable for me, even if they don't mean it to be. And what's even worse," Fatima added angrily, "this Christmas party is blowing a major chunk of the dorm's activities fund for the whole semester! *Our* money is helping to pay for a party that leaves us out."

QUESTIONS

1. Should Nicole and Fatima lighten up and go to the party, ignoring aspects of it that displease them, or are they right to feel hurt and excluded?

2. If their grievance seems legitimate, what should they do—find some other entertainment by themselves the night of the party, go to the party and protest the aspects of it that offend them, or do something else to raise others' consciousness of the problem?

3. Which ethical principles are at stake in this case, and how might Nicole and Fatima appeal to them in arguing for a more inclusive party?

4. Do the Rockwell Hall party planners have a responsibility to make the holiday party feel inclusive to everyone? If so, should they try to make the affair combine elements of different religious traditions, or make sure that it completely avoids references to any particular religion? Are there other options?

5. Is it possible to have a "holiday party" that doesn't offend any group?

6. Would the problem be alleviated if the money for the party came not from common funds, but privately from the pockets of a few wealthy students who invited all the rest?

CASE 3.8 *Racism or Self-Sabotage?*

Kweisi is an 18-year-old black freshman in his first semester at college, majoring in African-American Studies and apparently doing well. Nonetheless his freshman faculty advisor, Prof. James McWhorter, is concerned about Kweisi's future.

Professor McWhorter describes his worry to a colleague over lunch.

"This kid Kweisi came in and told me he considers himself 'black identified' and that he thinks the whole college is 'racist.' I tried to get him to tell me what had happened, why he thought that, but all he'd say was, 'it isn't one thing; it's everything.' And since then I've been thinking: You know, all of the classes Kweisi's taking are in the African-American Studies Department. He lives on an all-black dormitory floor. And as far as I can tell, every one of his friends is black, or a 'black identified' Hispanic. So Kweisi's completely separated himself from anyone or anything white at college—it's like he's stuck himself in some little black ghetto in the middle of campus! No wonder he thinks the place is racist." Professor McWhorter takes a sip of ice water and grimaces.

His colleague, Professor Satir, shrugs. "I think you're overreacting, Jim. Sounds to me like this student's just nurturing his cultural identity. Nothing wrong with exploring your roots. Or maybe he's inherited the fears of his ancestors, and he needs to build up some self-esteem by sticking to the community of people that fit his comfort zone."

"Pardon me, Mirium, but that is a load of cow dung," replies Professor McWhorter, abruptly putting his glass down. "'Self-esteem'! How's Kweisi ever going to get any real self-esteem—the kind you get by grappling with new ideas, new challenges, new people—if he stays stuck in his little 'comfort zone'?"

Professor Satir says placatingly, "Well, he is a freshman, right? He's only been here a few months. Give him time! Eventually he'll have to take other classes to fulfill his distribution requirements, and then he'll get exposed to different people and ideas."

"I wonder. The way he sees racism everywhere makes me doubt it. Seems to me it could easily turn into a self-fulfilling prophecy."

"What do you mean?"

"Well, if Kweisi is so determined to engage fully and sincerely only with blacks, then he's probably going to have trouble making any connections to whites. That means that later on he'll have problems getting internships and jobs. He'll blame his troubles on racism; his friends will agree; and he'll never even see his own self-victimization."

"'*Self*-victimization,' Jim? Don't you think racism is real?" Professor Satir arches her eyebrows.

"Yes, but not nearly to the degree that Kweisi does. Not nowadays. Look, it's like he's shooting himself in the foot: if he keeps on segregating himself from the larger society and blaming everything that happens to him on racism, he'll be socially and economically crippled, and never be able to reach his potential."

"But aren't you blaming the victim here? Seems like you expect him to just snap his fingers and forget all that people of color have suffered over the years."

"No, no, I don't expect him to forget that, but he also doesn't have to see himself as a victim in this time and place. He's not! If he'd get rid of his defeatist, separatist attitude and join the rest of the college community, he'd discover it's not nearly as hostile as he expects."

"Sure. We'd better eat," Professor Satir replies, "or I'm going to be late."

[Based on a situation described in *Losing the Race: Self-Sabotage in Black America* by John H. McWhorter (New York: Free Press, 2000/HarperPerennial 2001); see "Background Readings" for this chapter.]

QUESTIONS

1. What is your reaction to Professor McWhorter's argument? Would it make a difference to you whether he is black or white? Why or why not? Is your opinion influenced by your own political leanings, if any, either toward the left or the right? If so, how?

2. What kinds of ethical principles do Professor McWhorter and Professor Satir seem to base their lines of argument on? Could you join in their discussion with an argument based on a different moral principle?

3. McWhorter and Satir's argument is a fictionalized version of a real argument that is going on right now at the national level; it has to do with whether or not affirmative action and racial preferences in college admissions are good policies for our nation to continue pursuing. Many of the moral dilemmas in this book have wider policy implications. What positions do you suspect that McWhorter and Satir hold on affirmative action and racial preferences in college admissions?

CASE 3.9   *One of "Us," or One of "Them"?*

The professor in Mustafa's political science class had tried to be fair. The class had been discussing the global effects of terrorism, and she had been active in moderating the discussion. When a student, glaring at Mustafa, expressed anger about "those crazy Muslims and Arabs who are trying to destroy the West," she quickly pointed out that "of course we must remember that not all Muslims or people from the Middle East are behind acts of terrorism; only a fringe minority is." And when another student asked Mustafa to explain "why your people do these things," she had stepped in to say that it was not an appropriate question. But the teacher's attempts to protect him weren't enough, Mustafa thought; he had still felt that the whole discussion was very much "us" against "them"—with him being the sole representative of "them."

The class had never paid much attention to him before, and Mustafa had liked it that way. (He usually sat by himself toward the back of the room and rarely spoke, out of shyness about his slight stutter.) Today his anger and embarrassment were extreme as the other students kept turning around to stare at him during the discussion. Didn't they know how stupid they looked? He was as good an American as they were; maybe better. Why pick on him? But he thought it wiser not to try to explain their ignorance to them.

What followed after class was worse. The discussion had so stimulated the students that several of them hung around talking outside the classroom door even after the professor left. As Mustafa walked down the hall, he overheard a voice behind him say, "We should make all those towel-heads leave the country." Another replied, "Yeah, we'll never be safe until we've bombed them all." Mustafa's ears burned. Were those hateful words intended for him? He didn't wear a turban, but the remarks seemed to follow from the hostility in class. He wasn't sure who had spoken. Should he turn around and say something, or just keep walking? Either way, he couldn't see ever going back to that class.

QUESTIONS

1. Do you think that any of the students' comments to Mustafa were examples of hate speech? If so, which ones, and why? Can prejudiced comments be considered hate speech if they are not directed (at least not openly) at a member of the targeted group? If yes, should they be punished? How? If not, should expressing a prejudice that is unintentionally offensive be punishable? How should such speech be dealt with by the professor and other authorities?

2. How do you think Mustafa ought to respond to the students' remarks: Should he try to prove his patriotism and horror of terrorists? Should he try to explain some of the root causes of terrorism, or the teachings of the Qur'an on the subject, or the evils of generalizing and racism, or otherwise try to educate his fellow students? Should he refuse to lower himself to their level by answering them? Should he avoid the students and drop the course? Perhaps you can think of other responses as well. Does your answer differ depending on which ethical principle you use as a basis?

Oreo Intellectual CASE 3.10

"Oreo!"

The insult rang in Shimene's ears. You'd think she'd know better by now than to let anyone find out she was getting good grades; after all, in high school she'd been dissed by black classmates for taking Advanced Placement classes. But she'd thought college would be different.

Ears burning, she found herself apologizing for her academic success. "I guess I just got lucky," she faltered. "It doesn't mean anything."

"Huh. You know, girl, you better quit tryin' to act so white." Her roommate Alexis shook her head. "Else you gonna have noooo friends." She narrowed her eyes in disgust and left the room.

Shimene knew that Alexis's rap-inflected ghetto talk was just a pose; they'd both grown up in middle-class suburbs, and Alexis could switch into white English whenever she felt like it. But Alexis's hostile attitude toward schoolwork and academic success was not a pose, and what's more, it seemed to be shared by most of the other black students on campus. They spent their time talking about what party they were going to on Friday night or their favorite music or the football game, not what book they were reading or the professor's lecture.

Shimene sat down on her bed with a sigh.

Not for the first time she realized that it just isn't cool for black students to be interested in academics. Her whole first semester Shimene had tried to hide from her fellow students how much she was excited by the reading, and she'd held herself back from participating too much in class. When her peers complained about their assignments, she was glad that none of them knew she actually *liked* writing papers.

But maybe, she thought, I do finally have to choose. I can keep on doing well in school and be gradually shunned by other black folk, or I can lower my sights and have them as friends. Shimene felt depressed. Was it true that she couldn't be intellectual without "going white"? So how could she be true to herself as a black woman with a mind?

[Based on situations described in *Losing the Race: Self-Sabotage in Black America* by John H. McWhorter (New York: Free Press, 2000/HarperPerennial 2001); see "Background Readings" for this chapter.]

QUESTIONS

1. What should Shimene do? How might you use the principles of community, character growth, relationship, and the greatest good to explore her options? Do different moral principles suggest different courses of action for her? Is there any way to view the situation other than Shimene's analysis of it?

2. A similar situation could involve two Native American college students, in which case the insult used would not be "oreo" but "apple" (red on the outside, white on the inside). Are there cultural differences between Native Americans and African Americans, or differences in those groups' historical treatment by European Americans, that would lead you to analyze the case differently if it involved Native American students?

3. Some critics of McWhorter's book point out that the "anti-intellectualism" he describes as endemic to black culture and a source of "black self-sabotage" is in fact not limited to the black population.

   This is "not a country that's known for its embrace of intellectual pursuits," says Samuel R. Lucas, a black assistant professor in UC Berkeley's sociology department. "White students, Latino students, Asian students, and black students are all represented among the worst and among the best in terms of the grades they get, the seriousness with which they engage the materials, and the creativity they bring to the assignments." [from Leo Reisberg, "A Professor's Controversial Analysis of Why Black Students Are 'Losing the Race': a Review of *Losing the Race: Self-Sabotage in Black America* by John H. McWhorter," in *The Chronicle of Higher Education*, 11 August 2000.]

   Do you think your classmates in general are anti-intellectual, that is, do most of them consider it "uncool" to be very interested in their coursework? Do you believe there are differences between racial or ethnic groups on your campus (whites, blacks, Asians, Hispanics, others) in terms of how acceptable they seem to view the pursuit of academic excellence? Is this a racist question? Have you yourself ever modified your behavior in class for fear that others would think you were "kissing up to the teacher" or "showing off"?

BACKGROUND READING

"Political Correctness" on Campus

• Paul Berman (editor), *Debating P.C.: The Controversy over Political Correctness on College Campuses* (New York: Dell/Bantam Doubleday Dell, 1992). This book is a collection of excerpts from writers who cover the political and cultural spectrum of opinions about "political correctness." The excerpts are arranged in six sections: debating political correctness; politics and the canon; free speech and speech codes; the "Texas Shoot-Out" (see "Additional Materials" item 2 below); public schools; and diverse views. Berman describes the background of the debate over P.C. in his "Introduction" (pp. 1–26) and also precedes each excerpt with a paragraph summarizing its content.

• David Denby, "Annals of Education: Does Homer Have Legs?," in *The New Yorker*, 6 September 1993, vol. LXIX, no. 28, pp. 52–69. A self-described "middle-aged, middle-class white male" returns to college to attend a Great Books class at Columbia University, to see how the traditional Western canon is taught and justified. He also ruminates about how the books in the course affect him and the other students in the class (who are a young, ethnically diverse group).

• Dinesh D'Souza, *Illiberal Education: The Politics of Race and Sex on Campus* (New York: The Free Press/Macmillan, 1991), especially Chapter 6 pp. 157–193, and pp. 246–247. Gives examples of the controversy surrounding the canon and background on the debate over it.

• Louis Menard, "The Culture Wars: A Review of *Dictatorship of Virtue: Multiculturalism and the Battle for America's Future*" by Richard Bernstein (Knopf, 1994), in *The New York Review of Books*, 6 October 1994, pp. 16–21. This lengthy and largely negative review discusses a number of recent college and university cases of hate speech, "political correctness," criticisms of multiculturalism, and attempts at gender equity on campus, some of which are mentioned below under "Additional Materials." It also presents an argument against speech codes and even the use of "multiculturalist categories like race, gender, and sexual orientation" on campus (p. 18).

The Many Faces of "Multiculturalism"

• Jean J. Schensul and Thomas G. Carroll, "Vision of America in the 1990s and Beyond: Negotiating Cultural Diversity and Educational Change," in *Education and Urban Society*, August 1990, vol. 22, no. 4, pp. 339–345. This whole issue focuses on cultural diversity on campus. Schensul and Carroll's article introduces three other articles discussing the background of the current campus debate between advocates of multicultural studies and the traditional Western canon. The authors also summarize various responses American schools have taken to student diversity in the past, and they suggest a program of cultural pluralism and cultural transformation for the future.

• Alaka Wali, "Multiculturalism: An Anthropological Perspective," in *The Report from the Institute for Philosophy and Public Policy*, Spring/Summer 1992, vol. 12, no. 1, pp. 6–8. Wali discusses the "virtual meaninglessness" of the biological category of race and examines the reasons for and implications of racial and ethnic identification, particularly in current debates about multiculturalism.

• George Will, "A Kind of Compulsory Chapel: Multiculturalism is a Campaign to Lower America's Moral Status," in *Newsweek*, 14 November 1994, vol. 124, no. 20, p. 84. This article is an analysis of a list of "multicultural horror stories" that the conservative columnist culled from Richard Bernstein's *Dictatorship of Virtue: Multiculturalism and the Battle for America's Future*. Readers should be aware that others have challenged the accuracy of the facts in some of Will's descriptions. Will also favorably reviews Bernstein's book.

• See also Menard's review of *Dictatorship of Virtue*, above.

The Controversy Over Affirmative Action and Desegregation

• William G. Bowen and Derek Bok, *The Shape of the River: Long-Term Consequences of Considering Race in College and University Admissions* (Princeton University Press, 1998). Bowen and Bok are two former Ivy League college presidents who here defend affirmative action on the basis of a study of 45,184 students who entered 28 selective colleges in the fall of 1976 or the fall of 1989. This book has been lauded by many academics as the most comprehensive look ever at how students who benefited from racial preferences have fared both during and after college, but critics like McWhorter (below under Reisberg) fault it for ignoring the disadvantages of affirmative action in terms of how it affects blacks' sense of competence and ability to compete with other races.

• Gerald Early, "Understanding Afrocentrism: Why Blacks Dream of a World Without Whites," in *Civilization, the Magazine of the Library of*

Congress, July/August 1995, vol. 2, no. 4, pp. 31–39. This cover story seeks to explain why a growing number of African Americans reject the pro-integrationist stance of many blacks during the Civil Rights movement in the 1960s. It also defines the doctrine of Afrocentrism and explores its historical and psychological roots.

Along the same lines, see *"Brown* Blues: Rethinking the Integrative Ideal" by Drew S. Days, III, in *The Report from the Institute for Philosophy and Public Policy*, vol. 17, no. 4, Fall 1997. The *Report* is available on-line at www.puaf.umd.edu/ippp (The Institute for Philosophy and Public Policy's Web site).

• Robert K. Fullinwider, et al., "The Affirmative Action Debate: A Special Issue of the *Report from the Institute for Philosophy and Public Policy*," vol. 17, no. 1 and 2: Winter/Spring 1997. This whole issue of the *Report* is devoted to affirmative action. Article titles include: "Affirmative Action Status Report: Evidence and Options," "Civil Rights and Racial Preferences: A Legal History of Affirmative Action," "The Merits of Merit," "Diversity and Affirmative Action," "Diversity and Stereotyping," and "Affirmative Action as a Strategy of Justice." The *Report* is available on-line at www.puaf.umd.edu/ippp (The Institute for Philosophy and Public Policy's Web site).

• Norman Lockman, "Why the Results Were Surprising in a Poll of Black Americans," syndicated column in *The Ithaca Journal* (and other newspapers) on 7 March 2001, p. 11A. Lockman describes the results of a recent "national issues" poll of African Americans. "Most startling to me was the finding that 65 percent of those polled opposed racial preferences in hiring or college admissions," says Lockman, and he analyzes the "growing unease among black Americans about programs that make it look as though they are benefiting more from pigment than performance."

• Leo Reisberg, "A Professor's Controversial Analysis of Why Black Students Are 'Losing the Race': a Review of *Losing the Race: Self-Sabotage in Black America*" by John H. McWhorter (Free Press, 2000), in *The Chronicle of Higher Education*, 11 August 2000. McWhorter, a young black associate professor in Berkeley's linguistics department, believes that affirmative action contributes to a strain of "anti-intellectualism" in black culture and to a "deep-reaching inferiority complex" among African Americans that encourages them to consider themselves society's victims. This mind-set is what really causes black students of all social classes and income levels to lag behind their white counterparts, he claims. Thus while affirmative action and racial preferences in college admissions were "necessary evils" 30 years ago, McWhorter argues, they now "encourage defeatist thought patterns" that are "much, much more serious barriers to black well-being than is white racism," and should be abandoned. Reviews of McWhorter's book range from "absurdly simplistic" (black columnist Jack E. White in *Time* magazine, 3 August 2000) to "brilliant, sparkling, effervescent" (Stephen and Abigail Thernstrom, right-wing white critics of racial preferences in their book *Black and White: One Nation, Indivisible* [Simon & Schuster, 1997]). See also Ron Suskind, *A Hope in the Unseen: An American Odyssey from the Inner City to the Ivy League* [Broadway Books, 1999], for a personal narrative that is a powerful response to McWhorter's position.

- A number of Supreme Court rulings have affected desegregation of colleges. In *Missouri ex. rel. Gaines v. Canada* (1938), the Court ruled that if a state provides a graduate education in law to whites, it must, under the equal protection guarantee of the Fifteenth Amendment to the Constitution, offer a substantially similar education to blacks. Similarly, *Sweatt v. Painter* (1950) affirmed that a qualified black student has a constitutional right to a state-provided legal education equal to that offered to qualified whites. *McLarin v. Oklahoma State Regents for Higher Education* (1950) ruled that a black student admitted to an all-white university as a Ph.D. candidate cannot be assigned to separate seating in the classroom, library, and cafeteria. And although the landmark case of *Brown v. Board of Education* (1954) applied specifically to elementary schools, the ruling was taken broadly to mean that all segregated education is inherently unequal and thus unconstitutional. Later, amid concerns about the effects of "reverse discrimination" on qualified white students, the Court rather confusingly decided in *University of California Regents v. Bakke* (1978) that colleges and universities cannot use racial quotas in admissions decisions, but they can consider the race of applicants. This uneasy compromise has come under attack in a string of federal court cases challenging the use of racial preferences in college admissions, most recently at the University of Michigan's law school (March 2001). The Supreme Court will almost certainly have to deal with the issue soon.

Perspectives on Racism

- Paul Berman, "Reflections: The Other and Almost the Same," in *The New Yorker*, 28 February 1994, pp. 61–66, 68–71. This article presents a detailed analysis of the roots and meanings of tensions between black and Jewish Americans. It begins with a discussion of a Kean College, New Jersey, speech by a representative of Minister Louis Farrakhan and the Nation of Islam. It goes on to suggest the wider cultural implications of this campus event, which was widely seen as an example of hate speech.

For more in the same vein, see John Blake, "When Friends Feud," in *Atlanta Journal and Atlanta Constitution*, 5 June 1994, sec. G, p. 1, col. 2. This is the text of a roundtable discussion on relations between blacks and Jews that involved three participants (including a college student) from each group.

• Judith Lichtenberg, "Racism in the Head, Racism in the World," in *The Report from the Institute for Philosophy and Public Policy*, Spring/Summer 1992, vol. 12, no. 1, pp. 3–5. This entire special issue of the *Report* is devoted to discussions of ethical issues involved in "race, discrimination, and group identity." Lichtenberg analyzes the differences between individual racism, racist institutions, and racist societies, and argues that even if "racism in the head" disappeared, "racism in the world" would not. The *Report* is available on-line at www.puaf.umd.edu/ippp (The Institute for Philosophy and Public Policy's Web site).

• Lena Williams, "Growing Black Debate on Racism: When Is It Real, When an Excuse?" in *The New York Times*, 5 April 1992, sec. 1, p. 1, col. 1. This article examines an emotionally charged debate among African Americans today. An increasing number have become openly critical of the actions of black public figures such as Leonard Jeffries (see "Additional Materials" item 5 in this chapter), Mike Tyson, and Marion S. Barry, suggesting that the communal psychology that has long bound black Americans in unanimity is slowly dissolving. Such criticisms are being countered by other groups claiming that Jeffries, Tyson, and Barry are victims of the white establishment.

Hate Speech and Free Speech

• William A. Kaplan, "A Proposed Process for Managing the First Amendment Aspects of Campus Hate Speech," in *The Journal of Higher Education*, September–October 1992, vol. 63, no. 5. This lengthy article provides a legal overview of the subject of hate speech. Specifically, it defines "the character and harms of hate speech," explores the first amendment (freedom of speech) aspects of the topic, reviews judicial rulings on hate speech, and recommends a process for colleges and universities to follow in dealing with hate speech.

ADDITIONAL MATERIALS

1. Bernard Malamud, a Jewish novelist, has written a powerful novel, *The Fixer* (New York: Dell Publishing, 1968), about anti-Semitism in Russia. Many of his characters are anti-Semites who say things that should be viewed as hate speech, if anything should be. Is he guilty of hate speech? What does this tell us about the importance of context in making judgments about the meaning of speech?

2. For further information about the following case, see Louis Menard, "The Culture Wars: A Review of *Dictatorship of Virtue: Multiculturalism and the Battle for America's Future*" by Richard Bernstein (New York: Knopf,

1994), in *The New York Review of Books*, 6 October 1994, p. 20. See also section 4 of "The Texas Shoot-Out" in *Debating P.C.: The Controversy Over Political Correctness on College Campuses* (New York: Dell/Bantam Doubleday Dell, 1992). A controversy arose at the University of Texas at Austin over a proposal to force all sections of the required composition course to use readings on racial and sexual discrimination. Adherents saw the change as a needed counterbalance to racist and sexist undertones on campus and in society at large. Critics saw the proposal as an attempt to impose "thought control" on the 40 percent of Texas students forced to take the course. After increasing furor led to national attention, the proposal was eventually dropped.

Do you think the proposed course change would have closed down or opened up campus discussions? Why would you or wouldn't you want to take such a course? How might the principles of community and respect for persons be applied to both the course proposal and the controversy that followed it?

3. For further information about the following case, see Michael de-Courcy, "No Penalties for Black Students Who Took Magazines at Penn," in *The New York Times*, 16 September 1993, sec. B, p. 9, col. 4; and "Panel Says Penn Police Overreacted," in *The New York Times*, 28 July 1993, sec. A, p. 15, col. 1. A group of African American students at the University of Pennsylvania were long angered by a conservative student newspaper that they considered racist. Finally they confiscated all copies of one issue of the newspaper to protest a columnist's criticisms of Martin Luther King, Jr. and claims that the university gives preferential treatment to African Americans in admissions and disciplinary procedures. Campus police could identify only nine of the sixty students involved in confiscating the newspaper, and the university at length dismissed all disciplinary proceedings against them. The newspaper staff felt that although the university talked forcefully about protecting freedom of speech, it refused to punish those who violated it, or to guarantee police protection against the papers being stolen again.

Is confiscation of offensive material a legitimate or effective way to deal with it? Does it matter who does the confiscating, who the audience is, or whom the offensive material targets? You might think here of additional examples, such as pornography, or notoriously "dangerous" books such as Hitler's *Mein Kampf.* What other options might the African American students have had? Are the kinds of opinions expressed by the conservative columnist really examples of hate speech? How would you evaluate the university administration's response to this incident, in terms of finding a balance between banning hate speech and protecting free speech?

4. For more information about the following, see Terry Wilson, "New' Support Group Seeks to Offer Help to Gay Teachers," in *The Chicago Tribune*, 29 December 1994, sec. 2C, p. 7. col. 1. Some people believe that

homosexuality is somehow contagious. At least, that seems to be the reasoning behind a number of laws and social practices affecting gays. For example, teachers, professors, and college students studying to be teachers often fear being fired (or not hired) if they admit that they are gay, or if they present positive gay and lesbian role models to students. Do you think that gay teachers should be kept away from students (of particular ages)? Why? In the same vein, should the influence of gay student groups be limited by not allowing them to use campus facilities? University of South Alabama sophomore George Hite Wilson is pushing to overturn an Alabama law banning gay student groups from using public funds or facilities because they "promote a lifestyle" outlawed in Alabama's anti-sodomy statute. (For more information see Judy Sheppard, "Gays Need Not Apply," in *The Atlanta Constitution*, 16 August 1994, sec. A, p. 3, col. 2.)

A recent survey found a significantly higher percentage of gay men and women have college educations, compared to the general population (David W. Dunlap, "Gay Survey Raises a New Question," in *The New York Times*, 18 October 1994, sec. B, p. 8, col. 4). Do these figures suggest that homosexual teachers influence students to become gay (as some fear), that people with homosexual orientations tend to go to college proportionally more than their nonhomosexual peers, or that college raises gay students' consciousness and makes them more willing to identify themselves openly as homosexual? Can you think of other explanations for this difference? Should a purpose of the college experience be to help students discover or explore their sexual orientation? (See also Chapter 8.)

5. For further information about the following case, see "Watching Dr. Jeffries Self-Destruct," in *The New York Times*, 25 August 1991, sec. 4, p. 14, col. 1; Denise K. Magner, "In a Reversal, Court Upholds CUNY's Demotion of Afrocentrist," in *The Chronicle of Higher Education*, 14 April 1995, vol. 41, no. 31, p. A23(1); (Editorial) "Hate Speech and the University (Court of Appeals Upholds Loss of Leonard Jeffries' Chairmanship of Black Studies Program at CUNY for Remarks against Jews)" in *The New York Times*, 6 April 1995, vol. 144, p. A18(N), p. A30(L), col. 1; and Edward Felsenthal, "CUNY Free-Speech Case (Federal Appeals Court Rules that City University of New York Didn't Violate Constitutional Rights of Professor Leonard Jeffries)," in *The Wall Street Journal*, 5 April 1995, p. B4(W), p. B5(E), col. 6. Leonard Jeffries Jr., Chairman of the Black Studies Department at the City University of New York, has had a highly controversial career. He advocates a radical form of Afrocentric education that many critics see as racially divisive, hate-filled, and based on "misinformation." Among Jeffries' contentious theories are his assertions that Jews financed the African slave trade, that American Jews and Italian Americans conspired to denigrate and destroy African Americans in the movies, and that African Americans are morally and genetically superior to European

Americans. However, Jeffries has gathered strong support among his black students and many in the African American community, who feel that he restores their sense of self-worth and pride in their ancestry (see Jacques Steinberg, "Jeffries Misses Brooklyn Rally on Racial Issues," in *The New York Times*, 16 August 1991, sec. B, p. 3, col. 1; Steven Lee Myers, "500 Rally to Support Controversial Professor," in *The New York Times*, 12 August 1991, sec. B, p. 3, col. 3; Ellen Whitford, "Jeffries Stresses Heritage," in *The Atlanta Constitution*, 2 April 1992, sec. B, p. 4, col. 4; and "Professor's Remarks Reported as Bigoted," in *The New York Times*, 28 November 1994, sec. B, p. 3, col. 2).

The controversy over Jeffries began when he made an angry speech attacking Jews at the state-sponsored Empire State Black Arts and Cultural Festival on July 20, 1991. Then-Governor Mario Cuomo, other state officials, some top CUNY administrators, and many faculty members quickly assailed Jeffries' "anti-Semitism" and urged CUNY to take disciplinary action against him. But the CUNY Faculty Senate declined to censure Jeffries, and the university trustees merely put Jeffries on one-year probation as chairman of the Black Studies Department because they were "hesitant to dismiss him for fear of adding to racial tensions already high on campus" (Joseph Berger, "CUNY Board Votes to Keep Jeffries in Post," in *The New York Times*, 29 October 1991, sec. B, p. 1, col. 5).

Next, a student reporter from the *Harvard Crimson* claimed that Jeffries threatened his life if he used statements Jeffries made about two black scholars during an interview, and he ordered a bodyguard to seize his tape recording of the interview, which Jeffries had permitted, after Jeffries turned hostile. Jeffries continued to make contentious statements, and then on March 23, 1992, the CUNY Trustees replaced him with a far less controversial figure as Black Studies Department chair. Jeffries promptly sued CUNY for reinstatement, testifying that his academic freedom and right to free expression had been violated by the school. He also warned that his demotion would spark community resistance (Maria Newman, "Jeffries Warned of Unrest If Demoted, Official Recalls," in *The New York Times*, 24 April 1993, sec. A, p. 26, col. 5). A federal court ruled in Jeffries' favor on August 4, 1993, saying that CUNY violated his free speech rights. The judge further ordered the university to pay Jeffries $400,000 in damages and to reinstate him as head of the Black Studies Department. But in April 1995, the Federal Court of Appeals reversed this ruling, saying that CUNY did not violate Jeffries' constitutional rights.

How can a college ensure a civil, nonintimidating atmosphere while also protecting students' and faculty members' right to free speech? Should colleges even try to curb or censure racist or other hate speech, or only teach students how to respond to it? Are Jeffries' statements examples of (properly censured) hate speech, or of bigoted remarks that nonetheless might serve an important purpose in bolstering minority students' self-esteem? If his theories are false, what implications might this have for his students' raised self-esteem? Why should (or shouldn't) increasing self-esteem be a purpose of education?

For more information, see Edwin M. Yoder, Jr., "A First Amendment with Footnotes: Is the Supreme Court Preparing to Broaden Exceptions to Free Speech?" in *The Washington Post*, 18 December 1994, sec. C, p. 4, col. 1; "Editorial: Professor Jeffries' Speech," in *The Washington Post*, 16 November 1994, sec. A, p. 24, col. 1; "Editorial: Pity His Students," in *The Washington Post*, 9 August 1993, sec. A, p. 16, col. 1; Nathan Glazer, "Academic Freedom? Academic Farce," in *The New York Times*, 21 May 1993, sec. A, p. 27, col. 2; Lynne Duke, "Colliding Racial Beliefs Test Speech Limits at CUNY," in *The Washington Post*, 9 November 1991, sec. A, p. 1, col. 1 (interviews Jeffries and another professor); "Editorial: Words That Provoke," in *USA Today*, 19 August 1991, sec. A, p. 8, col. 1; and Roger E. Hernandez, "The New Racism," in *The Washington Post*, 16 August 1991, sec. A, p. 29, col. 1.

6. Until 1995, the University of Maryland offered the Benjamin Banneker scholarship to high-achieving black students. The program set aside scholarship money for about thirty such students each year. In these financially strapped times, white students have complained that race-based scholarships are unfair, and in fact the Supreme Court recently let stand a lower court ruling that such scholarships violate the equal protection clause of the Fourteenth Amendment to the Constitution. However, a study by the NAACP Legal Defense Fund indicates that "nationwide there is a plethora of scholarship programs that give financial aid exclusively to members of specific groups and that they have not been the subject of legal challenges." The scholarships are offered to groups such as "Jews, Chinese Americans, Italian Americans, foreign students, women, Greek Americans, men, Christians, lineal descendents of Confederate soldiers, Baptists," and so on (Steven A. Holmes, "Minority Scholarship Plans Are Dealt Setback by Court: Decision on Maryland Program Is Let Stand," in *The New York Times*, 23 May 1995, p. B9). Indeed, many scholarships and preferential admissions policies exclusively benefit two relatively privileged groups: student athletes, and alumni sons and daughters. Is there any reason race-based policies should be thought of differently?

Are such affirmative-action scholarships ethical? Why or why not? What moral principles might be useful in analyzing this issue, and how would you apply them? Are minority-specific scholarships in the best interest of the country as a whole, or only in the interest of the particular minority group being helped? Do colleges owe blacks or other racial or ethnic minority students some sort of compensation for past discrimination? For more information, see Holmes, "Minority Scholarship Plans Are Dealt Setback by Court"; and a transcript of the March 19, 1995 *All Things*

Considered broadcast on National Public Radio, which aired a debate between Banneker scholar Miesha Harris (a senior at the university) and a male freshman there.[6]

7. Ralph Frammolino, "Getting Grades for Diversity?" in *The Los Angeles Times,* 23 February 1994, sec. A, p. 1, col. 1. The Western Association of Schools and Colleges proposed to hold its member colleges accountable for fostering cultural diversity on campus, using accreditation as a tool for enforcing compliance. In other words, schools that did not meet the Association's diversity standards would not be accredited even though they met all other accreditation standards, and they would thus lose students and perhaps professors, and become ineligible for crucial government and foundation grants and private donations. Is bureaucratic enforcement of school diversity (either privately sponsored, as in the association, or publicly mandated, as in federal or state prohibitions against segregated schools) an appropriate way to ensure better education for minority students? Various university presidents reacted angrily to the association's proposal. But what differences, if any, are there between the association's plan to enforce diversity and federal and state statutes that refuse tax-exempt status to racially segregated schools? Should schools be punished for being unwilling (or perhaps even unable) to attract and keep traditionally underrepresented students? Why or why not?

8. In Dinesh D'Souza, *Illiberal Education: The Politics of Race and Sex on Campus* (New York: The Free Press/Macmillan, 1991), Chapter 5 describes the case of Reynolds Farley, who was "acknowledged as America's leading demographer in the field of race relations," a self-proclaimed liberal democrat, author of widely assigned sociology textbooks, and a popular professor on the Michigan State campus, when he was criticized in the student newspaper for remarks he made during a Sociology 303 class on racial and cultural contacts in the fall of 1988 (p. 148). Professor Farley was accused of showing "insensitivity" to Malcolm X and Marcus Garvey because he mentioned less-than-flattering facts about these black leaders. He was also castigated for quoting "prejudicial statements to the class," although he claimed that he used these to "help describe the history of race relations" (p. 149). A student in the class wrote that "Farley is insensitive to issues of racism and sexism" and "perpetuates a racism that's in the university as a whole." The student called for the course to have a different instructor in the future, "someone who's sensitive—preferably a person of color" (p. 150).

The Department chairman convened a faculty executive committee to meet with students and discuss their grievances. At the meeting, other faculty who defended Farley were themselves denounced for insensitivity.

[6] Available as a transcript or tape from "National Public Radio Tapes and Transcripts," Washington, DC 20036, or (202) 822-2323. See also www.npr.com.

However, no action was taken, and eventually the whole affair subsided. Farley nevertheless felt that his reputation had been "gravely damaged" by unsubstantiated, irresponsible charges. He was angry that the university hadn't stood up for academic freedom and open expression, and he decided never to teach the course again.

Farley's student critic seems to assume that only a person of color can be sensitive to issues of race, and thus that only a nonwhite professor should teach about subjects touching on race. Do you accept this reasoning? Why or why not? If you do, does this also imply, for example, that only women should write novels about female characters? Does it mean that black professors are never prejudiced against black students, or that female professors can't be sexist? If you don't agree, do you think that professors (of whatever color or sex) should still be evaluated at least partly on whether or not they bring a minority viewpoint to the classroom? Do colleges and universities have a duty to counter the dominant culture's racism and sexism in what and how they teach? If so, how can they best go about doing this? How might the principles of the greatest good, equal respect, and community apply to this case?

9. Most colleges and universities practice what they call "affirmative action." In admissions, affirmative action usually means that members of minority groups are given some additional consideration in the admissions process by virtue of their minority status. However, there is a new trend for states to enact policies under which affirmative action is illegal. For instance, in Florida the "One Florida" plan recently eliminated all forms of affirmative action. Affirmative action has also been banned by statute in California.

This confusion over the legality of affirmative action stems from the controversial and conflicted 1978 *Regents of the University of California v. Bakke* decision of the Supreme Court. In this case, the Court held that colleges and universities may not have racial quotas, but may take race into account in admissions. Since then that view has been rejected by the Fifth Circuit Federal Appeals Court and then recently affirmed by the Ninth Circuit Federal Appeals Court.

Many people view affirmative action as a kind of compensatory justice, an attempt to recompense minorities for their history of injustice and to help them move more quickly into the mainstream of American life. The Supreme Court's argument in *Bakke* was quite different. The Court claimed that it found only one justification for affirmative action powerful enough to warrant the use of race as a criterion in college admissions—diversity. Justice Powell, who wrote the majority opinion, argued that a university is a marketplace of ideas. As such it not only must prohibit censorship of any kind, but it also must take steps to ensure that people from diverse backgrounds are represented so that their voices can be heard. Representation of diverse perspectives improves the education of all students. Moreover, the value of diversity has constitutional standing; it is in the penumbra (the implications) of the First Amendment.

We will not ask you to evaluate this argument in legal terms. It is likely that the Supreme Court will revisit *Bakke* in the next few years. The law may be different by the time you read this. But do you agree with Justice Powell's argument as a moral argument? Is diversity of such importance that it justifies the use of race as an admissions criterion, if that is necessary to ensure diversity? Should we not consider compensatory justice as equally important? This latter argument is also behind the current debate about whether or not our government should give reparations to the descendants of slaves, as the German government has given reparations to Nazi victims (see question #10 below).

10. For more information about the following, see Pamela Ferdinand, "Free-Speech Debate Splits Liberal Brown: Anti-Reparations Ad at Center of Controversy," in *The Washington Post*, 21 March 2001, p. A03; John Leo, "Ivy League Therapy: An Ad in the Brown University Student Newspaper Against Slave Descendant Reparations Caused the Theft of the Paper from News Racks," in *U.S. News & World Report*, 2 April 2001, vol. 130, i. 13, p. 14; Robert Fullinwider, "The Case for Reparations," in *The Report from the Institute of Philosophy and Public Policy*, vol. 20, no. 4, Fall 2000; "Forum: Making the Case for Racial Reparations," in *Harper's Magazine*, November 2000, vol. 301, i. 1806, p. 37; and "Democracy's Rough Edges" (editorial), in *The Ithaca Journal*, 19 April 2001, p. 11A.

In the spring of 2001, conservative author David Horowitz sought to publish a full-page ad called "Ten Reasons Why Reparations for Slavery is a Bad Idea for Blacks—and Racist Too" in dozens of college newspapers, in an effort to sway students against a movement that has been gaining momentum among civil rights groups and others nationwide. This ad, with its unsettling and often offensive prose (samples: "If not for the sacrifices of white soldiers and a white American president who gave his life to sign the Emancipation Proclamation, blacks in America would still be slaves" and "[reparations are just] one more attempt to turn African Americans into victims") suggests that black Americans owe more to the United States than it owes them. The ad immediately ignited controversy on campuses across the United States. Many student papers refused to run it at all, including those at Harvard, Yale, Columbia, and Cornell. Others did publish it, often to the accompaniment of student protests and general uproar in the community; some, including the University of California at Berkeley, subsequently apologized for printing it.

At Brown University, for example, after Horowitz's ad appeared on March 13, a coalition of students demanded that *The Brown Daily Herald* provide free rebuttal space and donate equivalent ad revenue to one of the university's minority organizations. When the editors refused, all 4,000 free copies of the *Herald* were taken from campus newsstands within minutes of their delivery on March 16. The ensuing debate over race and free speech deeply divided Brown's liberal Ivy League community, with attention focused as much on the manner in which students protested the ad as on the merits of the ad itself.

The *Herald's* editors defended their decision to publish the ad as follows: "We don't print anything that is illegal or libelous. But other than that, we don't really reject advertising, and we certainly don't reject advertising on its political content," said editor-in-chief Brooks King. "It's disgraceful not to run an ad because people on your campus are going to disagree with it."

What do you think of this position? Would you agree with it if the material in question were personally offensive to you, such as an attack on people of your ethnic background, age, gender, or political beliefs? Why might the free exchange of ideas be important, especially on campus? Do you think the controversy over Horowitz's ad was at bottom an issue of hate speech, or of free speech? In other words, should students have the right to stop the distribution of ideas they find disrespectful and hateful? Should newspaper editors? Are such actions examples of "responsible civil disobedience," as the student protesters at Brown believe, or "campus fascism," as Horowitz believes?

4

PRIVACY AND DIALOGUE

TWO CASES: INVADING PERSONAL SPACE

CASE 4.1   *Incompatibility*

Yusif remembered the form he had filled out for Residence Life. It had asked him to indicate the qualities he wanted in a roommate. Because he had been on the cross-country team in high school and liked classical music, he checked off athletics and music as his interests, and he asked for a nonsmoking roommate. He had gone three for three. Fred was into sports—boxing, which he watched religiously on his TV. And he loved music—he played riffs on his electric guitar at high decibels. At least he didn't smoke.

Although at first Yusif didn't altogether hate Fred's feeble imitations of Stevie Ray Vaughan, his idea of music to study by ran more toward Mozart. Fred seemed to have no opinion about suitable studying music, because he appeared not to study. However, he was disciplined about practicing his guitar regularly, at high volumes, often until the wee hours of the morning. Maybe all that loud music had done something to his hearing, because it seemed that everything Fred did was loud: he always turned the volume up high when a match was on TV or when he played his stereo, and he even talked loudly. Fred had turned their room into a dormitory version of a nightclub. Fred's friends felt free to walk in anytime and hold a jam session or play a new CD they'd gotten. The loud music and conversation often went on until two or three in the morning. Because Fred usually slept until noon, he didn't seem overly deprived of sleep, but Yusif had an 8:00 A.M. lab. He could escape his room to study, but he had nowhere else to sleep.

At first Yusif tried polite requests, but these seemed lost on Fred and his friends. They just invited him to join in and have a drink. Fred pointed out, "This is my room, too. There's nowhere else we can play. And who are you to tell me when I can practice or what I can listen to?" When Yusif asked if they could play more quietly, Fred responded simply, "This music's got to be loud," and turned up his amp.

Finally Yusif yelled, "Couldn't we at least talk about this?" Fred just ignored him. That was when Yusif decided to ask for a new roommate, but the college was short on rooms. They said they'd see what they could do for him next semester.

In desperation, Yusif tried being a little more aggressive with Fred. He told him that he had had it with the loud music and that Fred and his friends should find a practice room somewhere. Unfortunately, this seemed to be a mistake. Up until this point, Fred had tolerated Yusif. But now Fred seemed to think that Yusif had challenged him, and he had to defend his honor before his friends. Yusif became the butt of increasingly nasty jokes. Fred often "accidentally" knocked Yusif's books and papers over or spilled soda on his things, and a couple of times he roughly shoved him. Yusif was in no hurry to get into a fight with a bunch of guys at once, so he always backed down, much to his humiliation.

By the end of the semester, Fred and his friends had turned Yusif-baiting into an art form. Yusif decided that if he couldn't get out of that room for the next semester, he would drop out.

QUESTIONS

1. Does Yusif have a right to tell Fred how Fred can use their room? How would you justify such a right?

2. Suppose that Yusif simply disliked the kind of music that Fred played and took the position that Fred should not play it whenever Yusif was in the room. Does Yusif have a right to demand this? Suppose that Yusif used the room only to study or sleep and insisted that Fred maintain complete silence whenever he was in the room. At what point would Yusif's demands for Fred's silence become unreasonable?

3. How could Yusif and Fred settle a disagreement about the use of the room? What should Yusif do if Fred won't discuss it?

Different Strokes CASE 4.2

Rachel and Judy shared a lot of interests and enjoyed one another's company, despite a noteworthy difference in their backgrounds: Rachel was Jewish and from New York City and Judy was the quintessential suburban WASP. They had learned to live together well. Neither was a neat freak, and neither was a slob. They had worked out a study schedule. They managed to know when to exit when the other was entertaining, and neither abused the privilege. Everything was great—until Rachel's parents invited Judy to visit them in Brooklyn for a weekend.

There was much that Judy enjoyed: new foods, fascinating places to visit, and the parade of friends and relatives who wandered in and out of Rachel's house at all hours. Rachel's mother held court in the kitchen, serving food and gossip to all who came. By late Saturday, Judy knew more about Rachel's family and her neighbors than she did about her own. All of the weddings, divorces, child rearing problems, and operations were constantly discussed and debated. Judy was astonished when Rachel's mother told her how much she and Rachel's father earned and how much they had paid for their house and various items in it. Advice was freely given by all to each, and hugs and kisses seemed to be offered equally generously. Judy found it all quite wonderful until it was her turn.

Judy's family honored their Scottish ancestors by making much of the virtue of privacy. They never gossiped; it was understood that the affairs of each member of her family were their own business. People could discuss their private lives if they wished, but "Don't ask, don't tell" seemed the rule. In Judy's family, prying was a major sin. And hugging, kissing, and displays of emotion in general were simply not done—she had not been hugged by her parents (or seen them hug anyone else) since she was a small child.

Judy didn't have much trouble with the first question asked of her, although it was accompanied by a squeeze of her hand (Rachel's mother seemed to touch other people constantly as they talked). She answered that her father worked for an insurance company and her mother was a chemistry teacher. However, she was uncomfortable about being asked how much her parents earned. Rachel's mother clearly couldn't believe that Judy didn't know, and because this was obviously an important fact about Judy's family, she pressed before reluctantly going on to other subjects.

Judy tried not to be impolite, but in fact there was much that Rachel's mother asked that she couldn't answer, and much about which she said less than she could have. And she couldn't help shrinking away from all the touching and hugging with people she barely knew; they even sat closer together than she liked. By the end of the weekend, Rachel's mother had once referred to her as "my Rachel's mute friend" and intimated that there must be something suspicious about a family with so many secrets.

Judy was embarrassed for Rachel. She felt that she ought to reassure her that everything was still all right between them, and that she hadn't really minded her mother too much, but she hadn't quite found a tactful way to broach the subject. Rachel beat her to it. Soon after they got back to the dorm, she said, "Judy, how could you treat my mother that way? She really put out for you this weekend. She treated you like her own daughter, and you just clammed up every time she asked you a question! And you hurt her feelings when you tried to shake hands instead of hugging her goodbye. How could you be so rude?"

QUESTIONS

1. Having written this case, we worried that the character of Rachel's mother might seem like a negative Jewish stereotype. Do you think it is?

2. Does it make a difference that one author of this case has a Jewish background, and the other has Celtic ancestry?

3. Why would it be unlikely for anyone to complain that Judy is a negative Scottish stereotype? What makes a stereotype?

4. Judy and Rachel come from families with different expectations about physical and emotional openness and the disclosure of personal information. Is there any reason to believe that either view is right?

5. Was Judy rude to Rachel's mother? Because she accepted the invitation of a family with different expectations, should she have been willing to accommodate them? Or should Rachel's mother have been willing to accept Judy's reluctance to discuss her family?

6. Would Judy violate any trust or obligation she has to her family by discussing family matters with Rachel's family?

7. Does a reluctance to talk about yourself suggest that you have something to hide?

ISSUES

Universities feel entitled to do something that would not be tolerated anywhere else (except prison and the military): they assign people to live in the most intimate of arrangements with total strangers. For students living in dorms with roommates, a little time to oneself, a little space of one's own, can be hard to find. Even apart from living arrangements, college life is often more "groupish" than life elsewhere. Students are frequently herded together in classes where they are expected to talk even if they do not wish to. Sometimes they are asked to talk about sensitive or personal matters. Perhaps this book has been a vehicle for such expectations. Is it reasonable for you to be expected to discuss your views on ethical questions of the sort we raise here, in a group situation with people you don't know?

College often subjects students to several kinds of intrusiveness. There is the kind Yusif was the victim of—overt and heavy-handed. Fred simply behaved as though Yusif's views about the use of the room didn't count, and as though Yusif had no right to either privacy or a say about the use of the room. The tension between Judy and Rachel is more subtle. They come from families with quite different views about privacy and intrusiveness. Questions and touching that Judy finds invasive are meant by Rachel's family as an offer of friendship, trust, and inclusion. What Judy sees as protecting her privacy, Rachel's family sees as rejection, coldness, and unsociability.

Somehow privacy seems important in both cases. What is privacy? Should we value it? Why? How does it fit into each case? Is there anything common to the two cases?

Perhaps what is common to the two cases is that both Yusif and Judy have a sense of their own space and feel that someone else has intruded into this space. Yusif's space is in one sense physical—a room. But it is more than that. It is control over space, time, sound, and conversation. Yusif isn't free to arrange the circumstances of his life even in his own room. For Judy the space is not so much physical as psychological. Judy has inhibitions about sharing personal information and being touched. While there is nothing wrong with her sharing personal information and hugging if she wishes to do so, she doesn't want to, and she feels pressured by Rachel's mother to do so. She is especially reluctant to talk about her family, knowing they would not wish it. Thus in both cases what seems at issue is control over personal space.

Perhaps you found the case of Yusif and Fred to be clear-cut. We hope that it is at least obvious that Fred has not treated Yusif very well. Nevertheless, some things may not be very clear. Let's see if we can make the case a little more ambiguous.

APPLYING ETHICAL PRINCIPLES TO THE CASES

First, let's try to see Fred's side of the story, using the principle of the *greatest good*. Fred shares his room with many of his friends, and it's very convenient for them to be able to use it. After all, there is no other handy place for them to practice their music: there are few available empty rooms on campus, and these must be reserved well in advance. Spontaneous jamming can't happen unless they can use Fred's (and Yusif's) room.

Many "goods" come from their jamming together. Playing music builds a sense of camaraderie; it provides a healthy outlet for tension; and it satisfies Fred and his friends' need for creative self-expression. So isn't it possible that Fred and his friends get more benefit from playing music in the dorm room than Yusif loses? Doesn't the principle of the greatest good for the greatest number suggest that if this is true, then Yusif should give way to Fred and his friends? Maybe Yusif should invest in some earplugs.

But if we accept this reasoning, wouldn't it result in Fred having unlimited control over Yusif's space, so long as he and his friends continue to benefit more than Yusif is harmed? Should Yusif have no say in the matter?

These questions can be raised in a more general way. Suppose that people have rights, such as the right to privacy, meaning a right to some control over their personal space. Then suppose that privacy or some other right turns out, under some circumstances, to go against the principle of the greatest good. What do we do then? Does a person still have rights even if, overall, more people benefit from overriding the individual's rights?

We can also apply the principle of *community* to this case. Fred and his friends are forging bonds of friendship and loyalty when they jam together. They are enjoying a shared creative activity and good times, and strengthening their sense of themselves as group. And they have offered to include Yusif. Yusif has a right to refuse and to continue being an outsider. But isn't he being selfish, and in violation of the principle of community, when he refuses to let the others use the room for their jam sessions? The loss of a place to jam could well disrupt their feeling of communal loyalty, and weaken their relationships with each other.

With the principle of the greatest good, the question tends to be, "Where do the individual's rights fit in among the claims of the majority?" With the principle of community, the question instead tends to be, "What protection does the community have from the individual's rights?" For example, how far can people extend their right to privacy and personal space when doing so will affect others in the vicinity? If we claim a right to control our own space, and the area we think of as "our personal space" is big enough, then at some point we begin to control our neighbors.

This point might be clearer if we rewrote the case slightly. Suppose that Yusif insisted there be absolutely no noise at all in the room while he was there, no matter how many people were present. Or suppose he was a "neat freak." Would Yusif have a right to expect Fred to make his bed? Would he have a right to expect Fred to dress "tastefully"? Would he have a right to insist that before people can come into the room, they must first brush their hair, apply some deodorant, and floss their teeth? Just how far can Yusif push his right to control his personal space? Surely Fred (and even his friends) should have a say. Are there principles we can use to decide the boundaries of our personal space?

Let's look at Rachel and Judy and see how these ideas apply to their case. Judy seems to want to control information about herself and her family, to maintain her right to privacy and personal space among strangers. But can she bring her right to control her personal space into Rachel's home? There seem to be good reasons why Judy should let go of some privacy and oblige Rachel's mother. First, Rachel's mother offered Judy hospitality and inclusion, and Judy has accepted. Isn't Judy being rude to Rachel's mother by maintaining her personal space and refusing to answer questions? Second, there is an old saying that "when in Rome, do as the Romans do." Since Judy is in Rachel's home, shouldn't she follow the cultural manners and behavior of Rachel's family? By not following her hosts' lead, isn't Judy saying that her own culture's manners and behavior are better? And third, it's unlikely that opening up to Rachel's mother would hurt Judy. In fact, much good might result. Judy might come to feel so included in Rachel's family that they would become very important to her. Why should she reject their friendship?

To explore these two cases further, we'll need to invent a theory of privacy. It will have to deal with the two central ideas that we've begun to develop above: that privacy involves control over personal space; and that the boundaries of personal space aren't always clear.

A Theory of Privacy

Let's start with a claim that we hope everyone will agree with: people own themselves. We belong to no one but ourselves. Children are not the property of their parents. Husbands do not own their wives, nor vice versa. Owning another person is slavery, and morally intolerable. (Perhaps self-ownership is one outcome of the principle of *equal respect*. Can you explain why?)

What does it mean to say that "I own myself"? Usually when a person owns something, she has the right to use it or dispose of it as she sees fit, without consulting others. An example: because I own my car, I can decide who drives it without calling my parents. Property confers the right to control. So if I own myself, I have the right to control myself.

But if we define "the right to control myself" too broadly, then no one has the right to tell me what to do—I don't have to listen to the police or any other authorities—and this violates the very idea of laws and government. When philosophers such as John Locke[1] emphasize that self-ownership is central to a free society, they don't mean that anything goes. They are saying that monarchy and slavery are wrong, and that democracy is the only ethical form of government.

The challenge then is to figure out how to support the idea of self-ownership without rejecting the very idea of government. Or to put it another way, how can we tell legitimate authority from tyranny? When is allowing others some control over us a good thing, and when is it slavery?

Perhaps owning ourselves doesn't mean we must have absolute control over all aspects of our lives. Maybe we should try to decide what areas of our lives are most important, the ones it would be worst to have someone else control. These central areas can form the core of our right to self-ownership, with other areas being negotiable—we might give (limited) control over them to someone else, or to our society's laws and government.

You may have your own ideas about which areas are most important to protect from control by others. Here are five suggestions:

• First, our *religions and cultures*. Because these things tend to make us the people we are, to be the basis for our deepest understandings of life, they are central parts of us. Self-ownership here means that we have a right to follow the practices and beliefs of our religions and cultures. And if we

[1] John Locke, *Two Treatises of Government*. Introduction by Peter Laslett. (New York: Cambridge University Press, 1960). Original work published 1690.

accept the principle of equal respect, we will respect other people's choices about such things as well.

• Second, our *aspirations*. Most people want to be something, to do something, to be like someone. They want to be philosophers, carpenters, CEOs, photographers, saints, parents, or athletes. They may belong to a group or be committed to some cause. Such aspirations may be crucial to their sense of self. Self-ownership here means that we have a right to our aspirations.

• Third, our *self-respect*. We deny people their self-respect when we subject them to circumstances that are degrading or humiliating, or when we force them to do something they consider wrong or meaningless. These are violations of the basic dignity everyone has under the equal respect principle. Self-ownership here means that we have a right to maintain our self-respect by being treated with consideration.

• Fourth, our *bodies*. Self-ownership here requires that we have a large degree of control over our bodies—with whom, and when, we will be sexual; when we will submit to pain at the hands of others (such as a doctor or a coach); by whom, and how, we will allow ourselves to be touched; and how we will use our bodies in work and play. Obviously we can't control everything that happens to us (illness, accidents, and death come to mind). But we should be able to say "no!" to others' unwanted intrusions on our bodies—the most personal space of all.

• Fifth, *information* about ourselves. What kind of information about us is shared, and with whom, and when, is often quite important to us. If I disclose something about myself to you, I am then vulnerable to you; I risk my self-respect in trusting you to respond appropriately. If I know something about someone else, then I'm in a position to damage her self-respect by criticizing or rejecting who she is, or by using my knowledge to influence others' attitudes toward her. Self-ownership here requires that we be able to control both information about ourselves and the circumstances under which we choose to reveal ourselves to others.

However, even if these five areas are the ones we most want to be able to keep private and have control of, self-ownership in them is not absolute. Respecting people's religion does not mean we have to allow human sacrifices. Respecting people's aspirations doesn't mean we have to employ incompetent workers, or find jobs for those who make things or provide services that nobody wants. But because privacy is a right, we should have compelling reasons for asserting any control over these areas of people's lives.

(Unfortunately, the poor cannot be said to truly own themselves in these five areas. Their right to privacy and self-ownership is effectively denied by the bureaucratic procedures they must follow to get aid, by the conditions of poverty itself, and sometimes by abusive police or other officials. What "compelling reasons," if any, do others use to assert control over the lives of the poor in these areas?)

Which of these five areas are under assault in the cases of Yusif and Judy? No one has attempted to deny them their religion or culture or aspirations. What seems to be first and foremost at stake for Yusif is his self-respect. Fred has essentially told him that his interests and needs don't count, denying Yusif's dignity.

For Judy, what seems perhaps most at stake is her control over information about herself. She was being asked, in effect, to make significant personal disclosures to someone she didn't know, to trust a stranger. Judy had no way of knowing how Rachel's mother would react to anything she might tell her, nor whether Rachel's mother would gossip about her and her family with people unknown. Would this harm Judy or her family? Rachel's mother, while well-meaning, has insisted on Judy disclosing personal information without first establishing a bond of trust between them. Such trust may have to be earned before it is fair to expect personal revelations and the risk to self-respect that they entail.

So far, we've used the ideas in the five areas of privacy to side with Yusif and Judy. But we still need to think about how to describe the boundaries of privacy. There may not be a way to use ethical principles to decide where my personal space ends and yours begins. Take the use of Yusif and Fred's room as an example. At the extremes, it's not hard to decide what to do: neither Yusif nor Fred may behave as though the space is theirs alone and the other person's needs don't count. But beyond that, principles offer little guidance. No doubt if Yusif feels neatness is important, Fred should try not to be too messy, and might help with an occasional cleaning. But how much, and when? And what's "too messy"? We don't know, and we doubt if there is any way to know.

WORKING OUT SOLUTIONS

There is a way to decide such issues, though. Yusif and Fred can discuss the matter and try to seek a mutually acceptable compromise. Yusif in fact proposed this, when he asked Fred to talk about their problems. Fred's refusal to talk may be his worst insult to Yusif's dignity. He's decided that since he can impose his will on Yusif, there's no need for him to consider Yusif's opinions. Fred is thus violating the principle of equal respect.

Fred and Yusif need to talk about how to share the room. If they don't, no fair solution can be reached. And if they want to work something out, their talk can't be a shouting match, either. It must be a *dialogue*. A dialogue, as described in Chapter 1, has two goals: mutual understanding, and consensus or agreement. Three elements must be present in their talk to reach these goals:

- First, the dialogue must seek *voluntary* agreement. An agreement that is coerced is no agreement at all. If Yusif is forced into agreeing with Fred, then Yusif will feel no responsibility to uphold the agreement. Talking until they reach a consensus would help ensure that neither Yusif nor Fred is coerced, and give the agreement moral force.

- Second, the dialogue must assume that all participants are equal. No one is allowed to decide the outcome by an act of authority—"because I said so!" Fred and Yusif's interests and opinions must count as equally important in the discussion.

- And third, the dialogue must work toward an agreement using all of the relevant facts and arguments. By talking together, Yusif and Fred can each uncover facts and arguments that they were not aware of by themselves. Fred might discover that Yusif is having trouble studying and getting sleep. Even more important, he might discover how Yusif feels about this. He might then be willing to explore a schedule for using the room. But facts and arguments are not enough in themselves to decide the matter. Even after the people involved know all there is to be known and have said all there is to be said, they may still disagree. Moral argument can't bring consensus on every issue. However, if both Fred and Yusif begin with the assumption that they have an equal right to use the room and that they will respect each other's dignity and needs, then talking together might very well let them reach a mutually acceptable solution—even if they don't agree about the importance of a particular fact or line of reasoning.

What makes such an agreement ethical? We assume here that one thing that makes something the right thing to do is that we have agreed to do it. An agreement is a promise, and we should keep our promises. Perhaps Fred and Yusif might agree that Fred and his friends can have jam sessions in their room from 8:00 to 10:00 P.M. while Yusif studies in the library. There isn't anything inherently right about this solution, but having agreed to do this, it becomes the right thing to do.

The need for dialogue seems equally pressing in the case of Judy and Rachel. These friends do seem to respect each other's dignity and needs, unlike Fred and Yusif. But they do not understand each other. Rachel doesn't understand Judy's desire for privacy. Judy doesn't understand the importance of sharing personal information in Rachel's family, and why her resistance seems rude. Perhaps these differences are rooted in different cultures, perhaps not. Yet there is nothing incomprehensible in either view. If Judy and Rachel just take the time and effort to try to understand each other's outlook, given good intentions and mutual respect on either side, they are quite likely to fix the misunderstanding between them. The point isn't that once they understand each other's positions, it will become clear just how much touching and self-disclosure are appropriate. But by talking together, Judy can come to understand Rachel's family better, and her willingness to talk about herself may increase; and if Rachel and her mother come to understand Judy's feelings, they will be less likely to press her.

Perhaps neither Judy nor Rachel will be able to explain her feelings clearly. They may both have to struggle to give a name to concepts such as self-disclosure, trust, or inclusion. But that is another reason for dialogue. It is a means to self-understanding as well as agreement. For all these reasons, "let's talk about it" is morally crucial to resolving differences.

EXAMPLES OF COLLEGE AND UNIVERSITY CODES ON PRIVACY

Students' Privacy Regarding Visitors

Forty years ago, most colleges limited the hours and places in which students could entertain guests of the opposite sex. Since the sexual revolution of the late 1960s, few colleges see themselves as acting "in loco parentis" (in the place of parents), and students increasingly are allowed complete freedom regarding visitors in their rooms. Colleges vary widely, however, in the freedom and privacy they allow students in this regard.

1. **Excerpt from the college policies handbook of Hope College[2]**

Guest Hours/Parietals

No person shall be in a living unit with someone of the opposite gender outside of the visiting hours listed below. [. . .]

Parietals govern the visiting privileges of members of opposite gender in the living units. Parietals exist to help create a safe, private, and quiet atmosphere in which students live.

Guest/parietal hours have been set as:

Sun.–Thur. 11:00 A.M. to 12 midnight

Fri. and Sat. 10:00 A.M. to 2:00 A.M.

Residence hall lobbies and basement common areas, and cottage or apartment living areas are the only open areas during restricted hours.

---

[2] *Handbook of Selected College Policies 2000–2001*, Hope College, p. 15.

2. Excerpt from the survival handbook of Antioch College[3]

Visitors and Guests

[. . .] In the past few years there have been some problems with 'permanent' visitors. If you have someone visiting you who is staying for more than one week you should clear this with the Housing Office first.

Students' Privacy Regarding Their Records

1. Excerpt from the student handbook of Tompkins Cortland Community College[4]

Public Notice Designating Directory Information

Tompkins Cortland Community College hereby designates the following categories of student information as public or "Directory Information." Such information may be disclosed by the College at its discretion, for any purpose.

Category I. Name, address, telephone number, dates of attendance, classes for which currently registered, enrollment status (full-time, part-time, new, continuing, transfer).

Category II. Previous institution(s) attended, major field of study, awards, honors, degree(s) conferred (including dates).

Category III. Past and present participation in officially recognized sports and activities, physical factors (height, weight of athletes), date and place of birth.

Currently enrolled students may withhold disclosure of any category of information under the Family Educational Rights and Privacy Act of 1974. To withhold disclosure, written notification must be received in the Office of the Registrar within the first two weeks of the semester. . . . The College assumes that failure on the part of any student to specifically request the withholding of categories of "Directory Information" indicates individual approval for disclosure.

2. Excerpt from the code of student ethics of Indiana University[5]

'Public information' is limited to name; address; phone; major field of study; dates of attendance; admission or enrollment status; campus; school, college, or division; class standing; degrees and awards; activities;

---

[3] *1994–95 Survival Handbook*, Antioch College (Community Government), p. 61.

[4] *2000–2001 Student Handbook*, Tompkins Cortland Community College (Dryden, NY), pp. 55–56.

[5] "Appendix 4: Indiana University Release of Student Information Policy," *Code of Student Ethics*, Indiana University (University Faculty Council, 29 March 1977), pp. 43–44.

sports; and athletic information. Records of arrests and/or convictions and traffic accident information are public information and may be released to anyone making inquiry. [. . . .]

[. . .] Public information shall be released freely unless the student files the appropriate form requesting that certain public information not be released. [. . . .]

[. . .] A student's record is open to the student, with the following exceptions:

1. Confidential letters of recommendation [. . .] [if they] carry waivers signed by the student relinquishing the right of access to the document.
2. Records of parents' financial status.
3. Employment records.
4. Medical and psychological records; [. . . .]

[. . .] Student records are open to members of the faculty and staff who have a legitimate need to know their contents [. . . .]

[. . .] Normally, records can be released—or access given—to third parties (i.e., anyone not a member of the faculty and staff) only at the written request of the student. Without the consent of the student, releases to third parties may be given only as follows:

i. To parents of students who are dependents as defined by IRS standards.
ii. To federal officers as prescribed by law.
iii. As required by state law.
iv. To research projects on behalf of educational agencies for test norms, improving instruction, etc. (provided that the agencies guarantee no personal identification of students).
v. To accrediting agencies carrying out their functions.
vi. In response to a judicial order or lawfully issued subpoena [. . . .]
vii. By IU Police to other law enforcement agencies in the investigation of a specific criminal case.

ADDITIONAL CASES

CASE 4.3   *The Assignment*

Brian has enjoyed his Women's History class and enjoyed being one of the few male students in the course, but the assignment for the final paper (half of his grade!) angers him. "Interview the women in your family (as many as possible) and write their personal histories, analyzing them in terms of the demographic trends and social categories we have discussed," it read.

After class, Brian tried to explain to the instructor why he couldn't do this. "First, I don't have any female relatives that I'm in touch with except my mother and my sister," he said.

"Fine! Just interview them," the instructor said. "Or maybe you could use this assignment as an excuse to get in touch with some of your other relatives!" she added brightly.

Brian tried to imagine how his intensely private and bitter mother, estranged from her parents for thirty years, would react to this idea (his father's parents were dead, and he had no aunts). He changed his tack. "Besides, I don't think it's appropriate for me to try to get my mother and sister to tell me their problems and innermost thoughts; we don't do that in my family."

The professor was not dissuaded. "This assignment might be just the way to open your family up, then. You'll probably learn a lot about them that will give you a new respect and empathy for them, and they will be touched that you care."

That was ridiculous, Brian thought. Rather than feeling "touched," they would be outraged that he presumed to violate their privacy just to get a grade, sharing their secrets with a complete stranger to mark up with a red pen. Brian gave one last try: "I don't feel comfortable putting them in little niches like the 'trends and categories' we've talked about—they're too complex for that, they're individuals."

The instructor clearly was starting to lose patience with him. "Just do the best you can," she said as she turned to talk to the next student waiting for her.

QUESTIONS

1. Brian sees the assignment as an invasion of his privacy, whereas his instructor seems to see it as a means to self-understanding and perhaps family therapy, in addition to measuring how well students have absorbed the concepts taught in the course. It is probably true that we can learn much from making connections between the subjects we study in school and our personal lives. But can such connections be mandated? Do teachers have a right to make students dissect their personal feelings or family backgrounds in class, or for a grade?

2. Do such assignments show a lack of respect for students' differing cultural backgrounds, or is it merely a matter of different personalities preferring different kinds of assignments?

3. How should a student respond when faced with an assignment he or she regards as overly intrusive?

4. More generally, can, or should, a college force students to analyze their opinions and become more self-reflective? Where does the professor's duty to stimulate reflection and critical thinking (and the right to grade students on their abilities in this regard) end, and the student's right to privacy begin?

CASE 4.4   *Raided!*

At 9:45 P.M. on Thursday, an unidentified number of students (wearing stockings over their heads to disguise their features) burst into Hamilton House, a small co-ed residence hall on the edge of campus. Screaming like maniacs, they sprayed shaving cream wildly, threw rolls of toilet paper into every open door, and then ran out again before their stunned victims could respond.

Maggie was hard at work studying in her room when the raid occurred. She knows that raids like this are supposed to be good clean fun and part of college life. But she, like Queen Victoria, Is Not Amused. In fact, she thinks raiding is pretty stupid and immature, and she's angry about having her studying disturbed. Not only did she completely lose her train of thought when the raid started, she couldn't get back to work at all that night because her housemates were so noisy and excited as they exclaimed over the mess and planned for a return raid on the suspected perpetrators, the inhabitants of Jackson Hall. Worst of all, the shaving cream left permanent streaks on the photographs Maggie hung on her wall. They are the only large prints she has of her best pictures, taken over several years, and many of them are irreplaceable. She's furious!

QUESTIONS

1. Maggie's housemates seem to feel that the best response to a raid is "Don't get mad, get even." Is this an appropriate response if they aren't even sure who raided them?

2. Even if some residents of Jackson Hall are responsible for the raid, is a retaliatory raid likely to prevent, or encourage, future raids? Is it fair to Jackson Hall students who may not have known anything about the original raid?

3. Because Maggie thinks raiding is "stupid and immature," presumably she won't want to participate in a retaliatory raid no matter how mad she is. What other options might she have for punishing the raiders and/or ensuring that no more raids take place?

4. The raiders would probably claim that they hadn't meant any harm and hadn't realized that the shaving cream would ruin some of Maggie's prized possessions. Does Maggie really have a right to get so bent out of shape about a very temporary invasion of her space (the raid took all of three minutes) and accidental damage of her property?

5. Because everyone at Maggie's college knows about the possibility of raids, is it Maggie's responsibility to protect her belongings from damage during a raid, perhaps by keeping her special photos in a drawer rather than on the wall?

6. Activities such as the raid have been part of the college experience for years. Most students appear to enjoy them. They are long remem-

bered. They seem to help build a sense of solidarity with one's peers, and even with the institution. Are these community-building activities? Is that a reason to tolerate them or even encourage them?

Searching   CASE 4.5

Sam had a rather lonely first semester at college. Actually, it wasn't much worse than high school, but all through high school he'd kept thinking that things at college would be different. He imagined college as the place where he'd have long talks about the meaning of life with people who thought about the deeper things. He'd read The Important Books and learn from fascinating professors. Perhaps he'd even meet a girl who cared more about ideas and spirituality than looks and popularity. However, it hadn't worked out that way. He was still searching.

Toward the end of Spring semester, his luck seemed to change when he met Rashelle and Ben. They were very friendly and outgoing, and somehow they got Sam talking about the missing spiritual dimension in his life, even though he hardly knew them. "You know," Rashelle said, "this weekend there just happens to be a spiritual retreat that we're going on. We went to one before, and I loved it—lots of good talk, good people, and good food. I bet you'd like it too." "Why don't you come with us?" Ben smiled engagingly. "It's a great way to meet people you can really talk to. And it will be fun—we'll camp out together, play volleyball, do the whole campfire thing."

And so it was that Sam found himself that weekend at an isolated campsite with about fifteen people he didn't know. At first, it did seem rather fun and adventurous. Friday night they played volleyball and had a campfire as advertised. But Sam soon began to feel that he had been misled. It rapidly became clear that the "retreat" was not just vaguely spiritual, but an intense indoctrination into a religious sect. The group sat in a large circle, where the campers took turns describing their spiritual failings and pressuring Sam to come up with similar confessions. This emotional discussion continued until late at night, when the talk turned to ways to be "saved." Sam was very tired, but they mocked him for wanting to sleep when his soul was at stake and badgered him to confess and be saved.

This intense pressure continued all weekend. Sam stayed up all night Friday and barely got any sleep at all on Saturday. By Sunday, he was so tired and had had so many heated exchanges about various points of belief and exhausting emotional ups and downs (he had been both hugged by everyone in the group and shouted at for over an hour) that he didn't know what to think anymore about anything. The group had convinced him that his life was lonely and alienated, and that perhaps the way to happiness lay in bonding with them and accepting their doctrines. So before he left on Sunday, he agreed to start coming to their prayer meetings on Tuesdays and Thursdays.

"I'm so happy you've seen the light!" Rashelle sobbed with tears streaming down her face. "I'll come pick you up at your room at 7:00 P.M. on Tuesday. Welcome, brother!"

Unfortunately, by Tuesday morning, when Sam had caught up on his sleep and had a chance to think things over, he was no longer at all sure that he wanted to be part of their group. But Rashelle and Ben seemed to read his mind. They found him in his room after lunch, and in their friendly way managed to stick near him until seven o'clock, when Sam found himself heading off with them to the prayer meeting.

The more they pressured him in the days ahead, the more resistant Sam felt. Finally he told them outright that he'd decided he wasn't interested in their group, and that they should leave him alone. But this did not seem to deter them. "You promised to try it out, Sam. Open your heart, and you'll never be sorry you did," said Ben. "We care about you!" Rashelle added. "A battle is going on in your soul, and we can't let you fight it alone. We're your friends, Sam!"

Sam thought with a shock, "Some friends. How am I going to get rid of them so I can figure things out for myself?"

QUESTIONS

1. Is intense religious proselytizing of this nature an invasion of privacy? How?

2. Did Rashelle and Ben deceive Sam, and if so, can such deceit be justified?

3. Sam volunteered to them that he was searching for something spiritual in his life, and he chose to go to both their retreat and some prayer meetings. Does this mean that he owes it to Rashelle and Ben to give their faith (more) serious consideration?

4. Are Rashelle and Ben really friends to Sam? Why or why not?

5. Which moral principles might be relevant to this case, and how would you apply them in giving Sam advice about what to do?

CASE 4.6   *Smooching in the Lounge*

Rita and Anna were in love, and radiantly happy. But at their small, conservative school, there were few opportunities for lesbian couples to hold hands, much less have sex. Like all first-year students there, Rita and Anna had each been assigned to live in triples, rooms they shared with two other roommates. They thus found themselves limited to long talks, hugs, and furtive kisses. And then late one night they were "caught" kissing in the residence hall lounge. Three students suddenly came upon them cuddling in a dark corner and immediately started hassling them. Anna knew one of them, Paul, who lived down the hall from her and her roommates, and she and Rita had seen the other two around the school. But the fact that they all vaguely knew each other didn't stop Paul and his friends from swearing and shouting at Rita and Anna. "This is disgusting! You dykes are polluting the lounge—get out of here! You make us sick!" and more in the same vein.

Anna and Rita were so embarrassed and taken aback that at first they didn't respond. But then Rita started arguing that what they did was none of his business and that they had every bit as much right to use the lounge as anyone else.

At this Paul grabbed Rita's arm and roughly yanked her off the couch. "You have NO right to be here, you dirty little creep!" he shouted menacingly. "God hates perverts, and you belong in hell!"

"C'mon Rita," said Anna, getting up too. "Let's get out of here before Mr. Religious does something really stupid."

QUESTIONS

1. Have Anna's and Rita's rights to privacy been violated?

2. Since the lounge is public space, can students forbid behavior they find offensive there, such as lesbians' kissing? If not, how should offended students deal with public affronts to their sensibilities and perhaps to their religious beliefs? If so, which students should get to decide what constitutes "offensive behavior"?

3. Would your answers be the same regarding straight couples' making out in the lounge at night? In other words, should public space be off limits for all sexual activity if it bothers some students, or should those students mellow out?

4. Because gay students are often ostracized and persecuted, do they deserve special consideration here?

5. Arguments about acceptable uses of the common lounge might be similar in some ways to debates in some communities over the use of (semi-)public spaces. Neighborhoods' attempts to ensure "standards of decency" in common areas can range from efforts to get rid of "adult" bookstores to the imposition of zoning and yard maintenance requirements on homeowners. In all these cases, the questionable behavior is legal, and probably not offensive to some members of the community. The question is how to balance the competing interests of a community's consensus on public morals and appearances, and individuals' rights to privacy and the pursuit of happiness. What is the fairest way to make decisions about the use of public space? How might the principle of the greatest good apply here?

6. How could dialogue between people with such radically different positions work?

CASE 4.7   *Telephone Harassment*

Laura likes to think of herself as a kind-hearted person who is sympathetic to the underdog and open to new people. But recent events have challenged her self-image. A couple of times last semester, she had listened sympathetically to a lonely guy named Dan who talked to her after class about his problems. Gradually, Laura realized that Dan seemed both to have a crush on her and to be slightly disturbed. So Laura smiled at him but made excuses not to talk any more. She didn't want to encourage him, but she also didn't want to hurt his feelings by rejecting him outright. Then Dan stopped waiting for her after class, and Laura was relieved. The school year was almost over, and she was busy with exams, papers, and goodbyes. She forgot about Dan.

Back at her parents' for the summer, Laura got a call late one evening. Her mother handed her the phone with a sharp reminder to have her friends call before 11:00 P.M., and Laura sleepily said, "Hello?" It was Dan. He'd gotten her parents' phone number and address from the Student Records Office, and said that he had to talk to her. He loved her and needed her; she was the only one who understood him. Laura tried to extricate herself from this embarrassing conversation and finally hung up, saying, "I'm sorry, I have to go to bed!" But Dan was not dissuaded; he called her right back.

This time Laura was firmer. "You can't call me this late!" she said. "I don't want to talk to you!" But as soon as she hung up, the phone rang again. This time, she turned the ringer off and let the answering machine pick up, but her heart was racing as she heard Dan's voice saying, "I know you're there! Talk to me!"

These calls turned out to be the first of literally hundreds. Dan called so often, at all hours of the day and night, that Laura's parents finally had to get an unlisted phone number. Now Laura no longer hears from him, but she is still angry and frightened. He has her address. What if he tries to come to the house? She has no idea how far away he lives or how likely he is to carry his telephone pursuit into a physical pursuit. He seems to be a harmless crank, but she wonders what might happen if his telephone harassment turns into something scarier. Her parents are worried, too, but also irritated with Laura. They seem to think that somehow she must have encouraged Dan's crazy attentions and "led him on." Laura feels sure she hasn't, but can't understand why he is picking on her. What will happen when she returns to school in the fall?

QUESTIONS

1. Is Laura somehow at fault for Dan's harassment, as her parents think? If you said yes, what could she have done differently?

2. Are her only future options either fearfully keeping to herself or being open to new people who may hurt or bother her? How might she protect herself from further harassment?

3. Does she have any duty to help Dan, perhaps by trying to get him into counseling or by finding out more about his life and why he thinks she, a virtual stranger, is the only one who understands him? Is dialogue with Dan a reasonable way for Laura to deal with him, or has he proven himself unsuitable for such an approach?

4. Colleges often allow all kinds of information about students to be divulged without the students' express permission (see the examples of college and university codes on privacy above). Students are usually told (in fine print) that they can forbid the release of personal information, but they must sign a special form in advance. And because the Records or Registrar's Office is often the only way to locate a long-lost college friend, many students hesitate to tell the college not to give out their home address or phone number. Other students never worry about this; in fact Laura never signed the waiver forbidding the Records Office from giving out this information. Alumni groups and other organizations also may have legitimate reasons for wanting to get in touch with the members of the class of 2006. How can colleges help prevent situations like Dan's telephone harassment of Laura? If you were a college administrator, how would you try to balance students' right to privacy with others' legitimate desires for information about them?

Apartment 3-G　　　　　　　　　　　　　**CASE 4.8**

Tameka, Tracy, and Juanita share an apartment with a common kitchen and living area, and each student has her own bedroom. The three women like each other personally, but their different sexual styles are driving them apart. Tameka is practically married to her boyfriend, Glenn, and he sleeps at the apartment regularly. Tracy occasionally has short affairs with men she brings home, rarely seeing the same one for more than a few nights. Juanita is a virgin and doesn't approve of having men in the apartment at all. At first Juanita was shocked that her roommates were having sex, but now she just resents having men around because their presence intrudes so much on her privacy.

When Glenn or one of Tracy's guys stays overnight, Juanita feels that she can't walk around in her underwear or eat breakfast in the morning before she's got her "face" on. They also seem so inconsiderate: men always seem to leave the toilet seat up; a guy once walked in on her in the bathroom without knocking; and she finds it distracting, to say the least, to hear sex through her wall when she's trying to sleep or study. She also hates the surprise of waking up to find some strange man (Tracy's one-night stand) sitting at the kitchen table. Glenn is bad in a different way. Although he's friendly, he never does chores around the apartment, and he leaves his clothes and books in the living room, or forgets the remains of a late-night carton of ice cream on the kitchen counter. Tameka has tried to pick up after him ever since

Juanita mentioned the problem, but Juanita thinks Glenn should pick up after himself. And she says that if he's going to be there so often, he should pay rent, too, and share household cleaning jobs and the phone bill.

In fact, Tameka, Glenn, and Tracy have agreed to share the apartment and split the rent if Juanita wants to move. Juanita does want to leave, but housing is tight and she can't move before next semester or perhaps even next year. Besides, she feels that she is being forced out by their inconsiderateness. They shouldn't just get their way and make her go through the hassle of finding somewhere else to live and moving all of her stuff. It's not fair.

QUESTIONS

1. Tameka feels that she's trying to accommodate Juanita by picking up after her boyfriend. Is this enough to make up for the inconvenience his presence causes Juanita? What else could, or should, Tameka, Glenn, and Tracy do?

2. Someone else might not be bothered at all by the men's presence and Tameka and Tracy's behavior. Does this mean that Juanita has no right to be upset?

3. Does Juanita have a right to insist that no men be allowed in the apartment, or is this too great an imposition on her roommates?

4. There is a difference between Glenn and Tracy's one-night stands in the inconvenience they cause Juanita. Should there be a difference in how she responds or what she asks of them?

5. Should Juanita try to talk with the bothersome men directly, or with her roommates, who are responsible for inviting the men there?

6. At least for now, the apartment is home to all three women. How can they accomodate each of their rights to privacy?

CASE 4.9   *Noise Pollution*

It's a beautiful spring day toward the end of the final exam period. Out in front of West Hall dorm, students are celebrating the end of exams by playing frisbee and hackysack to the sound of music blasting out of the open windows of their rooms. Like a giant amplifier, the front of the multistoried dorm picks the music up and sends it echoing out across the quad. Windows are open all over to let in the fresh air, glorious sunshine, and sounds of spring. The scene looks idyllic, except for one jarring detail: first one student, and then another, leans out of the dorm windows and shouts something at the celebrators that can't be heard, their faces contorted with annoyance and anger.

A few minutes later, several of the angry students are outside arguing with the music lovers. It seems that they can't study with the music playing, even when they shut their windows. The music players think that requests to turn the music off or way down are unreasonable. They want to be able to hear music on the quad as they celebrate. They point out that most students are finished with their exams and papers, and they suggest that the few people who aren't should go to the library if they need quiet. The angry students respond that they feel pressured enough without all the noise. They don't want to go to the library because they have too many books to lug, and it's not convenient. "We should be able to study in our own rooms!" they shout. The two groups seem at an impasse.

QUESTIONS

1. Should one group of students clearly have priority in this situation? If so, which one, and why?

2. How might they negotiate a compromise that respects everyone's interests? Might the principles of the greatest good, community, and equal respect suggest different solutions to this conflict?

3. Does the fact that noises and smells are less tangible invasions of one's space than the presence of other people mean that they are less important intrusions on privacy, or that they should be treated more leniently?

Smokers' Rights? CASE 4.10

Hippocrates Community College recently designated all buildings on the entire campus as "smoke free." Student smokers have vocally protested this decision. They see the College's action as an invasion of their privacy and freedom to make the choice to smoke. "It's just nosiness on the part of our obsessively health-conscious and paranoid administration," a sophomore named Sunil told the student newspaper. His view is apparently shared by a number of students, faculty, and staff (especially those with European or Third World backgrounds, who find Americans' obsession with secondhand smoke bizarre). Sunil went on, "What the administration is really saying is that 'smoking is morally bad,' although they pretend it's a health issue. If it were really just about secondhand smoke bothering some people, they would have places for smokers to go. But they really want to *punish* smokers and make them go outside in freezing weather for a smoke. They like to see smokers suffer for their 'sins.'"

QUESTIONS

1. Does Sunil have a point? Do smokers have privacy rights? That is, should they be able to smoke in private (say in their private rooms, or in a public bathroom when no one else is in it)?

2. The College might argue against allowing smoking anywhere not only because of the dangers of secondhand smoke for nonsmokers, but also because smokers should be discouraged from hurting their own health, and because of the danger of fire. But is harming your own health anyone else's business? Why or why not?

3. People have been smoking on the Hippocrates campus since it was founded forty years ago, and there have been no reported cases of fires being caused by cigarettes. Does this record mean that the administration has no right to use fire safety as a grounds for forbidding smoking?

4. Which moral principles might apply here, and how?

CASE 4.11   *Porn Assignment?*

Emily stared at the screen, but she couldn't concentrate on her Economics assignment. Out of the corner of her eye, pink and brown images of naked bodies squirming across the computer screen next to hers kept distracting her. Was that was she thought it was? She took a better look.

"Oh my God," she thought. "They *are* having sex!" She tried to shut the pumping figures out of her mind, but they wouldn't go. The guy watching them was breathing heavily. "This is disgusting," Emily fumed.

Emily tried to reposition her body so that she couldn't see the pornography. But the computer lab chairs were too close together to create much distance.

So she tried another tack. "Maybe if I stare at him, he'll have some shame," she decided. "I can't believe he's doing this right in the lab!"

She turned back to face him and glared. He was an ordinary-enough looking guy, not obviously perverted, and about her age—and he was glued to that hard-core screen with his mouth slightly open, paying no attention to her stare. "He looks like he's about to drool or something," Emily thought to herself. "What a total jerk." Then she noticed he had one hand in his lap. "Oh my God, is he actually . . . ?" Her face flushed. "I can't sit next to this!"

Emily saved her work and stood up, angrily slamming her books together. The porn-watcher didn't seem to notice. She meant to change to another computer, but as she crossed her station off the sign-up list, indicating it was now free, she discovered that all thought of the Economics assignment was banished from her mind. "I can't work on this anymore right now; I'm too upset," she realized. "Maybe I should go get a snack or something. And he'd better be gone when I come back!"

QUESTIONS

1. Would you have dealt with this situation differently if you were in Emily's position? What are some of the options she might have had, besides just glaring and then leaving?

2. Why do you think Emily didn't talk directly to the porn-watcher and tell him to stop? How might the idea of privacy apply here, both to her and to him?

3. You might well be able to apply several of the ethical principles we've discussed to this case. Which seem most useful here, and how would you use them to analyze the positions of Emily and the porn-watcher?

BACKGROUND READING

- David L. Kirp, "Proceduralism and Bureaucracy: Due Process in the School Setting," in *Stanford Law Review*, 1976, vol. 38, p. 841. This article discusses the advantages of "structured conversations" (slightly more formal versions of what we call dialogues) over the legal route of due process hearings and so on, for resolving disagreements, especially in college settings.

- The Family Educational Rights and Privacy Act of 1974 (20 U.S.C. 1232g, "The Buckley Amendment," subsequently amended and clarified by U.S. Senate Joint Resolution No. 40) is a piece of federal legislation that guarantees all students access to their personal educational records (with some limitations), allows them to challenge these records as "inaccurate, misleading, or otherwise inappropriate," and protects their privacy when a third party (other than a school official) wants to see their personal records.

- Several sources discuss the almost unnoticed loss of privacy that is occurring as society becomes more computerized and personal information becomes available to merchants, the direct marketing industry, social service workers, and various officials without our knowledge or consent. Such information includes material generally considered private, such as educational accomplishments and records, credit ratings, income levels, purchasing habits, health records, job histories, and psychiatric records. See Anne Wells Branscomb, *Who Owns Information? From Privacy to Public Access* (New York: Basic Books, 1994); Jeffrey Rothfeder, *Privacy for Sale: How Computerization Has Made Everyone's Private Life an Open Secret* (New York: Simon and Schuster, 1992); *Privacy Journal: An Independent Monthly on Privacy in a Computer Age* (P.O. Box 28577, Providence, RI 02908, (401) 274-7861); and Peter McGrath with Patrick Rogers, "Info 'Snooper-Highway' Privacy: As Computer Power Grows, So Does the Personal Information Available. Have We Compromised Ourselves?" in *Newsweek*, 27 February 1995, p. 61.

ADDITIONAL MATERIALS

1. "Student Sues College, Saying Party-Animal Roommate Drove Him into Therapy," in *The New York Times*, 27 May 1994, sec. B, p. 5, col. 1. This article relates the case of an Albright College freshman who requested a docile, studious, and philosophical roommate on the "compatibility" questionnaire the school sent out over the summer. Instead, he was paired with a football player who did not study, played loud music, and partied late. The student then dropped out after two months, claiming that he developed posttraumatic stress disorder because of his assigned roommate and had to go into intensive psychotherapy. He finally decided to sue the college for negligence, and his ex-roommate as well. If you were on a jury for this case, would you believe that someone could develop "posttraumatic stress disor-

der" as a result of two months with an incompatible roommate? Would you allow the college to be held financially liable for roommate incompatibility? Which moral principles might apply here, and how?

2. Bob Levey, "Holiday Question: Who Sleeps Where?" in *The Washington Post*, 13 December 1994, sec. B, p. 11, col. 1. This is the story of a student who refused to come home for the holidays unless his parents let him and his girlfriend sleep in the same bed at their home. The parents felt that in their house, their son should not sleep with a woman unless he was married to her. He thought this was hypocritical because they knew he slept with his girlfriend at school. Is the son's behavior an example of emotional blackmail, or a principled stand? The student and his parents obviously have different ideas about acceptable social norms regarding premarital sex. How can they respect each other's views and stay in the same house? Who should decide who sleeps where, and why should their views be given priority? How might this argument be framed in terms of competing rights to self-ownership?

3. Geeta Anand, "Waltham Police Appeal to Parents of Noisy Students," in *The Boston Globe*, 27 November 1994, sec. WW, p. 1, col. 1. In the two years since a new letter-writing policy began to deal with noise complaints, Waltham, Massachusetts police mailed twenty letters of complaint to parents of students at both Brandeis University and Bentley College. The letters drew outrage from students, who wanted to be treated equally under the law and not have the police go over their heads to their parents. Are such letters an invasion of students' privacy? Should students (or anyone else) lose their rights to privacy if they break laws or regulations like the Waltham noise ordinance? Do you think writing to parents would be an effective way to deal with noisy students? Is it fair? Why or why not?

4. Peter McGrath with Patrick Rogers, "Info 'Snooper-Highway' Privacy," in *Newsweek*, 27 February 1995, p. 61. "Last month, 28 Harvard students were mortified to learn that the campus newspaper, *The Crimson*, had identified them as consumers of pornography simply by tracking their Internet activities through the university's network." Did *The Crimson's* actions violate the students' privacy? Could there be any ethical reason(s) for publishing the names of students (or others) who "consume pornography"? Which moral principles might you use in analyzing this incident, and how? Is there anything wrong with the monitoring of Internet users' hobbies and interests by others for various purposes? What can computer users do to protect their privacy? For more information, see the third set of items under Background Readings in this chapter.

5. Kelly McCollum, "Hackers Attack Web Site Set Up to Nab Student Rioters at Michigan State U.," in *The Chronicle of Higher Education*, 23 April 1999, vol. 45, i. 33, p. A38. Privacy issues were at the center of a contro-

versy surrounding a Michigan State University Web site containing pictures of rioting students. The University posted riot photos at the site to solicit help in identifying the rioters, drawing criticism about nonparticipants featured in the photos. Then the site was hacked into, possibly to obtain the names of informants, which created additional privacy problems. What are some of the ethical principles involved in this situation? Under what principles might the University appeal for help in identifying rioters? Under what moral principles might the people featured in the photos object? And what principles might have motivated the hackers to hack into the site? Which moral principles do you feel should be paramount in this case, and why?

6. Leo Reisberg, "When a Student Drinks Illegally, Should Colleges Call Mom and Dad?" in *The Chronicle of Higher Education*, 4 December 1998, vol. 45, i. 15, p. A39(2). Many academic institutions, including the University of Delaware and Radford University, have an alcohol policy involving notification of a student's parents. Some colleges and universities, however, fear that sharing disciplinary records with parents would violate a law that protects students' privacy, the Family Educational Rights and Privacy Act. (Congress did pass an amendment to the Higher Education Act that allows colleges to inform parents if a student under 21 violates alcohol or drug laws.) Do you believe that informing parents about an offspring's illegal drinking invades that student's right to privacy? Is the issue important enough that such an invasion of privacy may be justified? Do you think calling parents is an effective way to deal with student drinking? Whose responsibility should it be when someone of college age breaks a law?

7. Robin Wilson, "Professor Cited for 'Amorous' Relationship with Student Accuses Appalachian State U. of Violating His Rights," in *The Chronicle of Higher Education*, 20 March 1998, vol. 44, no. 28, p. A13. Administrators at Appalachian State University accused an assistant professor of violating a 1996 policy that forbids "amorous" relationships between faculty members and the students they supervise. However, the professor in turn accused the University of violating his rights to due process and privacy, by seizing his office, combing through his electronic files, and planning to demote him to an instructor and cut his salary. Do you believe "seizing" his office and "combing through" his electronic files were appropriate actions to put an end to a forbidden professor–student affair? Would the University be justified in doing a similar search for some other violation of university policy, or for crimes punishable under state or federal statutes? What if University officials found nothing incriminating during their search of his computer and office—is such an action then less justifiable? Would there be any difference ethically between searching the student's computer files and searching the professor's? What are the conditions under which such an invasion of privacy could be justifiable?

5

LOYALTY, FRIENDSHIP, AND COMMUNITY

TWO CASES: UNITED WE STAND?

CASE 5.1 *Loyalty Test*

Barbara Stalking Bear is president of the Native American Student Association. Her friend Roger Turner is treasurer. They have been friends for the three years that they've been at Amigos Community College and have worked together on a number of projects for NASA—an acronym whose irony they both enjoy.

They became friends despite some significant differences in their backgrounds. Barbara comes from a middle-income family in a suburb of a large eastern city. Barbara's father teaches biology in the local high school. Her mother is a lawyer. Although her parents encouraged her to explore her heritage, they have not been active in any community of Native Americans, so Barbara's exploration of Native American cultures and history has been academic. Friends occasionally comment on her last name, but Barbara's father is two generations removed from being a functional part of a Native American community, and Barbara's mother has a French and Irish background with only a small amount of Native American blood. Until she went to college, being Native American was not part of who Barbara was. Roger helped change that.

Roger was born and raised on a Cheyenne reservation in Oklahoma. He grew up poor and angry. Barbara has learned something about Native American culture from her parents, but she has learned about the oppression and reality of Native American life from Roger. There are other differences. Barbara's Iroquois father's ancestors were from somewhere in central New York. Barbara supposes that the Iroquois and the Cheyenne share about as much common culture as the French and the Germans do—perhaps less; but she also thinks that solidarity among Native Americans is important and that discovering or even inventing a shared culture is worthwhile. Here, too, Roger has been her guide. He has many insights into Native American traditions and helps Barbara see themes and commonalities. Roger is a traditionalist, but he is quite willing to incorporate the wisdom of various Native American cultures into his beliefs.

Thus their friendship has developed despite the differences in their backgrounds. Roger has been the mentor, Barbara the devoted apprentice. Nor has their friendship been strained by one durable difference in their views of what is involved in being Native American. As Barbara learns about contemporary Indian life, she has come to see herself as a modernizer. She now thinks of herself primarily as a Native American, and she respects Native American traditions. She also believes that Native peoples need to become more integrated into mainstream society to escape their poverty and stigmatization. She wants to see them become doctors, lawyers, and business people. She wants them to avail themselves of opportunities off the reservations. Indeed, she quietly hopes for a form of life for her people in which reservations will disappear.

Roger, however, is not only a traditionalist, but a hard-core traditionalist. He is intensely committed to restoring the traditional values and lifestyles of Native Americans. This commitment has often led him into conflict with other Native Americans and with whites. He has actively resisted the emergence of casino gambling as a way for reservations to generate income and develop capital. He often criticizes other Native Americans on campus because they see their education more as a means to advance their careers than to improve the welfare of their people. In contrast, he views his college education as a way to "learn the white man's ways in order to resist white oppression."

The sharpest point of contention between Roger and Barbara has to do with spirituality. Curiously, both Roger and Barbara have been raised as Presbyterians. Barbara isn't sure how seriously she takes her Christianity. She rarely attends church anymore and doesn't miss it much. However, her lack of faith extends to religion generally. She isn't very interested in converting to one of the Native faiths, which seem puzzling to her and unsuited to the life she is likely to live after graduation. Roger, however, is deeply committed to the recovery of Native American spirituality. He has worked to discover what traditional Native American religions teach and to distill an understanding of spirituality that is authentically Cheyenne. He and a group of friends have begun to meet to discuss and practice what they are learning. Often they invite Native American leaders renowned for their high level of spirituality to campus to instruct them. Roger and his friends believe that spirituality is the foundation of everything Native American, and increasingly they make commitment to that spirituality the litmus test for who is a "real" Native American.

Barbara's friendship with Roger has survived even this difference. She has attended a few meetings and made polite and noncommittal excuses to avoid others. She respects Roger's commitment. As president of NASA, she has agreed to use some of the organization's funds to bring in those whom Roger identifies as spiritual leaders.

But now Roger has gone too far for her. He signed two large checks that, as far as she can see, were not approved by her or anyone else. After a little investigation, she found that the checks were apparently used to conduct a peyote ceremony. One went to the man who led the ceremony. The other paid for the peyote. Both checks were for nontrivial amounts, considering the modest budget of a student organization.

Barbara is stunned. A little checking reveals that the sale, purchase, or use of peyote is illegal in their state. Peyote is a controlled substance. Roger has very likely committed a felony and involved others in it. He has also used NASA funds without submitting the expenditures for approval. In short, he has stolen them, and because some of NASA's money comes from the college's student organization fund, he has very likely spent college money on an illegal activity. She earnestly hopes that she won't have to justify these expenses to anyone from the student activities office.

Her meeting with Roger is a disaster. He is utterly unrepentant. He claims to have "liberated" some of the "white man's money" and considers it reparations, but what bothers her most is his attitude toward her. He makes her support of his actions a test not only of their friendship, but also of whether she is a true Native American. "It's time you decide," he says. "Are you one of us, or an apple? You need to get a red soul to go with your red skin."

CASE 5.2   *Group Guilt*

Dean Wong decided that the problem might be solved by an approach that involved a little open discussion instead of a judicial hearing. The brothers of Tau Rho Epsilon were not known to be troublemakers. They didn't violate the university's liquor regulations. The TREs were normally good students. They were what a fraternity should be—harmless.

Except for their Christmas initiation rite. Pledges were expected to provide the fraternity's Christmas tree. There were only two rules: they had to cut it themselves, and they could not pay for it. No doubt there were a few legally cuttable trees in the nearby state forest, but they were not the right size or well shaped. Competition for sunlight did not a good Christmas tree make. Thus the TRE tradition effectively required pledges to steal a tree.

After a few years of this, campus security knew where to look if anyone reported that a tree had been molested, but it was difficult to do much. It was hard to prove anything, given that one Christmas tree was much like another. One year the pledges had gone so far as to purchase a second tree merely to be able to produce a receipt for the one they stole.

This year they went too far, and they were stupid. They didn't raid a rural resident's recent plantings or a "You Cut" Christmas tree farm. They cut a tree from the university arboretum. Not only that, they cut a rare tree. It had been given by a delegation from Nepal, and it was estimated to be worth several thousand dollars. The head of the arboretum was beside herself. She wanted something done to the perpetrators, apparently along the lines of *The Texas Chainsaw Massacre.*

The pledges didn't even get rid of the evidence. Custom required that the tree team cut off a few extra inches from the bottom of the tree when they brought it back so that there was no danger of the bottom of their tree matching the top of the victim's stump. This year's pledges had tossed the cutting into the dumpster behind their frat house, where it was discovered by the inquiring officer. They were dead meat.

The problem in prosecuting them was that the police had to charge someone, and they had no way of knowing who actually cut the tree. Nor was anyone talking. The TREs were good at solidarity. Thus there seemed no way to prove anyone in particular guilty. This was when Dean Wong opted for sweet reason. He had the following conversation with TRE's governing council:

Dean Wong: I'm not going to charge anyone, but I want to end this. I want you to see that it's wrong and stop cutting trees.

TRE Council: No doubt it is wrong. We hope you can persuade whoever's doing this to see it your way.

Dean W: Isn't there any way I can get you to be responsible about this?

TRE: Isn't it really the fault of the arboretum or Security? Everybody knows that someone cuts an occasional tree before Christmas. If they haven't got the brains to guard a valuable tree, it's their fault. Not ours.

Dean W: You really think it's all right to destroy other people's property?

TRE: No, we really don't. We aren't destructive people. But this is your rule, your tree, and your problem. We have our relationships with our brothers to worry about. We aren't going to rat on them, and we aren't going to do your job for you. Sorry, Dean.

QUESTIONS

1. Both Barbara and Roger are Native Americans. Do they have different relationships to the Native American community? In what ways?
2. Do the members of Tau Rho Epsilon have a still different kind of relationship to the fraternity? In what way?

3. How would you characterize the ways in which these communities are important to their members?

4. Loyalty and friendship are usually counted as virtues. What is the basis of loyalty? What kinds of obligations follow from it?

5. Should Barbara turn Roger in?

6. Should one of the TREs turn in whoever cut down the tree?

7. Should citizens support the law by informing on lawbreakers? If so, does this obligation change when the lawbreakers are members of one's group or are one's friends?

8. Suppose that the incidents described above were more serious. Suppose, for example, that there had been a murder. Would you feel differently about informing?

9. If everybody is equal, why should we be more loyal to those who are members of our group than to outsiders?

10. Do the demands of loyalty or friendship change depending on the group? Should we be more loyal to members of our race, religion, or culture, than to members of our age group, sorority, or softball team? Why should we be loyal at all?

11. It is usually viewed as prejudice if white people try to promote the hiring of other white people at the expense of members of other races. Is it similarly wrong for minorities to look out for the welfare of other members of their groups? Why or why not?

12. How does loyalty to or solidarity with members of our race, culture, or religion differ from prejudice?

13. What role does solidarity with a community play in our lives?

ISSUES

Human beings are communal beings. That's why our opening chapter included *community* among the five ethical principles we've chosen to help you think through moral dilemmas.

People form communities to accomplish various goals; they are also *formed by* their communities. The identity we get from belonging to a community may be central to our sense of who we are. And some of the qualities people most value, such as loyalty, solidarity, and patriotism, seem bound up in the idea of community. So community is important.

But the implications of the importance of community are complex. Suppose, for example, that we belong to a group, yet reject some of its values or actions. Should we support our community when we think it is wrong? Are there times when it is wrong to be loyal to our friends or our group? Does loyalty to particular people violate the principle of equal respect for all? The principle of community generates some hard questions.

Communities can be divided into different categories, according to their effect on their members' sense of self. On one hand, we belong to some communities that have little impact on how we define ourselves—credit unions, choirs, health clubs, study groups, and chat rooms on the Internet usually belong in this category. We join these kinds of communities because they are useful; they provide us with a service or allow us to pursue one of our interests. They are not likely to shape our character or personality. We will call them "merely useful communities."

On the other hand, some communities do shape us. This is likely to be true of a religious or ethnic community, especially if we were born into it. It is also true of our families. Such communities give us values and moral commitments that guide our choices and orient our lives. (Even if we try to abandon these values later, the strength of our rebellion reveals the importance of these communities to us.) So the very fact that we belong, or have belonged, to such a community helps make us who we are. We will call these communities that help to form us "formative communities."

Other communities are in the middle, such as sports teams and perhaps businesses. Colleges and universities may fit in this category as well. Students and faculty might attend a school because it is useful to them, a place to learn valuable skills or provide a paycheck. But students and faculty may also bond to their institution; this is often encouraged through the promotion of "school spirit." And for some, the intellectual community of a college or university can become transforming and life-defining. In college people don't only learn chemistry or philosophy or architecture; some of them also become chemists and philosophers and architects. These students come to identify themselves with the intellectual craft they are taught and with the teachers who practice it; for them, college is a formative community.

These differences between communities, whether we find them formative or merely useful, depend partly on the community, and partly on us. Look, for example, at Barbara and Roger's different relationships to the Native American community.

For Roger, the Native American community seems to be a formative community. He is not just a member of a group interested in exploring Native American culture. He *is* a Native American. This community defines him, and he does not seem to view his membership in it as a matter of choice.

Barbara's relation to the Native American community is less clear. She has an identity independent of her membership in the Native American community. If the Native community is to be a formative community for her, it will be by her choice—a choice influenced by her ancestry, but still a choice.

Roger, too, could make a choice about his relationship with the Native American community, but it would be a very different choice. His identity is already strongly formed by his being Native American. Could he choose not to belong to this community? What would that mean? Perhaps he could stop attending meetings with Native Americans or about Native issues. And maybe he could become an accountant or an engineer, take a job with an appropriate corporation, move to the suburbs, and try to take up a middle-class life unrelated to his Native heritage—one much like the life of Barbara's parents. But would that make him no longer a Native American?

This transition is not as easy as it sounds. For better or worse, we are heavily influenced and constrained by others' responses to us. To the extent that other people continue to see Roger as Native American and treat him accordingly, it will be difficult for him to be anything else. Another difficulty is that the more central being a Native American is to Roger's self-definition and understanding of the world, the harder it will be for him to abandon this identification. To become something else he would have to reconstruct much of his sense of self—his beliefs, his values, his orientation to the world, and his fundamental ways of thinking about it. Is this something he could decide to do? How can he decide to undergo a transformation that will change his reasons for making decisions in the first place?

The members of TRE have a very different relationship to their community. Their affiliation with the fraternity probably means more to them than belonging to a credit union or another merely useful community; it may even have some of the feeling of a formative community. Members may be strongly bonded to the fraternity and may have internalized much of its culture. They may feel quite loyal to each other. But it seems unlikely that TRE would be life-defining for its members in the way that being Native American is for Roger. Roger does what he does, in many cases, simply because he is a Native American and that is what Native Americans do. TRE members might say that they too do what they do because they are TRE brothers. But belonging to the TRE community motivates them to act in only some cases, such as following frat traditions or adopting a certain attitude toward college life. The rest of their actions and their outlook on life are influenced much more by family, ethnicity, religion, and so on—the frat brothers' true formative communities.

APPLYING ETHICAL PRINCIPLES TO THE CASES

The principle of *community* describes communities partly as groups that allow people to pursue shared values. These values are often central to the group's character, such as the theological beliefs of a religious community. Such underlying values are often described as the community's "culture." However, the fact that these values are central in the community does not mean they are clear, universally agreed upon, and unarguable. Roger, for example, actively debates his picture of Native American culture against that of others. He doesn't believe that the values characterizing Native culture are a package he must accept in order to belong to that community. So even in formative communities, "belonging" is often a matter of having a vague sense of something important in common with others, with whom you can then argue about how your shared values should be understood.

The values of a formative community are often discovered by their new members, rather than understood and agreed upon beforehand. Roger understood that being a Native American required a view of spirituality that was incompatible with being a Presbyterian. This was something he discovered about himself, rooted in his membership in the Native community; he didn't become a Native American because he found their spirituality truer. (Could he have? Or, for example, can white New Age religious seekers legitimately adopt Native American spirituality without having such heritage?) Barbara is also in the process of discovering what it means to be a Native American. She differs from Roger in that she also defines herself in other ways, and must balance her loyalties.

To be a member of a community is to be loyal to its values. This loyalty need not be mindless subservience. It is more a matter of being committed to a process of reflection and discovery that focuses on these values, rather than some others. And these shared values and common loyalty can lead to friendships among members, especially in communities that are more than merely useful to those involved. But even in merely useful communities, members tend to be preferred to non-members and given privileges that are not given to outsiders. For example, only members are usually allowed to participate in meetings about how the community will conduct its business. In formative communities, of course, members are bound by much stronger ties than these.

Thus our membership in communities of all kinds affects our sense of identity, our basic values, our loyalties, and our friendships. Communities play an important role in our ethical lives. They can also be the source of some of our most perplexing moral dilemmas. For few of us are members of a singe, all-encompassing community. Instead, we are members of a variety of groups, and we sometimes must decide which has our primary loyalty. For example the TREs are members of a fraternity, but they are also members of a university community and a civic community, as well as the different communities each brother is connected to by his upbringing and ethnic background.

Membership in differing communities can generate several different kinds of ethical conflict. One type is *identity conflict*. People who have strong attachments to more than one formative community may not know who they are. Barbara is not sure whether she is a Native American or a middle-class suburbanite.

Another type is *loyalty conflict*. Should the TREs be loyal to each other, or to the university community? Should Barbara be loyal to Roger, to the college, or to the civil society whose laws Roger has broken? And what action would count as being loyal to the Native American community?

Finally, there may be a *conflict of values*. Is there any sense in which Native spirituality is superior or inferior to Barbara's Presbyterian heritage? Is one her "real" heritage? Do the TREs have a moral obligation to support the civil society's anti-stealing values, or to be loyal to their fraternity brothers and frat tradition?

We might examine these conflicts by thinking about the difference made by taking an insider's perspective versus an outsider's. Roger, for instance, seems not to be bothered by the fact that he has violated the law and his college's regulations. He judges his conduct only in terms of how it affects or serves the Native American community. Since he doesn't consider himself a member of the college community or the civil society, and may even view them as oppressors or enemies, he feels no duty to abide by their laws. They are to him like the laws of Mongolia might seem to us: they may or may not be good laws, but they aren't ours, so we need not obey them.

The TREs (with less justification) seem to have taken a similar view toward the university: "This is your rule, your tree, and your problem." They seem to agree that stealing and destroying someone else's property are wrong, but they refuse to enforce these standards against themselves. In other words, they recognize the validity of the rule, but they feel entitled to violate it when it conflicts with their fraternity's traditions.

Why do Roger and the TREs view themselves as outsiders at college? It's not hard to see for Roger. As a Native American, he is rooted in a different formative culture than the one that dominates the college. Moreover, he quite reasonably views his status in American society as a consequence of a history of oppression.

Roger's us-versus-them position might be justified in other ways as well. Perhaps he believes that the state's laws banning peyote shouldn't apply to Native Americans. "What right do they have to regulate our religious ceremonies?" is a useful question for Roger (as well as the authorities) to ask. Peyote may be a hallucinogen, but its use in Native American ceremonies does not make the users drug addicts. Arguably context makes a good deal of difference here.

It might be more difficult to justify Roger's us-versus-them mentality regarding stealing the money. Roger is not in favor of stealing generally. Moreover, it is unclear whose money he has used—although it came from the college originally, it was currently NASA's. Has Roger used his alienation from the college and civil society to rationalize stealing NASA's funds? His attack on Barbara might be motivated by a need to cloak his guilt.

It's hard to see what justification the TREs have for feeling like outsiders. Culturally they are indistinguishable from the population of the rest of the college and the larger society. Many sociologists claim that such alienation is common among youth in our society, created in part by the extreme age segregation in our educational system. Youth, they argue, grow to adulthood in institutions where they are influenced much more by their age peers than by adults. The adult world is largely invisible to them, and as a result, they view themselves as outsiders in the adult world.

Perhaps the TREs consider themselves outsiders in their own society, too, and so experience its rules and laws as something imposed on them by adults—not as *their own* rules and laws. Do you think this reasoning explains the TREs' attitude toward theft and the destruction of private property? If so, does it justify their attitude?

Some moral ideals seem to apply broadly and generally. For example, the principle of *equal respect* applies to everyone who is a human being, regardless of personal characteristics. The equal respect principle also suggests that it is just as wrong to steal from someone, to lie to someone, or to murder someone who is not a member of our group as to do these things to someone who is "one of us." Dishonesty and murder seem wrong, period, no matter what communities the victim and perpetrator belong to.

However, not all moral ideals can be applied equally to everyone. Loyalty means nothing if we must be equally loyal to everyone. Is it wrong to give gifts to our loved ones without giving them to everybody? Don't we have stronger bonds of caring and obligation with our families and members of our formative communities than with strangers?

And sometimes moral ideals conflict with each other, such as loyalty and honesty. We believe we should be honest and help others—if we saw a stranger rob someone and then drive away, it would seem reasonable to write down the license number of the getaway car to report it to the police, and to help the victim. But the special bonds we feel toward our loved ones, friends, and the members of our formative communities can sometimes conflict with our belief in honesty. What if the offender is a friend, relative, or fellow member of our group? Do we still have the same responsibility to turn the person in?

You might say yes. You might argue that we must follow the principle of equal respect and treat everyone equally. So we should turn in the robber, regardless of whether or how we feel attached, because that's what fairness and justice demand.

You might say no. Suppose the robber was your parent or your partner, a brother or a sister, or a close friend. Do love and loyalty count for nothing? Society should not expect us to betray someone we love.

WORKING OUT SOLUTIONS

You may have noticed that we didn't tell you which answer is "right." That is because when faced with such conflicts between loyalty and honesty, we believe there are few clear rules. Should the TREs turn in those who stole the tree? We think that their leaders should at least acknowledge their own responsibility, but after that, we're not sure. Should Barbara turn in Roger? We really don't know.

We do think it is a rare case when loyalty justifies allowing the members of one group to harm the members of another. Turning in friends or community members when they have done something wrong may often be the right thing to do. Nevertheless, the reluctance we all feel at such an act reveals our loyalty, not selfishness or bias. And loyalty is praiseworthy.

How can we decide that a particular case is one where loyalty should trump honesty? One consideration might be the nature of the bond. For example, our society has made it a rule of law that one spouse cannot be forced to testify against another, no matter what the spouse did nor how crucial the testimony would be. The bond between husband and wife is viewed as important enough to override society's interest in uncovering the truth and prosecuting criminals. Another consideration might be the seriousness of the harm. If Roger or the TRE members had committed murder, we do think they should be turned in by members of their communities.

What can we learn from this? Since ethical situations are frequently not clear-cut, our judgment will depend on knowing the context and the particulars of the case. There are no rules for producing clear decisions in hard cases, and we will often need to balance conflicting principles. So we must rely on our judgment, compassion, and wisdom to make decisions. We can acquire these virtues through experience and practice, and also through talking with other people who can help us see what is at stake in a choice. For none of us is so wise that we can afford to overlook the moral wisdom of others.

ADDITIONAL CASES

CASE 5.3   *Hazing*

Although hazing is forbidden at the University of Eastern West Texas, several fraternities there practice it secretly. For example, Chi Chi Chi's initiation rites require that inductees prove their mettle by downing enormous quantities of hard alcohol during a special drinking game; and Sigma Epsilon Chi requires that pledges describe in vivid detail a love-making session with a girlfriend or date whom they must then bring to a large frat party.

In past years, XXX pledges have occasionally had to go to the hospital to have their stomachs pumped, and many have passed out for periods of time. Fortunately, no one has ever died, although death by acute alcohol poisoning is a very real threat from such a drinking "game." While SEX pledges run no such health risks in proving their devotion to their house, they do have to prove their loyalty at the expense of unsuspecting non-initiates, at least some of whom they may be supposed to care about. Other fraternities merely require members to wear strange uniforms, or be accompanied by a frat brother everywhere they go (even to the bathroom), or always walk around campus in a single file with other pledges throughout the rush period.

QUESTIONS

1. Hazing activities take place in the name of bonding and forming group loyalty. Of course, some fraternities substitute community service requirements or other more socially acceptable means for pledges to prove their commitment. Yet hazing persists on many campuses, despite being outlawed. Why is hazing so persistent, even when colleges attach severe penalties to any fraternities that are discovered hazing their pledges? What benefits might pledges and previous members of the frat get out of hazing that would motivate them to continue such traditions at all costs?

2. Do the hazing practices of the XXX and SEX frats violate different ethical principles? Is one type of hazing morally worse than the other?

3. If you were an XXX or SEX pledge, how would you respond to being told to do something potentially harmful to yourself or someone else because "it's a frat tradition"? Where do you think you would draw the line, and why?

Sharing Secrets CASE 5.4

Scott and Maya have been dating for two years, and they are very close; they will probably get married after they graduate. Scott is also very close to three other guys, and he regularly spends time hanging out with them when Maya isn't welcome. Maya accepts the exclusive friendship of "the Four Musketeers" because she knows that Scott needs time alone with his friends. Secretly, she is proud of never seeming possessive of Scott or grilling him about what he and his friends do together. "I'm too mature for that," she thinks to herself. All of Scott's and Maya's friends admire their relationship, which seems so strong that it precludes the petty jealousies and fights that trouble weaker matches.

However, now Maya is shocked to learn that Scott has told his buddies a painful secret from her past. Scott doesn't see a dilemma, saying, "I never promised that I wouldn't discuss something about you, because if I need to talk about you, they're the only ones I can talk to. And we were all talking about our relationships." Maya thinks he has no right to share her private life with people she hardly knows (or with people she knows well, either), especially without her permission. For the first time, she sees his male friendships as a threat to their relationship as a couple. And she feels that she can never trust Scott again.

QUESTIONS

1. Should Scott's loyalty to Maya override his loyalty to his male friends, or vice versa? Why?

2. Is telling someone else's secret always a breach of loyalty? Might it be justifiable in some circumstances? (See Chapter 4.)

3. Is discussing the details of an intimate relationship with someone out-side that relationship disloyal, or can it be a healthy way to learn from others' advice?

4. Is it "mature" to have close friends outside of a couple bond? What if some of those friends are of the opposite sex?

5. In addition to sexual faithfulness, what might "loyalty" mean for a couple?

CASE 5.5   *Ratting: A Roommate's Dilemma*

Ruth was caught buying a term paper from Ever-Ready Student Services, an organization that writes papers and take-home exams for college students in exchange for cash. Honoria College has been trying to locate Ever-Ready and get enough evidence to close it down, and unfortunately for Honoria junior Ruth, they finally conducted a raid just when she was in the Ever-Ready office, paying for "The Role of Market Factors in the Development of the Health Insurance Industry." Caught red-handed, Ruth had no choice but to confess. In her confession, she mentioned that many other students knew about Ever-Ready too; for example, her roommate Smita knew about her activities. Ruth quickly added in Smita's defense that Smita had urged her not to resort to Ever-Ready, but she'd ignored this advice.

Smita, Ruth's roommate, was president of the student body, a hard-working and ambitious student. She and Ruth were both well aware that Honoria College has a strict honor code requiring faculty and students to turn in any students they suspect of cheating. However, Ruth refused to reveal whether she knew anyone who used Ever-Ready's services.

When the Honor Board confronted Smita, she said that she had tried to get Ruth to write her paper herself, warning her that everyone knew the college wanted to bust Ever-Ready and catch its customers, but to no avail. She then had hoped that if Ruth got away with her cheating this time, the college would shut down Ever-Ready before she could be tempt-ed again.

Ever-Ready Student Services was the most blatant example of a persis-tent cheating problem on campus, and Honoria College wanted to make an example of any of its customers they could identify. Therefore, they expelled Ruth for the remainder of the school year, telling her she could reapply for admission after that. The college administration also wanted to send the student body a message that they must take seriously the honor code's requirement to turn in students who cheat. Because the administration felt that Smita had not fulfilled her obligations as a leader of the college com-munity in this regard, they asked for her immediate resignation as president. Her permanent college record showed that the resignation occurred as the result of disciplinary action. Smita's stellar record thus contained a black mark that could haunt her future career.

QUESTIONS

1. Are there situations in which one student ought to report another to the authorities? How would you decide which situations merit such "ratting" and which do not?

2. How might a student leader resolve the conflict between loyalty to a friend and responsibility to the office she holds? Which moral principles might she use, and how, in deciding what to do?

3. Was Ruth really a friend to Smita? What ethical principles did she violate, if any?

4. Should higher standards of behavior be expected of people in positions of authority and power, like Smita?

5. Do you think the college administration should give Smita (or Ruth) another chance?

6. Is the honor code requirement that students turn in other students unrealistic? (See Chapter 2.) Is it unfair to force students to choose between loyalty to their peers and friends, and loyalty to the college community as a whole?

Secret Abuse   CASE 5.6

Late one evening, several members of Pi Alpha Lambda sorority are discussing a shocking scene that two of them, Maureen and Chong-Ae, have just witnessed. Maureen and Chong-Ae were walking through the sorority parking lot after a late night at the library when they noticed two people fighting inside a car. The street light was fairly bright there, and they thought they saw a man punching a woman. Chong-Ae recognized the car; it belonged to Matt, a junior who is dating Leah, one of the sorority sisters. Chong-Ae and Maureen had argued about what to do, and then continued walking. The car windows had been pretty fogged up, so they couldn't be sure about what they'd seen, and they didn't want to butt in inappropriately.

Now that they're back in the House, Chong-Ae is feelingly increasingly bad about not interfering. "I'm sure I saw him hit her!" she exclaims. "And I think he's beaten her up before. Remember that time Leah had a black eye that she said she got from slipping on an icy sidewalk? Well, that was just after she and Matt were out together." The others soon add in their observations and suspicions.

It turns out a majority suspect that Leah is being beaten regularly by Matt, who otherwise seems likes a dream date: good-looking, charming, athletic, funny, polite. "We should do something!" says Chong-Ae, and they resolve to talk to Leah when she comes in.

A moment later, Leah does come in; but she runs up to her room before anyone has a chance to speak to her. When Chong-Ae and Maureen knock on her door, a muffled voice says, "I don't feel like talking right now. I want to be alone." It sounds as if Leah is crying.

Over the next few days, several PAL sisters try to talk to Leah, but she denies that anything is wrong. When they suggest that she try counseling anyway, because she often seems to cry after phone calls or dates with Matt, she gets angry. "Look, I appreciate the concern, but everything is fine! My relationship with Matt is really no one else's business. And I don't need some busybody counselor making trouble between us. Matt would never go to therapy, and if I even suggested it to him, or went by myself, he'd be really ticked off."

QUESTIONS

1. What should the women of PAL do if Leah doesn't want help?

2. Is it a breach of loyalty to her as their friend and sorority sister to go to a counselor or other knowledgeable person against her expressed wishes? Does loyalty to her require getting her help even if she doesn't want it?

3. What if the sorority sisters do convince Leah to go to therapy, and Matt beats her up as a result?

4. If, after weighing the good and the bad in her relationship with Matt, Leah has privately decided that an occasional beating is worth it to keep him as her boyfriend, can this be a legitimate decision?

5. Should Maureen and Chong-Ae have interfered when they thought they saw Matt hitting Leah? Is interfering in a case of suspected physical abuse a violation of the participants' privacy, integrity, and freedom to run their own lives?

6. Can you make an argument for why Leah's situation should be the legitimate concern of her PAL sisters? What ethical principles might you use?

CASE 5.7 *School Spirit*

Mountain College prides itself on being a small school in which students have a big sense of community and college spirit. Mountain spirit peaks during homecoming week, when the gold and blue school colors are everywhere, and all minds are on The Big Game with perennial rival and neighbor Plains College. Students express their loyalty to Mountain by spending weeks preparing floats for the big pregame parade, planning elaborate halftime programs, and of course arranging for the best-ever homecoming dance. Some of them also traditionally express their loyalty by getting into postgame fights with Plains students.

This year, the Plains Tigers beat the Mountain Bulldogs 14–13, and feelings were high when the game ended. Mountain sophomores Drew,

Jonathan, and Will were heading out of the stands, talking angrily among themselves about the unfairness of the referee's last call, when they saw several Plains students (obvious in their gray-and-red sweatshirts emblazoned with huge Ps) celebrating their victory. One of the Plains students banteringly shouted out to them, "Those Bulldogs suck!" This insult was too much for the Mountain sophomores. Not about to let such a challenge pass unanswered, they exchanged a number of blows with the Plains students before Security broke up the fight.

QUESTIONS

1. The flip side of loyalty to a school or group is often hostility toward outsiders. Are fights like the one involving Drew, Jonathan, and Will a natural outgrowth of (excessive) competition between schools?

2. Are such fights and other extreme shows of loyalty to a school somehow the fault of the institution, or only of the individuals involved?

3. Can a college promote school spirit without also promoting intense rivalry with other colleges? Why might sports be the primary means schools use to develop school spirit? Are there other possible ways to build a feeling of loyalty to a school?

4. Promoting a strong sense of loyalty is obviously beneficial to the college: school spirit often translates into alumni loyalty and financial donations to the school. Having school spirit also seems positive for students because expressing loyalty to their alma mater might make them feel a sense of belonging otherwise missing in their lives and give them the satisfaction of working with others for common goals. Are there negative aspects of school spirit (expressed, for example, at sporting events) for colleges or students?

5. Is school spirit a distraction from "the real point" of school (academics), or *is* it "the real point," as many older alumni seem fondly to recall?

6. What do you think of the school spirit at your college?

Stand By Your Man? CASE 5.8

Thorndike Community College is in an uproar over allegations by juniors Mindy Engelhart and Lisa Fernandez that Associate Prof. Joe Washington has sexually harassed them. (The students' names were supposed to be kept anonymous, but someone leaked them to the local newspaper.) Mindy and Lisa were talking to Professor Washington after one of his "Africa: The Continent and Its Peoples" lectures when, they claim, he made an obscene joke about the sexual abilities of women in a certain African tribe compared to American women. He then followed this embarrassing comment with a joking question, apparently addressed to them both, about their abilities in the same regard. Mindy and Lisa said that they were not the only ones to be embarrassed and humiliated by this exchange—their fellow students Latifa Lee, Charlene Johnson, and Janice Howard were standing nearby. However Latifa, Charlene, and Janice have refused to support Mindy and Lisa's story.

What actually happened between Professor Washington and the students has largely become lost in an ugly, campuswide debate. The hullabaloo seems to center on the fact that Mindy and Lisa are not African Americans, and Professor Washington (and Latifa, Charlene, and Janice) are. Charges of racism mingle with countercharges of sexism, as defenders of each party accuse the other of the lowest motives.

Latifa, Charlene, and Janice have had many soul-searching discussions with their friends about their mutual decision to deny Mindy and Lisa's report. The talks have been soul-searching because all three women did hear Professor Washington's obscene comments. Furthermore, they know other female African American students who have heard worse from Professor Washington, and even been propositioned outright by him. However, the three women have decided that they should support him because they feel that whites are always trying to keep African American men down by means of trumped-up sexual charges.

"Our men have a hard enough time without having us women attack them too, especially in front of whites," Latifa said. "Look how white people are always trying to pull down any black man who gets some authority."

Charlene agreed. "There are hardly any other African American professors on this campus, and we have to stand behind him, no matter how much of a jerk he can be."

"I don't think he really means any harm," added Janice. "He thinks he's being friendly, or funny, or something. You just have to ignore it."

Thus the three students resolve to lie to the college administration in order to defend Professor Washington. However, they do privately feel bitter about his harassment and about his stupidity in showing his crass character to white students and thus putting them in the difficult position of having to decide whether to be loyal to their race or their sex (not to mention to the truth).

QUESTIONS

1. Did Latifa, Charlene, and Janice make the right decision?
2. Might their argument that black women need to stand behind black men in a hostile white world have merit?
3. Are they as much (or more) victims of sexism as Mindy and Lisa are?
4. Are there times when lying may be justified by a feeling of loyalty to a fellow member of one's group? If you disagree that Latifa, Charlene, and Janice are justified in lying to the administration, would they be more justified if Professor Washington were their father or other close kin?

5. If the three women are not willing to accuse Professor Washington of harassment publicly, is there anything they can or should do privately about his behavior? Is there anything they can or should do (privately, if not officially) to support Mindy and Lisa?

6. Can you say whether your sex, your race, or your social class more fundamentally defines you, and thus ultimately demands your loyalty when push comes to shove?

7. Why might "the women's movement" consist primarily of white females, and "the gay movement" consist primarily of white males, rather than either "liberation" movement including a proportional number of people of color?

8. What factors determine our strongest group loyalties?

Flamed! CASE 5.9

Shawn can feel his face start to burn as he stares at the computer screen. Even though the insults he's now reading were written to him, instead of shouted at him, they have the same effect on his body: his heart is racing and his fingers tremble slightly on the keyboard. He badly wishes he could punch the !*$%*!! jerk who wrote them. And that moron is attacking Shawn for something he didn't even say! At least, nothing he *meant* to say. Can't the jerk recognize sarcasm?

Gee, Shawn suddenly thinks, maybe not. Do other people also think I'm an idiot? This flame is so public! A flood of humiliation washes away some of his anger.

Shawn forces himself to scroll down for other postings on the topic. Sure enough, there are already several. Thank goodness most people seem to take his side. Some urge him to tell off the flamer—"fight fire with fire!"—and warn him against wimping out; others counsel him to rise above the insults; and one recommends getting revenge by reporting the offender to block him from further participation in the list-serve community.

Now that he's a little calmer, Shawn doesn't know how he should respond. He can't just ignore the flame; everyone will think he's a coward, afraid of a jerk, or else see his silence as an admission of guilt. But should he address himself directly to the lunatic who flamed him? Is there any point in bothering to try to explain yourself to someone like that? Should he really try to get the jerk kicked off the list? Maybe it's possible that Shawn's original posting was ambiguous enough that others had reactions to it that were similar, if less vehement, than the flamer's. So does Shawn owe the community at large a clarification?

QUESTIONS

1. How do you think Shawn ought to respond to the flame? Why? What ethical principles might come into play here?

2. Email is so effortless to send that we don't always take the time to make sure we've really said what we mean. But, because the recipient can't read the sender's tone of voice or facial expression to see whether the person was joking or deliberately offensive, email can be difficult to interpret. And a nasty or hurtful message can't be "unsent." So what can you do to help ensure you don't accidentally flame someone?

   (Products that scan incoming and outgoing email for offensive words or phrases are available, but they wouldn't catch flames that avoid those words. See Daniel Greenberg, "Eudora Organizes Mailbox," in *The Ithaca Journal*, 27 February 2001, p. 6A; and Greg Wright, "Electronic Etiquette," Gannett News Service, in *The Ithaca Journal*, 27 February 2001, p. 6A.)

3. Flames raise broader concerns about how to participate effectively and considerately in an on-line community. First, it helps to know standard Internet jargon and rules of discourse (see www.netlingo.com, or AOL's *Offline Companion Guide*, available in many bookstores, for explanations). Second, we must always strive for clarity of meaning, especially when writing about sensitive topics, or when addressing people who don't know us in person. And third, we should ask ourselves if civility in on-line communication is just an "extra" we can ignore when we're in a hurry, or if it might be more essential. What do you think?

BACKGROUND READING

• Current information about hazing on college campuses can be found in Lynn Rosellini, "The Sordid Side of College Sports (Hazing and Initiation Rites)," in *U.S. News & World Report*, 11 September 2000, vol. 129, i. 10, p. 102; Susan Kelleher, "College Fraternity Hazing Remained Secret Despite Vows to Quit," in *The Seattle Times*, Knight-Ridder/ Tribune News Service, 27 July 2000, p. K6274; Leo Reisberg, "Fraternities in Decline" (statistical data included), in *The Chronicle of Higher Education*, 7 January 2000, vol. 46, i. 18, p. A59(4); Welch Suggs, "79% of College Athletes Experience Hazing, Survey Finds" (statistical data included), in *The Chronicle of Higher Education*, 3 September 1999, vol. 46, i. 2, p. A83(1).

These articles provide both anecdotal accounts of extreme hazing incidents that led to hospitalizations, lawsuits, police action, and even deaths, and some statistical and legal data on the high incidence of hazing nationwide. A national study found that hazing activities occur in every part of the country, cutting across sports, divisions, school size, and gender; they frequently involve dangerous alcohol abuse.

For more information, see www.StopHazing.org, a Web site that offers a wealth of information on hazing, including a list of relevant books; and

Hank Nuwer's *Wrongs of Passage* (Indiana University Press, 1999), which describes the long history of hazing and examines reasons for its persistence.

• James Coleman (United States President's Science Advisory Committee Panel on Youth), *Youth Transition to Adulthood* (Chicago: University of Chicago Press, 1974).

This is one of the first and best-known sociological accounts of youth alienation, which Coleman blames on the high level of age segregation in our educational system.

• The ethics of the use of peyote in Native American religious rites are explored in a documentary film, *The Peyote Road*, directed by Gary Rhine, Fidel Moreno, and Phil Cousineau. Other sources of information about the subject include Linda Kanamine, "'Good Medicine' vs. the Law," in *USA Today*, 11 August 1994, sec. A, p. 2, col. 4 (describes a Senate bill to lift the last barriers to Native American use of peyote in religious ceremonies, thirty years after the cactus was listed as a controlled drug); "For Indian Church, a Critical Shortage," in *The New York Times*, 20 March 1995, sec. A, p. 10, col. 4 (discusses the law regarding peyote use and cultivation and provides some background about the Native American Church of North America); and "The Mescal Religion" in Natalie Curtis, recorder and editor, *The Indians' Book: Authentic Native American Legends, Lore and Music* (New York: Bonanza Books/Crown Publishers, 1987), pp. 162–165 (a reference work that describes peyote ceremonies and provides historical background).

• Michael Lind, "To Have and Have Not: Notes on the Progress of the American Class War," in *Harper's Magazine*, June 1995, vol. 290, no. 1741, pp. 35–39, 41–47.

The author explores the idea that beyond race, sex, or religion, social class (especially for the "hidden" upper class) determines Americans' ultimate loyalties. He argues that the contentious divisions between various disaffected minorities in American society are really diversions encouraged by the upper class to keep potential rebellion down.

• "To Tell or Not to Tell: Conflicts about Confidentiality," in *Report from the Center for Philosophy and Public Policy*, Spring 1984, vol. 4, no. 2, pp. 1–5.

This article explores the ethics behind issues of confidentiality and loyalty in various situations. *The Report* is available from The Institute for Philosophy and Public Policy, School of Public Affairs, University of Maryland, College Park, MD 20742, (301) 405-4759, and on-line at www.puaf.umd.edu/ippp.

• The number of Americans who identify themselves as having a racially mixed heritage is steadily increasing. For the implications of this trend, see:

Judith Lichtenberg, Suzanne Bianchi, Robert Wachbroit, and David Wasserman, "Counting Race and Ethnicity: Options for the 2000 Census," in *The Report from the Institute for Philosophy and Public Policy*," vol. 17, no. 3, Summer 1997 (available on-line at www.puaf.umd.edu/ippp, the Institute for Philosophy and Public Policy's Web site). The authors argue that people should be allowed to choose as many racial categories as they like to describe themselves on the Census. Their argument includes a discussion of the policy issues surrounding racial and ethnic classification.

Barbara C. Cruz, "Why for Some Kids Being 'Mixed' Creates Serious Problems," special to *Newsday*, 4 April 2001. Professor Cruz, who is also the author of *Multiethnic Teens and Cultural Identity*, reports that "the percentage of children reported to be multiracial in 2000 is three times greater than that of adults. Researchers say that within one generation there will be one mixed-race child in every 35 American children born." She describes the alienation and "race dissonance" felt by many of these youth, who "often feel caught between cultures." But she also has hopes that "multiethnic people in the United States will be the 'cosmic race' of the 21st century and be the stimulus for the racial healing our country so desperately needs."

David R. Harris, "The Multiracial Count: What Does It Really Mean?" special to *The Washington Post*, 4 April 2001. Harris, a black sociologist with a white wife, describes his difficulty in categorizing his young daughter on the 2000 Census form. He points out that for mixed-race people, "one's race is constantly being negotiated"; different people put us in different categories. "Race depends not just on ancestry . . . but also on the verbal, physical, and cultural cues we project to others, their interpretation of those cues and the setting in which this exchange takes place."

Several Internet sites exist as discussion forums and sources of information for young people of multi-race heritage. Among them are the Cornell Hapa Student Association, www.rso.cornell.edu/hapa/[1]; *Mavin Magazine*, www.mavin.net; and "What Are You," by Pearl Gaskins, www.whatareyou .com.

ADDITIONAL MATERIALS

1. Fraternity hazing frequently tests pledges' loyalty to the frat against their friendships with outsiders. When the principle of community is pitted against the principle of relationships in people's lives, it is often the rela-

---

[1] "Hapa" is Hawaiian slang for a person of half-Asian, half-other ancestry. While it was once applied only to part-Asians, and used as an insult, today it is used by many people of varied mixed-race ancestry to describe themselves. Several student organizations on campuses around the United States use some form of the name. (David Hill, "Census' New Race Options Prompt Discussion," in *The Ithaca Journal*, 2 April 2001, pp. 1A and 4A, available on-line at www.theithacajournal.com.)

tionships that suffer. Why should this be? Can you think of examples of such a conflict, either from history or your own experience?

Two recent movies strive to portray the "reality" of fraternity hazing. One, first-time filmmaker Jonathan Flicker's *Followers*, examines a trio of friends whose loyalty to each other is threatened when one is rejected by a frat because he's black. *Followers* proved so provocative on campuses in 1999–2000 (it's based on a true incident) that indie distributor Castle Hill recently bought it for national distribution (*USA Weekend Magazine*, 13–15 October 2000). The other, an award-winning 1999 documentary film called *Frat House*, by Todd Phillips and Andrew Gurland, showed violent hazing rituals taking place in Muhlenberg College in Allentown, PA. But *Frat House* was later discredited as "inaccurate and concocted" because some scenes were staged (*The Chronicle of Higher Education*, 12 February 1999, vol. 45, i. 23, p. A43). Whether or not *Frat House* showed what "really" went on at Muhlenberg College, there is no doubt that violent hazing does occur every year on campuses across the United States. At times this hazing becomes so punitive and extreme that it leads to student hospitalizations and even deaths. (See the Background Reading in this chapter for details.)

Why might there be a tradition in some frats (as well as clubs and sports teams) to ask members to prove their loyalty in extreme ways? Why don't more pledges "Just Say No"? If you were being hazed, where do you think you would draw the line? Colleges often forbid hazing and enforce strict penalties against any group that practices it. Yet hazing continues. Why is it so hard to eradicate? What purpose(s) might it serve?

2. When people allow the principle of community to become their sole ethical standard, they become racists or nationalists. The recent Bosnian civil war offered a striking warning of the dangers of community run amok. What light do the moral principles we have discussed shed on the Bosnian conflict? Some sources of information about the moral and human side of the war in Bosnia include Tom Gjelten, *Sarajevo Daily: A City and Its Newspaper Under Siege* (New York: HarperCollins, 1995); Misha Glenny, *The Fall of Yugoslavia: The Third Balkan War* (New York: Penguin, 1993); Brian Hall, *The Impossible Country: A Journey Through the Last Days of Yugoslavia* (Boston: David R. Godine Publisher, 1994); and David Rieff, *Slaughterhouse: Bosnia and the Failure of the West* (New York: Simon and Schuster, 1995).

Can you think of illustrations of the destructive potential of the other principles (the greatest good, equal respect, relationships, and character growth) if taken to extremes? What does this suggest about ethical argument in general?

3. Many writers believe that the Internet is changing our sense of community and even how we define "community." See Peter Levine, "The Internet and Civil Society," in *Report from the Institute for Philosophy and*

Public Policy, Fall 2000, vol. 20, no. 4, pp. 1–8 (available on-line at www.puaf.umd.edu/ippp or from The School of Public Affairs, University of Maryland at College Park, MD 20742, (301) 405-4753).

Levine's article analyzes the Internet's effects on the sense of community in modern society. It addresses many related issues as well: equity of access to the Internet and information, and the power that it gives; the Internet's "thin social bonds" (Levine claims that connections people form over the Internet "may replace robust, durable, emotionally satisfying social bonds with superficial and contingent ones"); "Internet balkanization," by which Levine means "the proliferation of separate communities or conversations that are not in mutual contact," that is, groups of like-minded people who never hear opposing views or debate and thus lose their ability to participate in public deliberation; the Internet's encouragement of excessive consumer choice ("too much of a good thing"); and privacy concerns (the Internet allows more privacy in some ways; e.g., one can hide one's appearance, age, and gender in communicating via email or chat groups, but the Internet simultaneously dramatically decreases people's ability to keep information about themselves private from large organizations, businesses, and governments).

What role to you believe the Internet plays in creating, or damaging, a sense of community in modern life? Do you believe that the Internet makes you feel more connected to others, or less? If you agree with Levine's analysis of the Internet's potential dangers, what do you think could be done to limit them?

4. Judy Jolley Mohraz, "Missing Men on Campus," op-ed article in *The Washington Post,* 16 January 2000, p. B07.

Mohraz, former President of Goucher College, Baltimore, points out that men of traditional college age are increasingly avoiding higher education. "According to U.S. Department of Education statistics, the proportion of bachelor's degrees awarded to males has dropped from 51 percent in 1980 to 44.9 percent in 1996." This means, Mohraz explains, that the percentage of men who get a college degree has decreased, while the percentage of women who obtain a B.A. degree has gone up.

Mohraz advances several possible explanations for the trend and notes that many of these men have jumped directly into the labor force as well-paid "techno-wizards." They skipped college because they saw it as irrelevant to them, a waste of their valuable time.

But, Mohraz wonders, have these young men missed something important? Without a college education, will they be prepared for the ethical implications of new technology? Will they lack leadership ability? She quotes a corporate CEO complaining, "We really get in trouble when these techies who have had no broad-based education get promoted into managerial roles. They just can't handle the complexities and generally top out."

In contrast, a typical college education—especially in liberal arts institutions—requires students to take courses beyond the hard sciences to help build essential writing, speaking, and interpersonal skills.

Mohraz also worries that these well-paid "computer geeks" will not be as able and willing as college graduates to participate in the civic community. "Historically, college campuses have been laboratories for civic engagement, a setting where students can acknowledge and honor each other's voices and a place where they can experiment with, recognize and practice community values. It does not bode well for the future of our nation if males are absent from this training ground."

Do you believe a college education—your college education—helps prepare graduates to engage effectively in the civic community (meaning everything from office politics, to the PTA and other aspects of local municipal government, to national debates and political campaigns)? How, specifically, might it do so? Are there ways in which people who don't go to college can learn these skills? Do you agree with Mohraz that they are less likely to?

What implications might this trend toward an increasing gender imbalance among college students have for those students? How might it affect college social life and dating? How might it affect classroom atmosphere? Might men and women both be harmed, perhaps in different ways, by having significantly fewer men than women on campus? If this imbalance between the sexes continues to grow, might it somehow violate the principle of equal respect?

6

SEX, RELATIONSHIPS, AND POWER

CASE 6.1 *Seduction or Rape?*

Carlotta Gomez was stunned by Peter Andretti's blunt response to her question. "I don't rape," he had said, "I seduce." He was clearly proud of his "moral" outlook on the topic. After her interview with Peter, Carlotta summarized his view to herself as involving essentially two ideas. The first was, "If it feels good, do it"; the second was, "Let the woman beware."

Carlotta was a counselor in the Office of Student Services at Columbia County Community College. Her job at Four Cs was to provide both academic counseling and emotional support to Four C students. While the emphasis in her job was academic, she was a warm and open person who often achieved the kind of trust and rapport with students that led them to discuss more personal problems with her.

Jennifer Black was one of her students. She had been in several times to discuss her schedule and her academic problems. Jen was usually an adequate student. However, her family was not a model of stability. Her parents were divorced, and her father's support payments were irregular. Often Jen was unable to pay even Four C's modest tuition. Even when her father came through, Jen often felt that she had to turn over some of the money to her mother to keep the rest of the family going. The need to work and the stress didn't do much for Jen's grades.

The last few months had been a disaster. Jen was failing all of her courses. Carlotta called her in to see what was going on. Jen was clearly troubled by something, and for a while she was unwilling to discuss it. Finally she blurted out, "Ms. Gomez, I was raped."

The story, as Jen told it, was this: She was at a party with a few friends and ten or so other people whom she didn't know. They listened to some music and had a few beers. She met Peter Andretti there. She enjoyed his company and spent much of the evening talking and dancing with him. At about one in the morning, when the party was breaking up, Peter asked Jen if he could give her a ride home. Jen agreed. When they were in the car, Peter suggested that they go over to his place to talk and listen to a new CD that he thought she would like. Jen wasn't very interested. It was late, she was tired and a little tipsy, and she didn't really trust Peter. However, Peter drove to his apartment over her objections, saying that he would be glad to drive her home after they had listened to the CD.

After they got to the apartment, Peter put on the CD and opened a bottle of wine. About halfway through the CD and the bottle of wine, Peter became sexually aggressive. For a while Jen made light of it, joking with Peter while pushing him away and suggesting that she should go home. Peter, however, was persistent. Moreover, he belittled her resistance. He wanted to know why she was so frigid and hung up, asking whether she was religious, or a lesbian. He made both things sound like some disease. He made her feel as though she had to prove to him that she was a normal human being, and that the only way that she could do that was to have sex with him.

Jen was fuzzy about most of what followed. There was more wine. The tension of the situation had seemed to her to be a reason to drink more. The next thing she could remember clearly was waking up in Peter's bed, plainly after having had sex with him. She dressed as quickly as she could and fled into the street. She remembered his laughing at her distress.

Although Jen wasn't very clear about some of what had happened, she was clear that she had repeatedly told Peter that she wasn't interested in having sex with him. At one point she recalled having said, "Maybe I'm not a virgin, but I'm not a whore either. I don't sleep with people two hours after I've met them." Thus, she concluded, "he raped me."

Carlotta wasn't so sure. She wasn't a lawyer, and Jen wasn't clear about the facts. In any case, Jen was unwilling to take the matter to the police. She had thought about it for a while, and she had even read an article on rape prosecutions. It was clear to her that any lawyer who defended Peter would pay a lot of attention to the question of why she had gone to his apartment, and that there would be other questions about other romantic involvements. She was afraid she would end up looking like a slut, and she couldn't prove anything. She didn't want to deal with it.

Because Jen was unwilling to pursue the matter, Carlotta thought that she herself should drop it. It wasn't part of her job to inform Peter of the error of his ways. However, her anger and her need to find out what kind of person Peter was led her to call him in.

Much to her surprise, Peter willingly confirmed almost all of the details of Jen's story. He was obviously proud of his "conquest." He bragged that there were others much like Jen. And he added a few details of his own. He admitted that Jen had resisted coming to his apartment and having sex with him, but he also noted that at no point had he forced her to do anything. "I just kept at her until she said yes," he said. "She was a little reluctant; girls like to say no for a while. It makes them feel more valuable and less guilty. But she was certainly willing in bed. In fact you might tell her when you see her that she's a damn good lay. I'll be happy to accommodate her again. Besides, I'm sure she really wanted it, no matter what she says now. Why else would she come to my apartment? She just needed a little help to relax!" That was when Carlotta accused Peter of rape, and Peter smugly replied, "I don't rape. I seduce."

QUESTIONS

1. What's the difference between rape and seduction? Does rape necessarily involve force?

2. What makes rape wrong? Is seduction wrong? If both are wrong, should both be criminal offenses?

3. Suppose that Jen had been willing and eager to go over to Peter's apartment and have sex. Suppose also that both understood that their sex was a casual matter for the pleasure of the moment, and that no long-term relationship was envisioned. Is there anything the matter with that?

4. Often these days, talk about responsible sex emphasizes either the prevention of pregnancy or the prevention of AIDS. Are avoiding consequences such as unwanted pregnancy or AIDS the only reasons for resisting casual sex?

5. What do you think about "If it feels good do it?" Jen seems to feel that casual sex is wrong. Is it?

6. Is casual sex inconsistent with some benefits or desirable ends that can be achieved through sex? Does this question ask about what is right or wrong?

7. Many traditional religions frown on premarital sex and are strongly opposed to adultery. Aside from the question of whether these prohibitions might reflect the will of God, are there other reasons for opposing premarital sex or adultery?

8. Most marriages involve vows of faithfulness that are broken by adultery. Why should there be such vows? What value is added to sexual relations when they are expressed within a long-term commitment?

9. Suppose Peter had seduced a male student rather than Jen. Would anything about your answers to these questions change? Does anything prevent same-sex relationships from realizing the benefits possible in heterosexual relationships?

ISSUES

Probably nothing we discuss in this book is likely to be as controversial as sex, nor is there a topic about which human beings have had more, and a wider variety of things, to say. Here we can suggest only a few approaches and questions about the ethics of sex. First, we want to discuss minimal standards for sexual conduct. Second, we want to make a few suggestions about how one might think of sex as part of durable and meaningful human relationships, and compare this position to another view of the significance of sex.

In most Western societies, the minimal standard for sexual conduct between adults is that it should be consensual. Coerced sex (rape) is commonly criminalized. Why should this be the case?

One response is that forced sex is a form of exploitation. One person uses another person for his own ends. Thus forced sex violates the principle of *equal respect*. This seems true enough, but perhaps it understates the case. Rape seems a particularly serious and violent form of exploitation. The act itself can be experienced as highly degrading, painful, and intrusive, and often it has quite emotionally destructive long-term consequences for the victim. What is the basis of such feelings? Why is rape usually considered even more heinous than other crimes of violence?

Note that it seems clear that Peter has exploited Jen. Jen did not want to have sex with Peter. Nevertheless Peter put a great deal of effort into getting her to have sex with him. Why shouldn't Peter's behavior be considered rape? One response might be that Peter didn't use force. That seems to be the point of his comment that "I seduce, I don't rape." Buy why should the use of force define rape? Isn't the point that sex should be consensual? The very meaning of seduction, however, is that the victim is persuaded to do something against her will or better judgment, even though physical force isn't used. Peter got Jen drunk. He brought her to his apartment when she wanted to go somewhere else. He lied to her. He applied psychological pressure in manipulating her until she gave in. There seems little doubt that Peter had every intent of exploiting Jen. Then why not view his action as rape? Indeed, why distinguish between rape and seduction?

Perhaps we should not treat rape and seduction as different acts. What should define rape is not force, but more simply the lack of consent. This thinking lies behind the idea of criminalizing adult sex with minors (statutory rape). Statutory rape is considered a violation of a minor even when no violence or threat of violence is used, because minors are presumed to be unable to give meaningful consent to sex.

Another view, however, is that the idea of consent in this case is ambiguous. Jen did, it seems, give in eventually. When we say that she didn't "consent," perhaps we mean something like this. Giving in to Peter is something that Jen would not have done under reasonable circumstances, in which she had not been drinking and was not being pressured. Giving in seems a different thing from freely consenting from the outset. Yet she did give in. Is this "ambiguity about consent" a reason for distinguishing between rape and seduction? Does the fact (if it is a fact) that Jen became fully involved in the sex act change anything?

One might argue that rape and seduction are different for legal purposes, but not moral ones. They are different legally because the ambiguity about consent makes it difficult to know the extent to which sex was consensual. Consider, for example, that it has been common for women to marry men whom they would not otherwise wed for the economic security that such a marriage can provide. Is sex in such a marriage consensual? Some feminists have argued that all sex under conditions of gender inequality is a kind of rape, that in a patriarchal society, marriage differs little from prostitution in being an exchange of sex for needed economic benefits. If the idea of "consent" is ambiguous, perhaps the point of treating force as a defining characteristic of rape is that the use of force seems to make it clear that the sex was not consensual.

However, in this case it seems clear that Peter's intent was to exploit Jen. Should we then conclude that his behavior is every bit as immoral as rape, even if it is not every bit as illegal?

DIFFERENT PERSPECTIVES ON SEXUAL ETHICS

The questions and responses we have discussed above are part of what might be viewed as a *minimalist view* of sexual morality. We have raised questions about how people ought to be treated and what kinds of conduct are wrong. A number of other perspectives might be used in questions of sexual ethics. For example, we have hinted at, but not developed, *equality* as a feature of an ethics of sex. Not only should sex be consensual, but it also should occur under conditions of equality and reciprocity. This could mean a number of things. It might mean that sex cannot be fully consensual in a society in which women are likely to be economically dependent on men or in which they have less power than men. It might mean that standards of sexual conduct should not differ for men and women. The common assumption that men should take what they can get sexually and women should resist is an example of inequality in standards of conduct. It might mean that the benefits of sex should be equal. It might mean that men and women should share familial responsibilities equally. What else might it mean? Can you think of other examples of gender inequality?

Another perspective that we will not pursue here has to do with *lying and promise keeping*. Sex is often connected with love and expressed within a context of promises. We may feel that sex is more appropriate with someone whom we love or for whom we have at least some affection. Jen seems to feel this way. We may express our love not only through sex, but also verbally. We may also express fidelity and faithfulness in connection with sex. Some of the ethical issues here are simple and straightforward: It is wrong to lie. It is wrong to make promises you do not intend to keep, and to fail to keep promises you have made. Thus it is wrong to do these things in the context of sex. However, there are complexities: Is it all right to lie if my purpose is benevolent rather than selfish? May I break a promise if circumstances change radically or unexpectedly? Might such promises sometimes be coerced? You might wish to consider how these questions can apply to sex. But also note that these issues are primarily about lying and promise keeping; they are not, except by implication, about sexual relations.

"Responsible sex" offers another perspective on sexual ethics. When people talk about "responsible sex," they often seem to assume an ethical outlook something like this: Sex is valued largely because it is pleasurable. However, like some other pleasurable activities, sex can have undesirable consequences. Among these are unwanted pregnancy and sexually transmitted diseases, the most chilling of which currently is AIDS. "Responsible sex" is consensual sex under conditions that avoid these unwanted consequences.

In one sense, this picture seems entirely reasonable. Sex that is not consensual, or that unreasonably risks unwanted pregnancy or disease, certainly is not responsible. However, we also think that the framework for thinking about sex needs to be broader than this. Discussions about responsible sex appeal to a moral principle—perhaps a variation of the principle of the *greatest good*—that says we should not seek pleasure in ways that significantly harm ourselves or others. But this principle does not take a position about the significance of sex.

Another approach we might take is to examine some *traditional social beliefs and customs* about sex. Is premarital sex wrong? Why have many human societies wished to confine sex to marriage, and to insist on faithfulness in marriage? Are there clues here to the benefits or meaning of sex beyond immediate sensual pleasure?

At least two important influences affect the way we think about sexual customs and behavior.

One influence is beliefs about the kinds of relationships required to provide healthy and stable conditions for nurturing children. As you probably recognize, this is a hotly debated and most controversial topic. Although we think it is crucially important, we are not going to discuss it further in this book, because doing so would involve a long detour into sociology. But we do believe that no reflection on appropriate sexual customs and behavior is complete without addressing this area.

Another influence on our thinking about sex is religion. Many religions have historically taken a dim view of sex outside marriage. Are such views morally correct? This seems a matter for you to decide, given your own religious beliefs or lack of them. Here are some points to consider:

First, since our society emphasizes freedom of conscience, we have to be cautious about assuming that anyone's religious beliefs should be made into rules of sexual behavior for others. This doesn't mean that religious views can't be true or false, or that one religion is as good as another. But even if one religion's views of sexual behavior are the correct ones (however we define this), that is still not a sufficient reason for believers to use the force of law to make non-believers follow them. So while you may feel that those who violate your religion's teachings about proper sexual behavior do wrong, you don't yet have a justification for forcing them to do right.

Second, the connection between religion and ethics is not always as straightforward as it may seem. Many religious people seem to believe that what makes actions right is that God has commanded them, or at least permitted them, and that what makes actions wrong is that God has forbidden them. Now God may or may not have made various commandments; that is not the issue. The issue is that such thinking tends to trivialize religiously inspired views of sexuality, because most religions interpret the meaning of sex in terms of what we call the principles of *relationship* and *community*. If we look at sexual ethics solely as God's commands, we miss much of what religions have to say about relationships and community.

For example, some religions view marriage as a sacrament. Marriage is not only the union of two people in such cases; it is also a representation of the relationship between God and the individual, or God and the religious congregation. Marriage is thus sacred. This means both that it should not be undertaken or broken capriciously, and that sex has a deeper significance than simply producing pleasure or children.

But marital monogamy is only one way that religions have viewed the purpose of sex. For instance, some groups have considered non-marital, non-monogamous sex a way to establish meaningful connections among fellow believers. The very openness of sex among such groups was intended to allow practitioners to connect to the divine within each other; by not choosing partners based on erotic attachment or other "superficial" qualities, practitioners hoped to embrace them in their spiritual essence. Instances of such religiously (or semi-religiously) motivated polygamous sex include: sacred prostitution in the ancient world (male believers worshipped at temples by having sex with women representing the gods); Christians who took Christ's command to love one another literally, such as the 19th-century American Oneida community in which all male members were "married" to all female members; free love advocates such as anarchist Emma Goldman in the early 20th century; and poets such as Walt Whitman,[1] who wrote,

---

[1] Walt Whitman, "Song of Myself," line 524 from *The Norton Anthology of Poetry*, Revised Edition, ed. Alexander Allison et al. (New York: W. W. Norton and Co., 1970), p. 819. Originally published in *Leaves of Grass* (1855).

"Divine I am inside and out, and I make holy whatever I touch or am touched from." In this view, open sex can express the divine love that binds us all, in contrast to more "selfish" monogamous sex.

Our point in noting these cases is to emphasize that religious views of sex are rooted in understandings of human relationships, what a good life is, and the proper relationship between God and human beings. So when you are thinking about how religious views affect sexual conduct, try not to worry about what God may have commanded you to do or not do, and instead try to think about the view of sex and human relations behind those commands. Ask yourself: Do I understand and accept the picture of life and of sex that my religion teaches?

The rest of this chapter explores this question of the larger meaning of sex, and how it can fit into various views of what a good life is. To help in this discussion, we're going to describe two characters who will represent opposite views about the meaning of sex. We will call them the "Bonder" and the "Aesthete."

The Bonder

The Bonder brings the principle of *relationship* to bear on the question of the meaning of sex; he or she views sex primarily as a way to develop a special kind of relationship with someone. A Bonder knows that a sexually involved couple can form a bond so intense and valued that it can change their lives.

The concept of "privacy" can help us understand the Bonder's view of sex. Suppose we think of privacy as involving the right to control, or not to have to disclose, information about ourselves (see Chapter 4). Think of personal "information" broadly here—it involves more than just data about our incomes or our grade point averages. It may include how our bodies look naked. Perhaps one reason most people aren't comfortable going nude or dressing provocatively all the time is that this would make them constantly objects of sexual appraisal.[2] The right to privacy protects us from having to reveal information about ourselves that would let someone harm us or evaluate us, unless we choose to trust them.

And when we do choose to trust someone with personal information, we usually do so only if we believe it will result in some form of sharing. For example, most of us have told an embarrassing story about ourselves to friends. The sharing we hoped for was perhaps shared humor, or a recipro-

---

[2] Of course, definitions of "casual sex" and "dressing provocatively" can vary from one culture to another. In societies where topless or nude beaches are common, for example, being topless or nude on the beach is not experienced as sexually provocative; and people from more traditional societies often find the way American women dress quite indecent. What do you think "casual sex" and "dressing provocatively" mean in your social circle?

cal story, or maybe a joint recognition of mutual weakness. Perhaps we wanted to explore if we could trust our friends not to misuse the information. Revealing personal information both requires and builds trust.

Having sex might be thought of as such a self-revelation. Indeed, having sex is a particularly revealing kind of self-exposure, because during the encounter we are very vulnerable to embarrassment or humiliation. Perhaps this is why we often feel awkward in sex with an unfamiliar person. This is also why Bonders consider sex a valuable way to build trust and to cement a bond between committed partners.

Another approach to understanding the Bonder's view of sex lies in the observation that bonds between people are often strengthened by activities that are shared with one special person, and no one else. A feeling that "you are the one I do this with" builds relationships. The activity that is shared only with one special person can be anything from recalling childhood memories to fishing. But sex seems to be the activity with perhaps the most potential to help build a strong bond. Of course, sex can usually do this only if it is shared exclusively with one special person. Joint promises to be true, and a shared belief that these promises will be kept, are needed for an atmosphere of mutual trust—without which a relationship cannot prosper.

Please note that nothing about the Bonder's view of sex supports the idea that premarital sex, casual sex, or even significant promiscuity is morally wrong. (It doesn't say that these activities are right, either. The point is that social or personal beliefs about such matters depend on other kinds of arguments, such as the best conditions for nurturing children, or religious considerations.) The Bonder's view of the meaning of sex doesn't address the question of wrong or right. Instead, it expresses beliefs about the conditions necessary for bonding and the role that sex might play. Bonders believe that it is difficult to bond with their sexual partners as "that special someone" while also having many other partners.

However, the Bonder's view of sex is not an argument for marriage. The faithfulness that the view requires could be expressed in many ways. It says nothing about what kind of sexual behavior I should engage in before finding my special someone, nor about how long I should expect a special relationship to last. At most, it says that monogamy is a precondition for a certain kind of human good—a pair bond. What makes the Bonder's point of view distinctive is that it considers bonding the main point of sex, beyond immediate sensual pleasure.

The Aesthete

In contrast, the Aesthete thinks of sex primarily as a potential "art form" or as a means of self-expression. In addition, Aesthetes reject the idea of limiting sex to socially predetermined roles or behaviors; they think this constrains their personal freedom too much.

What might it mean to think of sex as an "art form"? Art forms often take an experience that is usually considered pleasurable or beautiful, and seek to enhance it by making it more complex, sophisticated, or varied. We enjoy art forms more than ordinary experiences because art forms allow us to use more advanced skills and knowledge, and to practice more sophisticated discrimination. The more skills, knowledge, and ability to judge quality that we have in an area—whether it's sports, music, computer games, or wine-tasting—the more fun we have in participating. (See Chapter 7.) Applied to sex, the Aesthete's view emphasizes that we enjoy having sex more when we enhance our skills and knowledge and learn to be discriminating about the nuances of sex. The ethical principle behind the Aesthete's view of sex might be *character growth*, but defined in a somewhat narrow way.

Aesthetes also think of sex as a form of self-expression or self-realization. We are, they would claim, sexual beings; sexuality may be central to our natures. Self-expression, in other words the expression of something that is central to our natures, is good. Denial or repression of this self-expression is bad or even harmful. For example, some have argued that sexual repression is the source of many neuroses. So being able to express ourselves through sex is one of the main meanings of sex to an Aesthete; and anything that prevents us from such self-expression is destructive and should be resisted.

So why can't someone be both a Bonder and an Aesthete? Why not bond with one special person, and treat sex within the relationship aesthetically? We haven't given any reason yet why you should have to choose.

What makes these views alternatives is that Aesthetes often believe that moral constraints about sex place arbitrary limits on enjoyment or self-expression. Sometimes they see conventional morality as a source of sexual inhibition or repression, and thus deeply contrary to their belief in sex as self-expression. Aesthetes value novelty and experimentation, anything that enhances the enjoyment of experience. So moral obligations, such as a promise to be faithful, or strong ties to other people—the kinds of commitments important to the Bonder—can seem overly restraining to the Aesthete. They are inconsistent with the emotional freedom necessary to live aesthetically.

Perhaps, however, the Aesthete's values are not as sharply opposed to those of a "liberated" Bonder. After all, over time people can move from one view of the meaning of sex to the other, as in the case of a twenty-year-old sexual Aesthete who "settles down" into marriage with children in his or her thirties. But we suspect that there is a real tension between even the most "liberated" Bonder and the Aesthete. The center of that tension is different views about what makes a good life.

For the Bonder, relationships are key. It is in being with others, sharing with others, caring for others, and enjoying with others that the Bonder finds the good life. Bonders can enjoy the pleasure of sex, but they are likely to subordinate that pleasure to the best interests of their relationships. The relationship matters more than the quality of the sex to a Bonder. Bonders feel that sex within a pair bond, even if not always ideal, ultimately provides a good life—one enriched by deep relationships.

In contrast to the Bonder, the Aesthete considers the enjoyment of experience central to a good life. Aesthetes can enjoy the benefits of relationships, but they are likely to subordinate them to the intrinsic quality of the experience. For an Aesthete, having great sex matters more than having a romantic relationship. A relationship that puts constraints on sex will be abandoned, because an Aesthete finds the good life in sexual and other experimentation and the experience of pleasure.

To illustrate this tension, let's suppose that X and Y are in a bonded relationship. And suppose that X finds Z, a willing sexual partner who has mastered some exciting technique that could significantly increase X's sexual experience and pleasure. Should X have sex with Z?

The Aesthete seems likely to answer "Yes!", while the Bonder would say "No!" For the Bonder, the relationship with Y has become essential to the value of sex. Faithfulness to Y, the partner in X's relationship, may be more important than any enjoyment that could be had from the novelty of a new sex partner. Or, if the bonding is advanced, faithfulness to Y does not even permit X to enjoy sex with a new partner—novelty is no longer desired. In contrast, the Aesthete may believe that novelty and new partners significantly enhance sexual experience, which is one of the Aesthete's goals in life. For the Aesthete, a feeling of commitment to Y becomes an undesirable constraint on sex with new partner Z. The Aesthete might even take such a feeling of commitment as another reason to go to bed with Z: "I'm starting to feel tied down with Y; it's time to shake off the chains and try something new." The fact that the Aesthete and the Bonder tend to value novelty so differently is another basic difference between them.

A final difference between the Aesthete and the Bonder is their different views of the significance of sex. The Bonder seems to seek the "deeper meaning" of sex, and finds it in relationships. "But," the Aesthete might ask, "why must sex have a deeper meaning? Why must there be anything beyond the experience? Does sex have to be part of something larger or deeper? Indeed, perhaps looking for something more just distracts us and detracts from the experience. Maybe all the meaning there is can be found in appreciating the pleasure and joy of the act." (The Aesthete may not value faithfulness or bonding, but does the Aesthete value casual sex? The aesthetic view seems to require that sex be studied and mastered: sex as a practiced art. Is this "casual sex"?)

The Bonder and the Aesthete in the Media

Unfortunately, we think, the Bonder's views of the deeper meaning of sex (and life) do not get much press in our society, and neither does the contrasting picture of the Aesthete. Instead the mass media generate strong pressure for casual sex ("casual" here meaning sex that is both outside of meaningful bonds, which offends Bonders, and unstudied, which offends Aesthetes). Advertising, television, and movies seem to promote the idea that casual sex is good because (a) it feels good; (b) it avoids commitments (and the ensuing "hassle" of working out a long-term relationship); and (c) it reassures participants about their sexual desirability, general attractiveness, and even basic self-worth. Any other significance of sex is largely ignored. Sometimes opposition to casual sex does make it into the media. But public opponents of casual sex are usually motivated by religion; they tend to exude confidence that they alone know what God commands about sex, while also revealing a surprising ignorance about the meaning of sex even within their own traditions.

Is the view of sex promoted by the media and advertising a third view? How does it contrast with the Bonder's and the Aesthete's? Can you describe its values and argue for them? To what extent does the media's portrayal of sex seek to manipulate both men and women (especially women) for commercial gain? For more about media manipulation in the areas of sex, relationships, and power, see Gail Dines (ed.) and Jean McMahon Humez (ed.), *Gender, Race and Class in Media: A Text Reader* (Thousand Oaks, CA: Sage Publications, 1995).

There are images (somewhat distorted ones) of the Bonder and the Aesthete in popular culture, however, even if their views of the meaning of sex get ignored. You may recognize the Bonder in the roles of clingy girlfriend or loyal wife in TV dramas and sitcoms, and the Aesthete as the wealthy playboy of movies (think James Bond). Are the Bonder and the Aesthete gender stereotypes—women being Bonders, and men Aesthetes? If you think so, do you believe these stereotypes represent an innate difference between men and women, or a difference created by our mass media culture, or something else? Of course, there are men in our society who consider bonding with their partners the main point of sex, and women who value hedonistic recreational sex as a form of self-expression. But they go against our societal images of how women and men "should" be. Can these images be changed and made more gender-neutral? How? Should they be? We have hinted throughout this chapter that sexual relationships ought to be egalitarian. What might this mean? Does it lead to a critique of popular culture?

Up to this point, we have tried to avoid any judgments about sexual beliefs and behaviors. We have favored a minimalist ethics of sexuality, one that emphasizes consent and little more, and described several deeper ways in which people understand the role of sex in a good life. Do any of these views provide a perspective for critiquing popular culture?

APPLYING ETHICAL PRINCIPLES TO THE CASE

In this chapter we've discussed how the principle of relationship applies to sexual issues, and touched on the principles of community and personal growth in this area. Do our other main principles—the greatest good and equal respect—suggest different perspectives on the meaning of sex, or on the picture of sex generated by popular culture? What kinds of virtues or ideals of behavior (such as self-restraint, openness, honesty, unselfishness, faithfulness, and so on) does each view of the significance of sex require of us if we choose to be sexually active? Do all of the views imply necessary virtues? If some do not, what might this suggest about them? Which view seems most compelling to you personally, and why?

We particularly suggest that you try to apply the principle of character growth to questions about sex. Peter, for example, in Case 6.1, "Seduction or Rape?" has adopted an exploitative stance toward women. Has Peter thus damaged his ability to form a meaningful and equal partnership with a valued partner? Has he harmed himself in the process? How might an unequal, exploitative, or casual attitude toward sex shape a person's character? Does popular culture damage people?

EXAMPLES OF COLLEGE AND UNIVERSITY CODES GOVERNING SEXUAL BEHAVIOR

1. Excerpt from the Antioch College policy on sexual offenses.[3]

Under the *Sexual Offense Prevention Policy:*

- *All sexual contact and conduct between any two or more people must be consensual;*
- *Consent must be obtained verbally before* there is any sexual contact or conduct;
- Silence is *never* interpreted as consent;
- If the *level of sexual intimacy increases* during an interaction (i.e., if two or more people move from kissing while fully clothed, which is one level, to undressing for direct physical contact, which is another level), the people involved need to express their *clear verbal consent before moving* to that new level;

---

[3] Excerpt from "Sexual Offense Prevention Policy" in the *Antioch College 00'–01'* [sic] *Survival Manual.* (Yellow Springs, OH: Antioch College Community Government, August 2000).

- If one person wants to *initiate* moving to a different level of sexual intimacy in an interaction, *that person is responsible for getting the consent* of the other person(s) involved *before* moving to that level;

- If you have had a particular level of sexual intimacy before with someone, you must still be sure there is *consent each and every time;*

- If you have a sexually transmitted disease, *you must disclose* this fact to a potential partner before engaging sexually;

- If anyone asks you to stop a particular kind of sexual attention or behavior, you must *stop it immediately*, no matter what your intentions are [. . .]

Don't ever make assumptions about consent; assumptions can hurt someone and get you into trouble. Consent must be clear and verbal (i.e., saying, "Yes, I want to kiss you, too.")

Special precautions are necessary if you, or the person with whom you would like to be sexual, are *under the influence* of alcohol, drugs, or prescribed medication. *Extreme caution* should always be used. *Consent, even verbal consent, may not be valid.* Taking advantage of someone whose judgment is substantially impaired is not acceptable behavior, and this is a time of high risk for something nonconsensual to happen. Providing someone with alcohol to get him/her drunk so that person will consent to have sex with you (figuring that you wouldn't "get as far" if that person were sober) is a violation under the Sexual Offense Prevention Policy (SOPP). If you are so drunk that you act inappropriately with someone (in a way that you wouldn't if you were sober), or if you are so drunk that you don't hear "no," you may be charged under the SOPP.

[. . .] Our standards of behavior may be broader than currently exist under state and federal laws. These community standards are part of Antioch's educational mission [. . .]

2. Excerpt from the University of New Hampshire's Policy on Harassment and Sexual Harassment[4]

[. . .] no member of UNH may engage in harassing behavior within the jurisdiction of the university that unjustly interferes with any individual's required tasks, career opportunities, learning, or participation in university life.

The requirements of federal and state law determine the definition of discriminatory harassment. The relevant body of law stipulates that any behavior may be considered to be harassing when: 1) submission to or rejection of such behavior by an individual is used as a basis for employment

---

[4] *University of New Hampshire 2000–2001 Student Rights, Rules & Responsibilities* (University of New Hampshire, May 2000), pp. 35–36.

or academic decisions affecting that individual; 2) submission to such behavior is made either explicitly or implicitly a term or condition of an individual's employment or academic work; or 3) such behavior unjustly, substantially, unreasonably, and/or consistently interferes with an individual's work or academic performance or creates an intimidating environment.

[. . .] Discriminatory harassment does not include comments that are made in the classroom that are germane to the curriculum and a part of the exchange of competing ideas. A single incident that creates a distracting and uncomfortable atmosphere on a given day does not constitute discriminatory harassment. However, isolated or sporadic acts that are severe may. It is possible for a series of individual incidents, each minor in itself, to have the cumulative effect of becoming pervasively harassing behavior.

[. . .] Every instance of alleged discriminatory harassment must be considered in the context of its specific and unique circumstances. However, the following are examples of behavior that may be judged to be harassing: [. . .] repeatedly sending unwelcome, sexually explicit email messages; taunting a person about his or her sexual orientation [. . .] ; making unwelcome sexual propositions; repeatedly telling derogatory gender-based [. . .] jokes; displaying sexually suggestive objects or pictures in the workplace except as those items may be part of legitimate pedagogical pursuits; giving unwelcome hugs or repeatedly brushing or touching others.

3. Excerpt from the student handbook of Hope College[5]

The College is committed to fostering an environment in which all persons have an equal opportunity to work and pursue learning freely, whether in group settings or in close relationships between individual students, faculty, and staff. This entails an obligation to protect the dignity, safety, and self-respect of all students, faculty, and staff. As an academic community valuing the moral teaching of Jesus Christ, Hope College is committed to the belief that each individual is of unqualified worth. God values each person, female and male, as a unique work of divine creation. Therefore, the College condemns covert and overt acts which interfere with this commitment and will not tolerate any form of intimidation, abuse, or harassment.

Description and Explanation

Sexual harassment is a form of discrimination. It includes any inappropriate or unwanted conduct of a sexual nature which has a negative effect on the educational process, employee benefits, campus climate, or opportunities of any student or employee. [. . . .]

[5] "Sexual Harassment Policy" in *The Handbook of Selected College Policies 2000–2001* (Hope College, Holland, MI), pp. 5–6.

An abuse of privilege or power, sexual harassment can threaten a person's academic status, economic livelihood, sense of safety, well being, and personal dignity. The effects of sexual harassment may include feelings of anger, resentment, embarrassment, humiliation, fear, and lowered self-esteem. [. . . .] Nothing in this policy should be construed to limit the scholarly, educational, or artistic content of written, oral, or other presentations or discussions. Academic freedom should be extended to all members of the academic community. Sexual harassment includes the following categories:

A. Actions Which Create a Hostile Environment

    1. Generalized Sexist Remarks or Sexist Behavior

       This involves demeaning remarks or actions serving no scholarly, artistic, or educational purpose that are directed at individuals or groups because of their gender or sexual orientation.

    2. Sexually Offensive Remarks or Behavior

       This includes lewd, obscene, or sexually suggestive remarks or actions serving no scholarly, artistic, or educational purpose, which would be found offensive by a reasonable person in that situation. This category also includes the public display of sexually offensive audio and visual materials serving no scholarly, artistic, or educational purpose.

B. Sexual Advances

    1. Sexual Advances Without Intimidation

       This includes repeated unwanted requests for a social or sexual encounter. It also includes unwanted or inappropriate touching or kissing.

    2. Sexual Advances With Intimidation

       This refers to sexual advances that are accompanied by the threat of punishment or the promise of reward.

C. Sexual Assaults

    This includes sexual advances that are accompanied by actual or threatened physical violence. [. . . .] [It] also applies to any of the following, if lacking explicit verbal consent: physical contact with groin, genital area, inner thigh, buttocks, and/or breasts; penetration that involves sexual or anal intercourse; cunnilingus; fellatio; or placing any other object in the genital or anal opening. [. . .]

Romantic Relationships Between Employee/Student

A. Implicit in the concept of professionalism is the recognition by those in positions of authority that their relationships with students include an element of power. It is incumbent on those with authority not to abuse, or seem to abuse, the power with which they are entrusted. Therefore, the initiation of or consent to a romantic or sexual relationship between an employee of Hope College and any current Hope College student for whom the employee has a direct professional responsibility is unacceptable. [. . . .]

C. The initiation of a romantic or sexual relationship is strongly discouraged even where there is not a direct professional responsibility. In these situations, there may still be an element of power or authority which could diminish the individual's freedom of choice. Additionally, a change in the situation may establish a direct professional responsibility between the individuals. [. . . .] Furthermore, for individuals who enter into a relationship where a power differential exists, it will be difficult to prove immunity on grounds of mutual consent if a complaint alleging sexual harassment is lodged.

D. Such romantic or sexual relationships frequently can have a detrimental effect on other students or employees who share a work or classroom environment with the involved parties. [. . . .]

4. Excerpt from *The Logger 2000–2001* student handbook of the University of Puget Sound[6]

Sexual assault as defined by this policy with reference to applicable criminal law consists of any actual, attempted, or threatened form of nonconsensual sexual intercourse or other sexual contact of a forcible, threatening, or otherwise nonconsensual nature. Sexual conduct is of a nonconsensual nature if the complainant objected or manifestly attempted to object to the conduct, or if his or her capacity to consent was substantially impaired by reason of physical force, threat or intimidation, lack of opportunity to object, physical or mental disability, drug or alcohol consumption, or other voluntary or involuntary cause.

ADDITIONAL CASES

CASE 6.2 *Pregnant!*

Lorraine and Aidin are sophomores who have been dating for several months when Lorraine finds out that she's pregnant, despite the fact they've been using some contraception. Both are very upset by the news. After thinking long and hard, Aidin promises to help support the child and to marry Lorraine. Lorraine, however, has settled on having an abortion. She knows that she isn't ready to be a mother, she wants to finish school, and she doesn't want to marry anyone yet, including Aidin. Even though he no

[6] "Sexual Harassment Policy" in *The Logger 2000–2001* student handbook of the University of Puget Sound in Tacoma, WA, p. 110.

longer goes to church, Aidin's Catholic childhood rises up to remind him that abortion is a mortal sin. He pleads with Lorraine, but she remains firm through both of their tears.

QUESTIONS

1. Please note that this case does not ask you to discuss the morality of abortion. Instead we want to focus on the issues of power involved in this dilemma. Which member of the couple should have the deciding vote about whether or not to terminate the pregnancy, and why? Would your response differ if Lorraine wanted to have the baby and Aidin wanted her to get an abortion?

2. Do Lorraine and Aidin have an obligation to tell their parents about their predicament? Why or why not? If you believe that they don't, would you change your mind if they were fourteen instead of eighteen years old? Why?

3. If you were counseling Aidin and Lorraine, what would you tell them (separately and together) to do?

Best Buddies   CASE 6.3

Mark and Demetri have been close friends since the beginning of the semester. Leaving a party late one night, as they stumble drunkenly home together with their arms around each other, Demetri confesses to Mark that he loves him. At first Mark takes Demetri's declaration as an excess of drunken male bonding, but when Demetri stops and looks deeply into his eyes and says, "I really mean it, man, anytime you want . . . ," Mark's stomach turns over. He keeps his voice under control as he asks, "Are you gay or something?" After Demetri's quiet "I think so," Mark wants to run away and throw up. How could he not have realized?! Everyone else probably knows and is talking about them behind his back!

The next day Mark starts shunning Demetri and spreading vicious rumors about his ex-friend. Demetri is crushed by Mark's cruelty and feels lonelier than he ever has in his life. He's also angry with himself for having seen cues in Mark's behavior and body language that apparently weren't there—or did Mark "lead him on" and not have the courage to admit it, even to himself?

QUESTIONS

1. What do you think of Mark's reaction? What concerns seem to be motivating him? How would you analyze his behavior in terms of the principles of equal respect, relationships, and personal growth?

2. If you were Demetri's friend, therapist, or minister, how would you counsel him? Would your advice change, depending on which role you assumed?

3. Can a person "lead someone on" without being really aware of it? If so, should people be held ethically responsible for things they do without being fully conscious of them? (Other examples might be unwittingly hurting a friend's feelings or making a racist or sexist comment without intending any insult.) Another way of asking this is, are we morally responsible for our feelings (whether of love, hate, jealousy, lust, snobbery, and so on) and any "unconscious" behaviors they inspire, or only for acts we have consciously planned?

CASE 6.4   *Cheating*

Nick and Katie have been a couple for two years, and despite some minor fights, they feel firmly committed to each other. They often talk about getting married eventually and have even planned many details of their future life together. One night when Katie went out with her girlfriends, Nick met Olivia at a party. Olivia was very sexy, exotic, temperamental, and rather wild—everything that Katie was not. Nick and Olivia began an affair almost at once. Nick knew, even while he was "in lust" with Olivia, that he had no intention of dropping Katie for her. Katie was the person he wanted to marry someday, and Olivia was merely the person with whom he wanted to do unprintable things right now. Therefore he took great care to avoid making Katie suspicious, and he saw Olivia only on the sly, when Katie thought he was studying or out with his friends.

In fact, no one knows Nick's dirty little secret except for Linda and Omar, mutual friends of Nick's and Katie's who saw Nick and Olivia embracing passionately under a tree. Linda and Omar argue about whether or not to tell Katie what's going on. (They don't know Olivia, and they feel no loyalty to her.) Omar thinks it's none of their business; perhaps Katie already knows about it and has decided to ignore the affair until it blows over. "We'll just embarrass them both if we tell her what we saw," he says. "And maybe this is something Nick just needs to get out of his system."

Linda disagrees. "He has no right to treat Katie like this! When I see Katie with Nick, I'm sure she doesn't know. And she would never forgive us if she found out that we knew and didn't tell her."

QUESTIONS

1. What sort of duty does Nick have to Katie, and to Olivia? If the affair with Olivia doesn't mean much to him compared to his commitment to Katie, is it then less, or more, important for him to be honest with Katie about it?

2. If it turns out that Nick's affair with Olivia is brief and Katie never finds out, is any harm done?

3. How might Nick's character and his relationship with Katie change depending on whether or not he admits his duplicity?

4. Do friends have an obligation to tell friends painful truths, or should their role be only supportive? In other words, is it kinder to tell Katie something she will find painful, or to let her remain in ignorance and support her if and when she finds out? Should Omar and Linda tell Katie what they know?

5. Should they go to Nick, tell him what they saw, and ask him to tell Katie himself if he doesn't want them to? Is it fairer to Nick to approach him directly, or is this a kind of blackmail?

6. Consider the fact that the risk of AIDS (and other sexually transmitted diseases) increases exponentially with every new sexual partner a person has. Does this affect your answers?

7. Would your responses to any of these questions be different if Katie were the one having an affair behind Nick's back? If so, why?

Dating in the Age of AIDS **CASE 6.5**

After several dates, Cheryl and Ray find themselves in bed together. Ray has a condom in his wallet, but he's embarrassed to bring it out because then, he thinks, Cheryl will know he's been planning on having sex with her, which might insult her. Besides, a condom would really ruin the spontaneity of the moment. For her part, Cheryl has had little sexual experience. She feels shy and uncomfortable about sleeping with Ray, even though she's powerfully attracted to him. Like Ray, she is too embarrassed to mention contraception or safe sex until it's too late. It's almost as if she can tell herself that she isn't having sex (being a slut, as her mother would say) if she doesn't make any preparations for it.

After the deed is done, the two of them lie quietly side by side. Finally Ray works up the courage to say that he really cares about Cheryl and hopes they'll "get together" again, and next time, maybe they should use some contraception. Cheryl agrees, relieved. After a pause (during which she is thinking about pregnancy and AIDS and whether this might be the start of a long-term relationship), Cheryl asks Ray if he's had a lot of girlfriends. Ray knows that Cheryl has had only one boyfriend before him. He doesn't want her to think that he's slept around as much as he has, so he claims to have slept with only two women before her.

He wonders if Cheryl is worried about AIDS. He rationalizes lying to her with the thought that his ten or twelve previous partners "weren't the kinds of girls who get AIDS," although he knows that the risk of AIDS increases with the number of partners one has. "I really should get HIV testing," he thinks to himself. But he says none of this out loud, because he doesn't want to scare Cheryl away.

QUESTIONS

1. Ray has begun his relationship with Cheryl with a lie. What repercussions might this act have?

2. Do sexual partners have a moral duty to report honestly on their pasts, no matter how unsavory, or are their past relationships their own business?

3. Do we incur ethical obligations by having sex with someone, even if only once? If so, what kinds of obligations?

4. How might practicing safer sex, getting tested for HIV, and talking together about the results affect Ray and Cheryl's personal growth and the health of their relationship?

CASE 6.6   *Sexual Harassment I*

"Dick Reynolds gives me the creeps!" Helen Takahashi told her friends. "I try to avoid him, but it's hard, because he's in two of my classes. I think he's been trailing me, and I've caught him spying on me! No matter where I go, he keeps walking up behind me and muttering stuff like 'you turn me on, baby' and making lip-smacking noises, then running away. I'm going to report him. He's such a disgusting, immature jerk!" Helen's friends were sympathetic, but they reminded her that Dick hadn't done anything Helen could officially complain about. Besides, everyone knew he had a "thing" about Asian women, and the other girls he pestered just ignored him.

Then one night Dick exposed himself to Helen while they were both on a deserted floor of the library. After he dropped his pants, he immediately pulled them up again and ran away, but Helen was still scared, embarrassed, and upset for many minutes after the incident. Finally she went downstairs to the pay phones and called one of her roommates to come and walk her home. The next morning she reported Dick's actions to the dean of students, expecting that he would be quickly punished.

Instead it seemed that Helen was the one who was punished. She had to spend many weeks and considerable emotional effort in following up the matter. She had to give humiliating testimony, twice, before a faculty review board. One member even said, "Some women would consider Mr. Reynolds' actions flattering. He never actually touched you or threatened you, so what's the problem?"

Finally the board told her that Dick would be leaving the college. Helen was relieved until she found out that the school hadn't expelled him. Instead the administration had told Dick that if he left voluntarily, nothing would appear on his record and he'd have no trouble applying to another school. Helen also found out where Dick was transferring to, and she decided to write them a warning letter about him. But it seemed that everyone, from the board to her friends, thought that Helen should drop the matter. "He's been punished enough by having to change schools," they said. "Leave him alone and get on with your life."

QUESTIONS

1. Has Dick been punished enough for what he did to Helen (and, perhaps, to other women) by having to transfer?

2. Does the fact that Dick was known to "have a 'thing' about Asian women" make his harassment of Helen less, or more, offensive and actionable? Why?

3. If he never touched or threatened anyone, but did bother women and make some of them feel uncomfortable or scared, is he still guilty of harassment?

4. Can he be accused of sexual harassment if he is a peer of those he bothers, rather than their professor or boss?

5. Does Helen (or her school) have a duty to the unknown members of another college community who might be bothered by Dick, or should she (or the school) let him start over there?

Sexual Harassment II   CASE 6.7

Professor Kulbrick is the only professor at Melissa's large, impersonal college with whom she has ever had a private conversation, and he gave her her only A last semester. Now that Melissa wants to transfer to a smaller school, he seems the logical person to ask for an academic recommendation. However, he sometimes makes her uncomfortable. Once when she'd gone to his office to talk about a paper, he extravagantly flattered her, intellectually and physically, and made a double entendre comment about her "endowment." Melissa was embarrassed and didn't talk to him alone again, although she continued to participate actively in his class discussions.

Now, because she wants his recommendation, Melissa again finds herself alone with Professor Kulbrick in his office. He says that he would be happy to write a recommendation, but again he embarrasses her. He sits very close to her, touches her arm and leg several times while they talk, and makes a suggestive joke about "uncovering her secret abilities." Finally Melissa gets out the door with his promise to write the recommendation.

Six weeks go by, and Professor Kulbrick hasn't written Melissa's recommendation. Feeling uncomfortable about seeing him again, Melissa calls him to see whether he's forgotten his promise. He assures her that he plans to write the recommendation and suggests that she meet him again so that he can "get more background information." Melissa makes excuses for not being able to meet him, but she's feeling anxious—she's counting on his reference, and time has almost run out. She leaves him notes several times to remind him, but nothing seems to happen. Finally Melissa mentions the situation to her parents. They are outraged by what they regard as Professor Kulbrick's sexual harassment of their daughter, and Melissa's father writes a letter to that effect to the dean.

Two days before the final submission date for all the application materials, Melissa calls the professor one last time. He is furious and claims that he never harassed her. "You crazy, sex-starved bitch!" he shouts. "Do you know how much trouble you've gotten me into? You made up all this crap just to entrap me! Your recommendation," he adds nastily, "will be waiting for you with the department secretary, but I doubt it will be much help."

QUESTIONS

1. Do you believe that Professor Kulbrick's behavior (prior to the final telephone call) counts as an example of sexual harassment, or was this all a big misunderstanding? If he were genuinely unaware that he was embarrassing Melissa, would this matter?

2. Could Melissa have handled the situation differently? If so, what should she have done?

3. The professor retaliated by writing a bad recommendation. Is this action sexual harassment, unprofessional in some other way, or an understandable reaction to what he saw as Melissa's harassment of him? How might he have better handled the situation?

4. Do you think that if she wanted to pursue the matter, Melissa would have enough evidence to be able to win a sexual harassment complaint against Professor Kulbrick? What might the evidence be?

5. Suppose that Melissa had offered herself sexually to Professor Kulbrick as a bribe for a good recommendation. What, if anything, is wrong with an exchange of sex for an improved grade or recommendation?

6. Can a student who sexually pursues a professor despite the professor's objections be considered guilty of sexual harassment, or does "harassment" necessarily imply that the harasser has some sort of power over her or his victim?

CASE 6.8 *The Affair*

"I can't believe you're having an affair with Professor Woolf!" Rosa exclaimed to her friend Patsy. But actually, now that the cat was out of the bag, she *could* believe it; with hindsight she could see that there had been signs all semester. She remembered now that Patsy had confessed to having a crush on Professor Woolf when they'd both been in the archaeological field work seminar for only a couple of weeks. Then there were all those times Patsy and the professor seemed to catch each other's eyes during class discussions and talk after class, and Patsy did seem to know a lot of obscure details about cultural anthropology for a junior.

"I've wanted to tell someone for weeks; this whole thing's been like an incredible dream come true!" Patsy gushed. "It's been so hard keeping such a big secret and sneaking around all the time. It started that day Grant and I—"

"'Grant'?"

"You know, Professor Woolf. It started the day he took me out to look at the site by myself. We had this amazing long talk about Mound Builder culture, Indian history, mythology, the supernatural, everything in the universe—and then he told me about how lousy his marriage is, and how he wished he could talk to his wife the way he can talk to me. Then, well, one thing just led to another, as they say," she giggled. "Actually, I'm really flattered that he confides in me; and I'm learning so much from him. He's so sophisticated! And he makes me feel really attractive."

Rosa thought to herself that of course Professor Woolf found Patsy attractive; stunningly beautiful was more like it. Rosa was surprised to feel herself growing angry. "Am I jealous?" she wondered. "Shouldn't I be happy for Patsy?" Out loud she asked, "But you said he's married—what about his wife?"

"Oh, he's been very honest with me. He told me he wouldn't leave his wife, and she doesn't suspect anything. But I know how unhappy he is. She doesn't understand him or support him, and he really needs me. We're in love!"

Rosa didn't know what to say. She couldn't pretend that she shared Patsy's enthusiasm. In fact, she felt betrayed by both Patsy and Professor Woolf, although she couldn't say exactly why. This whole secret relationship just didn't seem fair to her and the rest of the class, or, of course, to Professor Woolf's wife.

QUESTIONS

1. If Professor Woolf weren't married, would there be any harm in Patsy's having an affair with him?

2. Patsy seems to be learning a lot from Professor Woolf. What might be the long-term effects of the affair on her intellectual development, emotional life, and character growth?

3. Is there anything wrong with students and professors' sleeping together? Is a student having an affair with a teacher ethically different from an employee sleeping with a boss, or with a May–December romance between any consenting adults? Would it make a difference if Patsy were a graduate student around the same age as the professor?

4. What are the effects on the class and the college community of an affair between a student and a professor? Are the other students in the class being harmed?

5. Would it make a difference if Patsy were doing an independent study with Professor Woolf, so that he wasn't grading other students with her?

6. In addition to being a grader, Professor Woolf is also a learning resource for his students. How might his secret affair with one of his students affect the learning of the others? If everyone knew that Patsy and the professor were romantically involved, would there still be a problem?

7. Is a private relationship between Patsy and Professor Woolf Rosa's business? If so, does her duty lie with her friend, who has confided an important secret to her, to the other students in the class, who don't know about the affair, or to Mrs. Woolf, whom she has never met?

8. What should Rosa do?

CASE 6.9 *First Comes Love, Then Comes Marriage . . .*

Seniors Jerome and Wendy are deeply in love, but they may have to break up with each other. Although they share the same conservative religion, Jerome takes their religion's prohibition against premarital sex much more seriously than Wendy does. He decided years ago that he would remain celibate until he married, and he's not ready to get married yet (although he may want to marry Wendy eventually).

Wendy thinks it's important for potential life partners to have sex before they commit themselves to each other. She feels that they can't know how compatible they will be in the long term until they have an intimate relationship. She believes that sex is a powerful way to both show their love and increase their intimacy. But Wendy also respects Jerome's feelings about sex; she even finds his devotion to religious duty admirable, if frustrating. However, she cannot promise to wait indefinitely until he feels ready. At this point in her life, she wants to get serious about someone, and for her, "getting serious" means having sex as well as considering marriage. Jerome loves Wendy, understands her reasoning, and doesn't want to lose her, but it's important to him to save sex for his wedding night. As Wendy tearfully asked Jerome, "It seems bizarre to say, 'I love you so much, but I have to look for someone else!' Isn't there some way to save our relationship?"

QUESTIONS

1. Do Jerome's views about virginity and sex have merit? That is, should a believer remain faithful to his religious convictions and traditional ideas about sex in a situation like this? Why or why not?

2. If Jerome's desire to remain celibate until marriage were based on nonreligious beliefs or feelings, would it be less defensible?

3. What other arguments might Jerome and Wendy use with each other for and against the idea of sexual abstinence?

4. Using the ethical principles we've discussed throughout this book, what would you advise Wendy and Jerome each to do?

BACKGROUND READING

• The increasingly active abortion debate on campus is discussed in David Crary (Associated Press), "Rival Forces Heat Up Abortion Debate on Campus," in *The Ithaca Journal*, 21 April 2001, p. 2B. Crary reports that Jill Ireland, President of the "pro-choice" National Organization for Women (NOW), and Gregg Cunningham, Executive Director of the "pro-life" Center for Bio-Ethical Reform, have been touring college campuses and organizing rallies to galvanize students around the issue of abortion. NOW and the Center for Bio-Ethical Reform are only two of the rival groups that have been increasingly targeting college students, whom they see as "ambivalent" and "vulnerable" on the issue.

For more information on the two sides in the debate, go on-line to www.now.org for the pro-abortion rights Web site of the National Organization of Women, and to www.prolifeaction.org/gregg-cunningham.htm for the anti-abortion Web site of the "Genocide Awareness Project."

• Current rates of pregnancy, contraceptive use, and abortions among American teens and college-age women are available in "National and State-Specific Pregnancy Rates Among Adolescents—United States, 1995–1997" (from the Centers for Disease Control and Prevention) in *JAMA, The Journal of the American Medical Association*, 23 August 2000, vol. 284, i. 8, p. 952, available on-line at www.census.gov/population/estimates/state/5age9890.txt; Steven R. Murray and Jessica L. Miller, Mesa State College, "Birth Control and Condom Usage among College Students" in *Research Quarterly for Exercise and Sport*, March 2000, vol. 71, i. 1, p. A-42; "Sad But True: Teen Motherhood Is as American as Apple Pie," in *U.S. News & World Report*, 5 March 2001, vol. 130, i. 9, p. 8; Thomas Kean and Isabel Sawhill, "More Teens Just Say 'No'" (op-ed), in *The Washington Post*, 5 September 2000, p. A25; and Marianne Lavelle, "Behind the Teen Birth Decline," in *U.S. News & World Report*, 8 November 1999, vol. 127, i. 18, p. 22.

Beginning in the early '90s, rates of teenage pregnancy, abortion, and births have been declining steadily—led by less sexual activity and better contraceptive use. The most recent figures show teen pregnancy rates lower than at any time since statistics were first tallied in 1976. A record low of 40 percent of college freshmen (down from 52 percent in 1987) believe that "if two people really like each other, it's all right for them to have sex even if they've known each other for a very short time," according to an annual survey conducted by University of California at Los Angeles. Yet the United States still leads the developed world in teen pregnancy; almost one million U.S. teenagers (four out of every ten girls) get pregnant each year.

• Joan Blythe, John Boswell, Leon Botstein, William Kerrigan, and Jack Hitt, "Forum: New Rules about Sex on Campus: Should Professors Be

Denied Admittance to Students' Beds?" in *Harper's*, September 1993, vol. 287, no. 1720, pp. 33–42.

This is a lively discussion of sexual harassment versus sexual freedom and privacy, carried out by several professors and administrators over dinner. Attitudes range from "students and professors are both adults, and some students only want to lose their virginity to a professor like me," to "a fair amount of data shows a long tradition of abuse of students by professors."

• Catherine MacKinnon, *Only Words* (Cambridge, MA: Harvard University Press, 1993). This work offers a deliberately shocking and graphic description of the harm done to women by pornography. It argues against giving pornography free speech protection because "social inequality is substantially created and enforced—that is, *done*—through words and images." Similarly, the author defines sexual harassment broadly ("unwelcome sex talk is an unwelcome sex act") and makes legal arguments for punishing verbal as well as physical sexual harassment. She finds that colleges (and workplaces) are sites of confrontation between women's rights and free speech arguments protecting harassment and pornography, because college and the workplace both "crucially enforce inequality and crucially guarantee equality."

• Gertrude Himmelfarb, "New Victorians Don't Earn That Label," in *The Wall Street Journal*, 12 January 1994, sec. A, p. 10, col. 3.

The author discusses the use of the word "Victorian" to describe the school of feminism led by Catherine MacKinnon. She critiques feminists who would prohibit pornography, censor "hate speech," punish sexual innuendos on the grounds of sexual harassment, prescribe detailed codes of sexual conduct, make "date rape" as odious an offense as violent rape, and subject offenders to "sensitivity" and "consciousness-raising" sessions.

• Karen Lehrman, "Has Sexual Correctness Gone Too Far?" in *USA Today*, 4 April 1994, sec. A, p. 15, col. 2.

The author explores the deleterious impact that bloating the definitions of "sexual harassment" and "date rape" has on the notions of romance and courtship, particularly in the workplace and on college campuses, as a result of the debate's focus on the extreme rhetoric and policies of "some radical feminists."

• Katha Pollitt, "Not Just Bad Sex: a Review of *The Morning After: Sex, Fear, and Feminism on Campus* by Katie Roiphe (Boston: Little Brown, 1993)," in *The New Yorker*, vol. LXIX, no. 32, pp. 220–224.

This author castigates what she sees as the excesses of the movement on campus to control sexual behavior through conduct codes and harassment policies. However, as an avowed feminist, Pollitt has different reasons for opposing this "climate of fear" than does Lehrman.

- The ethics of faithfulness and infidelity within a pair-bond are explored in Bonnie Steinbock, "Adultery," in *Report from the Center for Philosophy and Public Policy*, Winter 1986, vol. 6, no. 1, pp. 12–14. The *Report* is available from The Institute for Philosophy and Public Policy, School of Public Affairs, University of Maryland, College Park, MD 20742, (301) 405-4759, or on-line at www.puaf.umd.edu/ippp.

ADDITIONAL MATERIALS

1. Richard Bernstein, "Guilty If Charged," in *The New York Times Review of Books*, 13 January 1994, vol. xli, nos. 1 and 2, pp. 11–14; Jeremy Rabkin, "Rule of Law: New Checks on Campus Sexual-Harassment Cops," in *The Wall Street Journal*, 19 October 1994, sec. A, p. 21, col. 3; Anthony Lewis, "Time To Grow Up," in *The New York Times*, 14 October 1994, sec. A, p. 35, col. 1; and Joanne Jacobs, "College Professors Are Compelled to Tiptoe Around Student Sensitivities," in *The Atlanta Journal*, 5 October 1994, sec. A, p. 8, col. 1.

J. Donald Silva, a tenured English professor at the University of New Hampshire, was found guilty of sexual harassment in 1993 and severely punished. He was suspended from his job without pay for "at least one year," ordered to undergo a year of "weekly counseling sessions" with a "professional psychotherapist approved by the university," to "reimburse the university $2000 to cover the cost of setting up an alternative section of his course," and to "apologize, in writing, for creating a hostile and offensive academic environment." What had he done? (a) In class, he said that "Belly dancing is like Jello on a plate with a vibrator under the plate" as an example of a simile. (b) He explained the concept of "focus" by comparing it to sex ("you zero in on the subject . . . you move from side to side . . . you bracket the subject and center on it . . . you and the subject become one"). (c) When a female student said, "I guess I'll jump on a computer before someone else does," he replied "I'd like to see that!" (d) When he saw a student at the library, pulling out a card index on her hands and knees, he joked that "you look like you've had a lot of experience on your knees."

Do you think these are examples of sexual harassment? Do you agree with the University of New Hampshire's definition of sexual harassment (above under "Examples of College and University Codes Governing Sexual Behavior")? What role might generational differences (Silva was late middle-aged; his students were young) play in perceptions of sexual harassment? Is mandatory psychotherapy an appropriate punishment for convicted harassers?

2. Laura Miller, "May I Touch You There?" in *The San Francisco Examiner*, 19 December 1993, pp. D1–D4; Comment: "Different Strokes," in *The New Yorker*, 29 November 1993, vol. LXIX, no. 40, pp. 8–10; and Edward Felsenthal, "Campus Dilemma: The Risk of Lawsuits Disheartens

Colleges Fighting Date Rape," in *The Wall Street Journal*, 12 April 1994, sec. A, p. 1, col. 1.

Antioch College's Sexual Offense Policy (see above under "Examples of College and University Codes Governing Sexual Behavior") has become notorious recently. Is the policy an unwarranted intrusion into private life or a legitimate and helpful way to prevent the crime of date rape? Does the view of sex implicit in the policy make women into automatic victims? If so, could this attitude be harmful to women, or to men? How? What other implications might such a policy have?

3. How big a problem is (date) rape on campus? Different sources disagree. Some claim that one-fifth of all college women are victims of date and acquaintance rape and one-quarter experience either attempted or completed forced sex: Carol Bohmer and Andrea Parrot, *Sexual Assault on Campus: The Problem and the Solution* (New York: Lexington Books, 1993), p. 26. These sources describe the "typical" victim of a college sexual assault as a female freshman who has been drinking alcohol, especially during a frat party drinking game; she is unlikely to report the rape to the police or even to the college administration (ibid., p. 19). Fraternity pledges are the students "most likely to rape in college." Fraternity members in general and basketball and football players at NCAA colleges are significantly more likely to assault women sexually in college than are male members of student government or students not affiliated with other organizations (ibid., p. 21). Other sources say the estimate that 20–25 percent of women are victims of sexual assaults in college is inflated; few rapes are reported at least partly because women don't consider what happened to them "rape," and if they don't know they've been raped, it isn't rape (Neil Gilbert, quoted in M. Collison, "A Berkeley Scholar Clashes with Feminists Over the Validity of Their Research on Date Rape," in *The Chronicle of Higher Education*, 26 February 1992, vol. 38, no. 25, pp. A35, A37).

Looking at these figures in the context of the debate about date rape (see "Background Reading" above), what might be some of the problems involved in collecting accurate rape statistics? Should the actual number of campus rapes affect rape-deterrence policies? Aside from sexual conduct codes and anti-harassment policies, what can colleges and students do to help prevent (date) rape? Which methods seem the fairest to all involved, and why? What aspects of fraternity life might support a climate in which rape is tolerated or even encouraged? What can women do to protect themselves from rape? For more information, see Bill Hendrick, "Rape a Big Problem for Freshman Women," in *The Atlanta Constitution*, 18 May 1994, sec. A, p. 9, col. 1.; Bill Brubaker, "NCAA Intensifying Effort to Educate Athletes on Issues of Sexual Responsibility," in *The Washington Post*, 13 November 1994, sec. A, p. 24, col. 1; Bohmer and Parrot, *Sexual Assault on Campus*; Ruth G. Davis, "How to Talk Your Way Out of a Date Rape," in

Cosmopolitan, December 2000, vol. 229, i. 6, p. 261, and "What Is This So-Called Date-Rape Drug and What Effect Does It Have on Women?" in *Ebony*, July 2000, vol. 55, i. 9, p. 22.

4. Tamar Lewis, "If Flames Singe, Who Is to Blame?" in *The New York Times*, 25 September 1994, sec. 4, p. 3, col. 4; and Tamar Lewis, "Dispute over Computer Messages: Free Speech or Sex Harassment?" in *The New York Times*, 22 September 1994, sec. A, p. 1, col. 1.

Several students at Santa Rosa Junior College in California recently complained about a computer network flame that they considered sexually harassing. Can someone be sexually harassed via computer, rather than in person? How should computer users respond to sexually harassing (or racially intolerant, or otherwise offensive) messages on-line? How much responsibility should computer networks take for potentially offensive words posted on their bulletin boards? How might colleges try to balance computer users' freedom of speech with their right not to be intimidated or harassed?

5. "Date Rape and a List at Brown," in *The New York Times*, 18 November 1990, p. 26; and Bohmer and Parrot, *Sexual Assault on Campus*, p. 13.

A number of female students at Brown University believed that the University didn't take complaints of rape seriously, so they made a list of male students whom they claimed had raped them and wrote it on the bathroom walls to warn other women on campus. What consequences might such a list have for the rape victims and their assailants? Would you expect such a measure to be effective in preventing further rapes? What if a man's name was put on the list by mistake, or because of rumor, or because a woman wanted to "get him" for a reason unrelated to sexual assault? What are the ethics of taking matters into your own hands, bypassing official channels for punishing suspected rapists or other criminals?

6. Acquaintance rape has been the subject of a powerful motion picture (*The Accused* [1988], starring Jodie Foster, who won an Academy Award for her performance), and a made-for-TV documentary that focused on date rape on college campuses ("Against Her Will" [1989]), narrated by Kelly McGillis on Lifetime cable network). Compare these or other depictions of date rape; analyze how the moviemakers assign blame for the rape and its aftermath and the solutions they suggest. To what ethical principles do they seem to appeal? How is the victim "supposed" to act? You might contrast these more recent portrayals with older images of acquaintance rape, such as a 1979 portrayal on the soap opera *General Hospital*. Luke raped Laura, and Laura left her husband to marry him (cited in Bohmer and Parrot, *Sexual Assault on Campus*). How has public opinion about date rape, at least as reflected in television and the movies, changed?

7. Andre Dubus, "Townies," *Finding a Girl in America* (Boston: David Godine Publisher, 1980), p. 37. In this short story, Dubus paints a disturbing portrait of college acquaintance rape (and in this case, murder) from the assailant's point of view. He seems to suggest that class differences help explain such violence. Do you accept this explanation? Might class or gender differences contribute to a communication gap that results in date rape, or does this type of reasoning remove individual responsibility?

8. Ben Gose, "Court Allows Former Student to Sue Brandeis Over Its Handling of Rape Allegation," in *The Chronicle of Higher Education*, 15 October 1999, vol. 46, i. 8, p. A60. A complicated campus rape prosecution has resulted in a court ruling that students can sue colleges for unfairly administering their own student conduct codes.

In 1996, a female student charged junior David Schaer with raping her while she slept. (She admitted in a deposition that she did originally want to have sex with him, and had invited him to her room for this purpose.) A campus disciplinary board composed of six students and two professors found Schaer guilty. No criminal charges were pressed, but Schaer was punished by being barred from campus for the summer, so that he couldn't do his biomedical honors project, and he was placed on disciplinary probation for his senior year. Schaer requested a new hearing before an appeals board; his request was denied. He then sued the university for damages. His suit was overturned by a lower court judge. He took his suit to a higher court, and in 1999 the Massachusetts Appeals Court's three-judge panel unanimously ruled that Brandeis had violated its own student judicial code by allowing irrelevant and inflammatory evidence against Schaer, by failing to make any record of the five-and-half-hour disciplinary board hearing, and by rendering a decision "without clear and convincing evidence." (The full text of the decision is available from *The Chronicle's* Web site at http://chronicle.com.)

Some of the "evidence" admitted against Schaer at the original college disciplinary board hearing included statements such as "Schaer is a self-motivated egotistical bastard with no respect for women," and that his accuser "looked like a rape victim" when she brought charges against him one month after the alleged incident. Should statements about the personality or looks of an alleged rapist, or of a rape victim, have a bearing on a rape trial? Why or why not? If a person invites someone to have sex but then changes his or her mind during the act, and the partner will not stop, is this "rape"? Can someone legitimately decide that he or she was raped a month (or years) after the fact? Do you believe a rapist could be genuinely clueless about the criminal and unethical nature of his or her behavior? If so, would it still be rape? Popular and legal definitions of rape have evolved over the years (see some current examples of college codes governing sexual behavior at the beginning of this chapter). Is there a consensus among your peers about what behavior counts as "rape"?

7

DRINKING AND LIVING THE GOOD LIFE

The Drinking Survey

Avi Fisher, a senior at Bacchus University, always had a perverse interest in drinking. After all, it was a major factor in his life. His father's alcoholism had broken up his family, impoverished him and his mother, and made his teenage years unstable and unhappy. Maybe he'd overreacted to his dad's drinking, but Avi hadn't had so much as a beer since he was fifteen. He was a compulsive nondrinker.

Perhaps his experience and attitudes also explained the direction Avi's job had taken. Avi was an undergraduate dorm counselor for a freshman and sophomore dorm. He quickly learned that his charges' drinking behavior heavily influenced his job. Alcohol seemed to be behind a significant number of the fights he had to deal with, as well as his occasional trips to the college clinic with an injured or ill person. Just last week he had to call Security to provide a ride for a student who had broken his leg in a drunken fall.

These experiences led Avi to investigate undergraduate drinking for a term paper on the topic of why people drink. The dean of students encouraged his study and agreed to consider it part of Avi's paid work. Avi first tried to gather some data on alcohol-related incidents on campus. He interviewed a number of other undergraduate counselors, combed the campus and local newspapers, and interviewed people at the clinic as well as at campus security. Following are some of his findings:

- Campus security estimated that they received ten to fifteen alcohol-related calls a week, involving automobile accidents, fights or disturbances of the peace, or illnesses or injuries. One officer described these calls as "probably the tip of the iceberg." Most incidents, she assumed, either were not reported or were handled by someone else.

- The health clinic similarly saw a steady flow of alcohol-related illness and injury. Most of these were not serious: sprains, abrasions, and contusions. However, the clinic had dealt with several potentially life-threatening incidents, in which students needed to be revived after a binge with the bottle.
- Most of the incidents occurred on weekends. Bacchus University was a fairly demanding place; most students worked hard at their studies during the week. Those who partied continuously or who had serious alcoholism problems usually didn't last to become sophomores.
- The local papers provided a sample of alcohol-related incidents from the past few years:
  - One student died while trying to walk on top of a five-foot brick wall. He fractured his skull when he fell.
  - A second student died after being induced to drink nearly a liter of vodka at a fraternity initiation.
  - A third student nearly died of asphyxiation after being painted green from head to toe by a group of partiers who, after consuming more than a case of beer, decided that this would be a cool way to celebrate St. Patrick's Day.
  - One student appeared to have eased her path to suicide by washing down a bottle of sleeping pills with a large quantity of wine.

These findings suggested that many students abused alcohol. However, Bacchus University had more than twenty thousand students. Avi supposed that a majority of them drank, but few had these kinds of problems. Avi himself often went out for a beer with friends (even though he had a soft drink), and there were never any incidents. He decided to conduct a survey of undergraduates. He rounded up a group of students to serve as his sample and asked them three questions: (1) Do you drink? (2) When, where, and how much do you drink? (3) What are your reasons for drinking or not drinking?

In answer to the first question, Avi found that a majority of students drank. Underage students were only slightly less likely to drink than were older students.

Students tended to drink largely on weekends. Although a few might have a beer before going to bed, most drank while partying with their friends. Some students drank with their friends at bars, but most partied with friends at fraternity or sorority houses or in their dorms or apartments. When students drank, they drank a lot, averaging five or six drinks. A great number seemed to go on drinking binges.

Following are some of the reasons they gave for drinking:

- It's cool.
- To get drunk. I like being trashed.
- There's nothing else to do on weekends.
- It helps me escape the tension of this place.
- Everybody drinks. If you don't, you're a tool.
- It helps me have fun with my friends. It helps us let go.
- It helps me get into the music.
- It helps free me up.

Avi was a bit surprised at the absence of a few reasons. No students said that they enjoyed the taste of what they drank, or that drinking enhanced the taste of food. Although some students said that drinking helped them have fun with their friends, they seemed to mean either that they enjoyed having someone with whom to get drunk or that it helped them to be more uninhibited. They were willing to do some things when they were drinking that they wouldn't do when they were not. But no one said that it made conversation better or improved his or her sociability

Avi had expected mostly answers like these, but the more he thought about them, the more puzzled he became. None of these reasons for and against drinking seemed very convincing to him. For example, what does "cool" really mean? Why should the fact that lots of other people do something be much of a reason to do it yourself? Some of the reasons were escapist: people wanted to escape boredom, stress, or their inhibitions. But why would you want to lose your inhibitions? Is losing them a good thing? Having fun or enjoying music seemed more like good reasons to Avi, but he noticed that the students didn't seem able to define what was fun about their actions when they drank. And how does drinking help you enjoy music?

The few nondrinking students said that they avoided alcohol because:

- Drinking makes people act like jerks.
- I resent the peer pressure to drink.
- I can entertain myself just fine without drinking.
- I like to be in control, and drinking makes me lose control.
- Someone could take advantage of me sexually if I drank.
- I hate the taste.

Avi was surprised at the nondrinkers' resentment about the topic. The loosening of inhibitions, which motivated some people to drink, was viewed by nondrinkers as a very important reason for not drinking. Was it all really about self-control?

In search of more satisfying reasons for drinking (or not drinking), Avi went to talk to Dr. Sanchez, the instructor of a wine-tasting course. This class was one of the most popular at Bacchus, and every semester the university had to have a lottery to see who would be able to take it. He asked the instructor what she was trying to accomplish. She responded that she tried to enhance the appreciation of experience. "Drinking wine is like any other experience. You have to learn to appreciate what's good. You learn to appreciate good music or good art by learning to see and to hear more discriminatingly. This is true for food and drink, too. Good food and good wine are characterized by complex and subtle tastes. You need to learn to experience them."

For Avi this was a new thought: you have to learn to enjoy good things. He had always assumed that you liked what you liked and that was all there was to it. But Dr. Sanchez clearly had a different view. "Taste," she said paradoxically, "is not a matter of taste."

Regardless of whether Dr. Sanchez was right, Avi thought that this was the kind of insight about drinking he had been looking for when he'd conducted his survey and interviews. Dr. Sanchez had a view of how wine fit into the picture of a good life. That's what Avi had missed in his list of reasons for or against drinking. Only a few of those he'd talked with seemed to have an idea of how drinking could enhance experience. Was that the right question? Avi wrote in his notes, "So is there a difference between a hedonist and an epicurean?" and congratulated himself on having remembered something from his philosophy class.

QUESTIONS

1. Many conversations about drinking seem to emphasize the "bads" of drinking. Certainly there are some, often associated with injury or disease. As the label on any beer bottle will tell you, drinking can harm a fetus and impair one's ability to drive or operate machinery. Addiction is also a "bad." We haven't said much about these negative aspects because we suspect you've heard them all before. Are there other, less often discussed, "bads" to drinking? What might these be?

2. Do these same concerns apply to the use of other drugs?

3. Underage students often find ways to drink. They are frequently helped by older students. Should students be concerned about obeying the law simply because it is the law, or more because they might get caught? Why?

4. In his dialogue "Socrates' Defense (Crito)," Plato describes Socrates as willing to die rather than violate the law of Athens, even though Socrates could escape and believed that he had been unjustly condemned to death. Socrates says that the laws have nurtured and protected him, so he will obey them to the bitter end. Is there anything to be said for Socrates' view?

5. Discussions of drinking, at least the kinds that schools promote, often emphasize the bads rather than the goods of drinking. What are the goods?

6. Have we covered the kinds of reasons you or your friends might have for drinking? What have we left out?

7. Dr. Sanchez expressed a particular view of what makes drinking wine a good. Would Dr. Sanchez criticize the kinds of reasons the students gave in Avi's survey? If so, how might she criticize their reasons or their way of drinking?

8. Estimates of the harm done as a consequence of drinking are always enormous. They include thousands of deaths every year, and the loss of billions of dollars from employee accidents, absenteeism, and poor on-the-job performance. Thousands of families are destroyed through addiction. Are there goods that outweigh these bads?

9. Why not have prohibition? Why was Prohibition (the Eighteenth Amendment to the Constitution, which lasted from 1920–1933) repealed? Are there issues of personal freedom involved? What are they?

10. If you use alcohol, how would you describe your drinking pattern? Is it what you want? If not, what could you do about it?

11. One point of disagreement in the case involves the issue of self-control or loss of inhibition. Is loss of inhibition a good thing or not?

12. When something is described as "cool," what kind of reason for doing it is implied?

ISSUES

As you might guess, we could discuss a large number of issues in connection with drinking. We might talk about how drinking affects *relationships*. We might talk about how drinking affects one's health or sense of well-being. Such a discussion might look at drinking from the perspective of the *greatest good* principle. These are worthy and important topics, but we suspect that you have heard much about them. Instead we want to address some different questions, which might seem less familiar. The first one has to do with the issue of self-control. Curiously, there seem to be two quite different perspectives here. Some people think that alcohol liberates them from their inhibitions, and they describe this as being "freed up." Others view the relaxation of inhibitions as a loss of self-control and, perhaps, a loss of freedom. They tend to believe that the removal of inhibition puts them under the control of dangerous forces within themselves that should stay suppressed.

A second issue concerns the way alcohol fits into the quality of life, specifically, how it can enhance or detract from our enjoyment of experience.

A third issue, and one that seems intertwined with the first two, has to do with the idea of moderation. Some philosophers (for instance Aristotle, from whom many of the ideas in this chapter derive) have argued that good living depends largely on our ability to discover a middle ground between extremes. For example, we might think of the virtue of courage as a middle position between foolhardiness and cowardliness. Moderation, or finding a middle way between self-denial and overindulgence, might be a helpful way to think about the use of alcohol.

We hope you have noticed that these issues have to do with much more than drinking. In fact, we think that considerations about self-control, quality of life, and moderation apply broadly to a wide range of activities, from child rearing to sports. They are among the issues that you will need to consider when you reflect on what constitutes a good life for you. (Some additional questions are posed in Chapter 8.) Also, each topic has something to say about what we have called the principle of *character growth*. We want to encourage you to take a long view of your life. We don't mean by this that you need to plan your life in detail right now. Rather, we want to remind you that your choices and actions today help form your future character and personality. Many people delude themselves into believing that they can always change if they want to, can always be more honest, kind, brave, selfless tomorrow, when it's important. However, as we noted in Chapter 1, dishonest (or cruel, or cowardly, or selfish) choices harm not only others, but also the chooser, by building an unethical character.

You might think of this as an issue of freedom. Certain choices can make us into the kinds of people who are less free to choose in different ways. The use of potentially addictive substances such as hard drugs, alcohol, or tobacco can provide graphic illustrations of this point. Someone who chooses to smoke often and regularly becomes less free to choose not to smoke. But these habits are also misleading examples because of the physiological mechanisms behind addiction. Dishonesty is not an addiction in the same way. Nevertheless, it may he harder for the habitually dishonest person to choose honesty.

One way to think about our discussion in this chapter is that it broadens the range of ways to apply the principle of character growth. The idea that in acting you choose the person you are to become turns out to apply not only to whether you will become honest or kind, but also to whether you will become someone with good taste and developed sensibilities, someone who can enjoy or appreciate what's worthwhile. The basic idea is the same. When you choose, you should always keep in mind that you are also choosing to be a certain kind of person.

Autonomy and Self-Control

Among the reasons students gave for drinking was that drinking was "cool" and that nondrinkers were "losers" or "dorks." These are curious reasons.

What does it really mean to be "cool" or "a loser"? We suspect that these mean virtually nothing beyond vague approval or disapproval. How can they be reasons?

Other words, such as "good," may be similarly vague. If I say "That's a good movie," my comment won't tell you much more than that I liked it, unless we also agree about what makes a movie good. Perhaps, then, when we hear a reason that suggests little beyond approval or disapproval, we should ask, "Do I know what that person means by 'cool,' 'dorky,' and so on, and do I agree?"

Why care? We can suggest two related reasons. First, it is difficult to evaluate words that merely indicate approval or disapproval unless you understand *the reasons for* the approval or disapproval of the behavior or person. Second, we suspect that such words are often used to manipulate people. Perhaps they convey a pleasant or desirable feeling while also preventing you from questioning that feeling. Perhaps they convey an image. Perhaps they are a vehicle of social pressure or peer pressure. (Note how often vague, approving words like "cool," "excellent," "improved," and "new" are used in advertising.)

Following are some questions you might ask when someone gives you a reason containing such a word:

1. Do I understand exactly what the word means? How can I tell when it is used accurately?

2. If I can tell exactly what the word implies, does it seem like a good reason for the behavior or the purchase of the product it describes? Do I agree with it? Why?

3. If I can't tell whether or not the word is being used accurately, how does the word influence me? Does it make me want to buy or do something I would not otherwise have wanted? Such words might suggest that:

   I will be part of a group to which I want to belong.

   I will be popular or attractive.

   People who don't go along will be undesirable.

Not only can others use language of this sort to manipulate us, but we can also use it on ourselves. All of us sometimes have to confront arguments or evidence that we don't want to consider. We can dismiss such arguments with vague vocabulary that allows us to reject a claim without considering it. For example, saying a person (or position) is "really lame-ass" dismisses him as unworthy of consideration. Does such dismissive language have a role in our moral reflection? After all, we can't consider every claim and every claimant. Do we sometimes use such language because we are afraid to examine ourselves or our conduct?

Notice that these questions imply that you should have reasons for what you do, and be able to discuss your reasons. These questions also assume that it is bad to be manipulated, and good to be independent or autonomous in your decision making. Do you agree? Might these commitments to rationality and autonomy interfere with spontaneity, doing the will of God, or being deeply committed to a community? Is autonomy linked to some of the moral principles we have discussed, for example equal respect, but inconsistent with others, such as community? Are there times when we should relinquish our autonomy in order to belong? (Some of the issues in Chapter 5 may change if reconsidered in this light.)

Another set of reasons for drinking involves self-control. Some of the students Avi surveyed said that they drank to lower their inhibitions or free themselves up. Others viewed drinking as a kind of social lubricant—something that eases conversation or makes social situations more comfortable. On the other hand, some associated drinking with a worrisome loss of self-control. We want to develop these ideas a little by sketching two positions that we call "Plato's story" and "Freud's story" (although Plato or Freud might not have agreed with everything we put into their mouths).

Plato's story.   Plato (427–347 B.C.) described three parts of the soul: a rational part, a spiritual part, and the appetites. For him, a life was well ordered when reason ruled over the other aspects of human nature. Plato wasn't arguing that either our spiritual sides or our appetites should be suppressed. He did not want a life devoid of enthusiasm or full of self-denial. There is no evidence that he objected to drinking, and much to suggest that he enjoyed it. His point is rather that reason should be in charge. Students who worry about losing control when they drink seem to be expressing a similar idea. They may be suggesting that when they drink, reason no longer rules their conduct.

Freud's story.   Freud (1856–1939) believed that we often repress many of our wants and desires, meaning that although we have them, we are not consciously aware of them. Not only that, but in some sense we are also responsible for the fact that we are unaware of them. We have hidden them from ourselves, or we refuse to admit to them. Freud thought that one reason we repress some of our desires is that we strongly disapprove of them. We cannot simultaneously think of ourselves as good people, or be the kinds of people our parents want us to be, and admit to ourselves that we have evil desires. Thus we repress them and make them unconscious.

For Freud repression is an ambiguous thing. Perhaps we should repress some things, such as a death wish or the desire to have sex with our parents. On the other hand, our repressed desires often find subtle ways to express themselves; too much repression can lead to neurotic or even psychotic behavior. Some of Freud's followers and popularizers saw repression as an unmitigated evil, perhaps because they had more optimistic views of human nature than Freud did. They thought that people needed to be freed from the constraints of social convention to express their true natures and desires. (The Aesthete we described in Chapter 6 seemed to think this way about sex.)

Freud's and Plato's stories seem to offer different advice about ridding ourselves of inhibitions. Does losing inhibitions mean silencing the voice of reason and giving reign to dangerous uncontrolled passions, as Plato would say? Or might it mean ridding ourselves of burdensome social conventions and becoming able to express our true selves, as some Freudians suggest? Students who drink to become freer seem to be telling themselves a version of Freud's story. They may feel that sometimes they can't act the way they want to because they are "too hung up." Perhaps using alcohol to get rid of "hang-ups" such as shyness, insecurity, or an oppressive sense of social conventions frees us to be who we really are, or to do what we genuinely want to do. People who claim that drinking helps to improve conversation or to have more fun at a party may be saying something like this.

Are these stories compatible? Might one be true in some cases and the other in other cases? How can we tell?

Recall again the two previous cases from Chapters 3 and 6 that involved excessive drinking. In both cases, people did something when drunk that they would not have done sober. In "Hate Speech" in Chapter 3, Jake yelled racial insults when he was drunk; in "Seduction or Rape?" in Chapter 6, Jennifer had sex with Peter when she'd drunk too much. What story would Freud tell about these activities? He might suggest that Jake and Jen did what they really wanted to do, or that their behavior reflected their true (unconscious) natures.

If we agree, we probably also have to accept the following: First, our true nature comes out only when we lose our inhibitions; our unconscious desires are what we really want to do. Second, it is good to do what we really want to do and to express our true, or unconscious, natures. Finally, inhibitions are bad because they prevent us from doing what we really want to do or from expressing our natures. Do you agree?

We suspect that Jake would not agree, at least in the case of hate speech. He may have gotten drunk and behaved in a racist way, but he probably wants to deny that his "true nature" is racist. He might ask, "Why assume that what I do when I'm drunk is a better indication of what I'm really like than what I do when I am sober and can make decisions reflectively, in full control of myself? Maybe there is a part of me that is racist, but that is a part of me that I want to keep in check."

Remember that Peter's excuse in his seduction of Jennifer was that she really (unconsciously) wanted sex with him. Peter might claim that he helped Jen kick her sexually repressed hang-ups. Getting her drunk helped her to express her sexuality without those hang-ups; thus he did Jen a favor by liberating her from her inhibitions.

We don't think that Freud's story is very plausible in these cases. If we drink and then do something we wouldn't otherwise do, it may be true that some part of us wanted to do it. It does not, however, follow that this is what we "really" wanted to do or that it expresses our true natures. Why should we treat these unreflective urges or desires as more real or more truly "us" than what we choose to do or to be when we reflect about our conduct? Aren't our reflective judgments also a real part of who we are? Even if our unreflective urges are somehow more basic to us, it is unclear that it is always a good thing to act on them.

When we call something a "hang-up" we seem to mean that it is an undesirable or unreasonable restraint on what we wish to do. A clear example might be a phobia. One of us has a fear of heights that makes walking near steep drop-offs difficult. Because he is also an enthusiastic hiker who frequently finds himself in such positions, he finds this "hang-up" both irrational and frustrating. That's the nature of hang-ups; they are unreasonable and we don't choose them. People often label most restraints "hang-ups," especially when others' inhibitions are inconvenient for them, as Peter did in "Seduction or Rape?" But are inhibitions against promiscuous sex or racist speech "hang-ups"? Perhaps instead they are reasonable restraints on our conduct, on the way we wish to behave, upon reflection.

We are not suggesting that Freud's story is always wrong, even about drinking. Suppose that instead of looking at cases of racist speech or seduction, we consider the claim that drinking helps make socializing freer and easier. Is this implausible? Our conversation with others may very well be restrained by "hang-ups." Maybe we're overly concerned that others will find us foolish or stupid; perhaps we automatically feel embarrassed or tentative in social situations. It may well be that a moderate amount of alcohol can reduce these restraints. Are there other cases in which removing inhibitions may be desirable?

Thus while the "Hate Speech" and "Seduction or Rape?" cases seem to point to Plato's story, there is something to say for Freud's story as well. How to decide which story to tell when? We suggest that you ask these questions:

1. On sober reflection, is the way I act when alcohol has dissolved my inhibitions the way I want to act?

2. If someone else behaved the way I do when my inhibitions are dissolved by alcohol, would I like their behavior, especially if I were its recipient?

The first question suggests that while we think that Freud's story has a point, we think that Plato's story is more important here. You should decide, when your judgment isn't affected by alcohol, how you wish to behave when you drink. The second question is the Golden Rule rephrased for drinking.

It reminds us that the way we wish to behave when drinking should take into account the rights and welfare of others.

Another observation we might make about Avi's discoveries of people's reasons for drinking is the noticeable difference between the students' reasons and the view of drinking held by the instructor of the wine-tasting course, Dr. Sanchez. The principal goal of Dr. Sanchez's course was the development of a refined taste for wine. Avi's question to himself about the difference between a hedonist and an epicurean expressed this view as well.

Many philosophers who believe that pleasure or happiness is the ultimate good also hold two additional ideas. One is that what we might call the "higher" pleasures are better, more enjoyable, than "baser" pleasures. The second is that one has to learn to enjoy the higher pleasures. John Stuart Mill says this succinctly on page 410 of *The Utilitarians*.

> It is better to be a human being dissatisfied than a pig satisfied; better to be a Socrates dissatisfied than a fool satisfied. And if the fool, or the pig, are of a different opinion, it is because they only know their own side of the question. The other side of the comparison knows both sides.

Let's consider an example of this philosophy. Suppose we imagine a conversation between Dr. Sanchez and an undergraduate named Mike.

Mike: You know, Dr. Sanchez, I really like getting ripped. I feel great when I'm blitzed.

Dr. Sanchez: I can understand that. I've felt high a few times; but you can't understand what it's all about until you have a chance to enjoy a good Chardonnay with a well-prepared seafood dinner.

Mike: That doesn't really do it for me, Professor Sanchez. I've had wine before, but a glass or two with a meal doesn't give me anything like the good feeling a buzz does.

Dr. Sanchez: That's because you haven't yet developed the capacity to appreciate fine wine. You need to learn what to look for. That's what I can teach you in my class.

Mike: No thanks. Why should I want to learn to appreciate something I don't care about now? Why is what you like better than what I like? Aren't you being elitist?

Dr. Sanchez: Maybe I am, Mike. But I know that enjoying a good wine is better than a good buzz, because I've had both experiences. You know how to use alcohol only to get high; you haven't learned to appreciate good wine, so you can't judge which feels better.

Mike: Maybe not; but I still have the right to like what I like.

It isn't easy to say who's right. We'd like to make the case for Mill and Dr. Sanchez, but first we need to emphasize that we do agree with Mike that he has the right to like whatever he wants to like. Even when he might be better off if he liked something else, or when this something else, whatever it might be, is genuinely better than what he likes, Mike should not be coerced. We can only try to persuade him to change his mind.

Mill and Dr. Sanchez argue for the superiority of "higher pleasures," which result from activities or experiences that require a significant degree of learning to appreciate. Let's consider two examples by comparing chess with tic-tac-toe, and a good wine with a sweet soft drink. Wine and chess have a number of characteristics that soft drinks and tic-tac-toe lack: they are complex and varied, and their potential for novelty is not easily exhausted. Thus they can maintain our interest. Another significant feature is that they both engage and develop our capacities. Playing chess or enjoying a good wine requires that we develop skill, judgment, and discernment. We grow and learn. We become better (more skilled, sophisticated, interesting, and interested) people. And as we do, these activities allow us to express the increased capacities they have helped us acquire.

Often more complex activities are also occasions for forming desirable human relationships. When we have learned a complex activity, we often enjoy discussing it or participating in it with others. Thus such activities often form the basis of friendships and help us to enjoy the company of other people. Consider this point in connection with the principles of *relationship* and *community*, and contrast it with getting drunk, which, even when done with other people, tends to be an isolating and solitary experience.

We have used chess and enjoying wine as examples of higher pleasures, but many other kinds of activities, such as sports, crafts, and making music, have similar characteristics. Although there is something cognitive about all of these activities, "higher pleasures" need not be primarily contemplative or intellectual. Someone who can visualize the whole floor in basketball or who can see a beautiful sweater in a pile of yarn has acquired an enhanced capacity for experience much like that of someone who can read the situation in a game of chess or evaluate the nuances of wine. Similarly, making a good pass or a beautiful sweater are as much forms of self-expression as is making a good move in a chess game. When we say that there is something cognitive about these activities, we mean that they involve judgment, discernment, and a sophisticated way of seeing, not that they are passive or merely intellectual.

The fact that these enjoyments depend on judgment, discernment, and a special way of seeing also explains why they depend on learning. As anyone who's watched small children knows, we don't need to learn to enjoy sweet tastes. Similarly, there is little we need to learn to play tic-tac-toe.

This leads to Mill's and Dr. Sanchez's second point. How do we know that the "higher pleasures" are more enjoyable? It seems the only way to know that something is enjoyable is to note that people enjoy it. We must consult others' experience. However, Mill and Dr. Sanchez also want to say that not everyone's experience counts equally. They reason that without having acquired the right kinds of capacities, we cannot have or appreciate some kinds of experiences. These kinds of pleasures are learning-dependent. They conclude that when we compare the pleasure of different kinds of activities or experiences, we must consult those who have acquired the capacity to enjoy both. Only they are in a position to make a fair comparison. And Mill and Dr. Sanchez are confident that, given such a comparison, people prefer the higher pleasures.

Are they right? We suggest that you consult your own experience, but that you do so with their perspective in mind. Are there things you have learned to like? Are there things you like that have been enhanced by learning about them? Are there things you like that are dependent on learning? How do they compare with other things you enjoy?

Are there things you enjoy that do not depend on learning? We enjoy bicycling, hiking, spending time with our families, canoeing, dancing, gardening, drawing, karate, and singing. Do all of these things qualify as "higher pleasures"? Perhaps not. For some of these activities, enjoyment seems to come mainly from the exercise, relaxation, solitude, or excitement involved. Yet people who enjoy bicycling, for instance, often find the activity enhanced by learning about riding techniques or studying bike components. Hiking is more fun when you learn about the plants and animals you might encounter. Singing is more pleasurable when you learn to control your voice and notice musical subtleties. The urge to infuse our activities with cognitive elements and with the opportunity to display skills seems strong.

Moderation

People are often advised to use alcohol in moderation. No doubt this is good advice, but what does it mean? And why should we be moderate?

Moderation is often taken to mean "restraining pleasure." It might seem an old person's virtue, suitable only for someone who lacks the energy or drive to pursue life with gusto—to have it all, now. However, perhaps to enjoy life fully and have real freedom, moderation is important. Let's explore this idea further.

The word "moderation" is sometimes used as an adverb, as in "drink in moderation," and sometimes as a noun. As a noun, "moderation" is one of the character traits that used to be called "virtues": traits such as honesty, charity, fairness, and courage. Virtues are positive behavioral patterns that become habitual, part of one's nature. (Similar, negative, behavior patterns are labeled "vices.") They may also be thought of as excellent characteristics that, when present, make something a praiseworthy example of its kind. Just as strength and flexibility are excellent characteristics in a piece of steel, moderation, courage, charity, and fairness are excellent characteristics (or virtues) in human beings.

Many philosophers have argued that various virtues are essential to leading a life that is fulfilling, enjoyable, or satisfying. One reason is that virtues such as honesty enable people to pursue various worthwhile goals in association with others. They believe that many of the most important goals are social, in the same way that singing in a choir is social, and that they cannot be pursued apart from those virtues that assure mutually satisfying cooperation. It has also been argued that people who fail to acquire virtues, or who acquire vices, harm not only others, but also themselves. They argue that people who are greedy damage themselves in their pursuit of material things even if they succeed. Is this true? How might you argue for this?

One argument is that greedy people, like people with other vices, are ruled by their wants and needs. No matter how much they have, they want more; thus, even when they get what they want, they cannot be happy, because they never have enough. However, people who moderate their desires can be satisfied. Do you agree? Does this reasoning apply to other virtues and vices?

Moderation can also be seen as a capacity for avoiding the extremes of overindulgence or unreasonable self-denial in seeking enjoyment or pleasure. Both extremes interfere with leading a good life. Overindulgence eventually debases pleasure, and we become sated. Either we can no longer enjoy the experience at all, because it has become boring, or we must seek a particular pleasure in increasingly larger amounts or in more extreme forms. Overindulgent people end up going to great extremes to find any pleasure at all, rather as the addict requires ever more of a drug to get even a maintenance high. Ultimately over-indulgers find that they can't enjoy anything at all; they might even find themselves enslaved to something that no longer gives them any pleasure.

Those who practice excessive self-denial, in contrast, seem to reject out of hand the idea that a good life involves the enjoyment of experience. They lose the ability to appreciate even simple pleasures or the beauty around them. They, too, seem to have unreasonably diminished the worth of their lives. (Question: Does this sense of diminishment also apply in the case of religiously motivated self-denial? For example, stories of the lives of Catholic saints or holy people from other religious traditions are often filled with extreme self-denial, yet practitioners seem to feel closer to God the more they suffer. Why might this be? For some ideas, see William James, *The Varieties of Religious Experience: A Study in Human Nature* (1902; reprint, with a foreword by Jacques Barzun, New York: Mentor Books/New American Library of World Literature, 1958).

Both overindulgence and self-denial are vices that disrupt communities and relationships. Overindulgent people often end up sacrificing friends to the pursuit of ever less attainable pleasures. They use other people in their search for enjoyment and eventually become incapable of real friendship. Those who practice unreasonable self-denial also tend to be lonely because friendships are usually built around shared enjoyment.

This chapter focuses on drinking, and drinking seems a good example of something that over time best enhances experience when done in moderation. However, the virtue of moderation is a virtue in many areas of life. Unrelenting desires for money, status, popularity, or power become vices when pursued to extremes. When overindulged, they have consequences very similar to those of the over-consumption of alcohol: we crave more and more while enjoying it less and less. The single-minded pursuit of any desire disrupts friendship, marriage, and family.

To say that moderation is a virtue is thus to say two things about it: One is that it is essential to a successful and good life in association with others. The other is that it must be made a part of our character.

We can now summarize the central points we have wanted to make in this chapter. Issues such as drinking are often presented as a matter of making good choices, and a good way to think about making choices is by making lists of reasons for and against them. Of course we are not opposed to making good choices or weighing the pros and cons of a choice. But we think that this approach misses two important things. The first is Mill's point: what you now enjoy, and what you might enjoy if you learned how to appreciate various kinds of experiences, can differ. Moreover, it may be that the experiences and activities that require further learning to be fully appreciated are also among the most enjoyable. Evaluating choices in terms of what you now enjoy doesn't tell you what you might come to enjoy.

Second, making lists of pluses and minuses often overlooks the fact that in making a choice, you are also choosing your self. Little by little, your choices shape your personality and your character. You become a person predisposed to act as you now choose to act. Thus our central point is that you should learn to think of leading a rich and fulfilling life not so much as a series of choices, in which you always try to select the optimal one, but as a project in which you gradually make yourself the kind of person who can enjoy a fulfilling life. You are your most important project.

Questions

1. Is there such a thing as moderation in the use of heroin or crack cocaine?

2. Are there other areas in which moderation seems difficult, impossible, or undesirable?

3. Suppose that you could be attached to a machine that would sustain your life indefinitely and would also constantly stimulate the pleasure centers of your brain. Would that constitute a good life?

EXAMPLES OF COLLEGE AND UNIVERSITY CODES ON DRINKING AND DRUG USE

1. Excerpt from the student handbook of Hope College[1]

Hope upholds state and local laws regarding the possession and consumption of alcoholic beverages. The concepts listed below are for your consideration:

a) Michigan's drinking age is 21; therefore, most college students cannot drink alcohol legally;

b) alcohol inhibits individuals from functioning at full capacity;

c) alcohol abuse has a negative impact upon the learning environment of the College;

d) peer pressure may intimidate and compel persons to change their behavior to "go along with the crowd";

e) alcohol use has the potential for leading to alcohol abuse;

f) there is a high correlation between alcohol use and sexual assault.

While the College affirms that the decision to drink or not to drink is a matter of individual choice, it has established the following regulations regarding the use of alcoholic beverages in order to maintain an atmosphere supportive of its educational purposes:

1) The possession and/or consumption of alcoholic beverages on College property, College housing units, or College vehicles is prohibited. Any alcohol which is found on campus or in campus residence facilities will be confiscated and disposed of by the Residence Life Staff or Public Safety. [. . .]

2) The use of College or organizational monies to purchase alcoholic beverages is prohibited;

3) The availability of alcoholic beverages may not be used to promote an event;

4) The possession of alcoholic beverage containers is prohibited in campus housing units; this includes "collectable" empty or full alcohol containers. [. . .]

[. . .] It is important that the student be aware of the potential for legal responsibility when furnishing alcoholic beverages to other persons. If the individual to whom the beverage was furnished subsequently has an accident attributable to the beverage, then the furnisher may be found legally liable.

---

[1] College Regulations on Alcoholic Beverages, *Handbook of Selected College Policies 2000–2001*, Hope College, Holland, MI, pp. 13, 23.

2. Excerpt from Howard University's Student Code of Conduct[2]

A. The sale, service, possession, or consumption of an alcoholic beverage in academic facilities, including classrooms, studios, theaters, auditoria, and/or laboratories is prohibited.

B. Consumption of alcoholic beverages in the residence halls, not in accordance with District of Columbia laws [. . .], is also prohibited.

C. Student organizations affiliated with schools and colleges may not serve alcoholic beverages at events without the expressed approval by the academic dean of the school or college and the Director of Student Activities [. . .]. If approved, alcoholic beverages may not be consumed outside of the designated areas for the event.

D. Student organizations serving alcoholic beverages at off-campus events may not identify these events as University-sponsored or sanctioned.

E. After consuming alcoholic beverages students must assume full responsibility for their conduct as it relates to the need for good judgment, moderation, respect for the rights of others, and the legal regulations of the jurisdictions involved.

Drugs/Controlled Substances

The University has a "zero tolerance" policy on the improper use of controlled substances that expressly prohibits:

A. The illegal possession, use, distribution, and/or sale of a controlled substance.

B. The illegal possession, use, distribution, and/or sale of drug paraphernalia.

C. Aiding or abetting the illegal possession, use, sale, or distribution of controlled substances or drug paraphernalia.

ADDITIONAL CASES

Alcohol and the Real Me   CASE 7.2

Like her friends, Seema drinks at social events. Unlike them, she recognizes that she needs to drink to relax socially at all. Drinking at a party is not only fun for Seema; it's necessary. She wishes this weren't the case, but it is. Seema knows that when she's tipsy, she's much funnier, sexier, and more self-confident than when she's not. In fact, she even wonders whether her friends would like her much if they didn't see her mainly when she's had a few drinks. She's afraid that someday they'll realize the "real," sober Seema

[2] *2000–01 Howard University Student Handbook & Planner,* Office of Student Activities, Howard University, p. 106.

is a shy and boring fool, because she can never think of much to say when she runs into them at the cafeteria or after a class. However, no one seems to have noticed yet, and Seema is careful to avoid nondrinking situations that might reveal what a dork she is.

Because Seema only drinks at parties, she doesn't think her dependence on a few beers is a problem—at least she can always count on a buzz to turn her into Ms. Partygirl. And who knows? Maybe someday she'll learn how to be funny and self-confident without drinking. Right now, however, she's grateful that she's discovered a way to escape her shyness when it matters most.

QUESTIONS

1. Is Seema's "real" personality the tipsy, uninhibited party animal, the shy and insecure nondrinker, or some combination of the two?

2. Is there anything wrong with using alcohol (or other drugs) to let out a side of yourself that you like better than your ordinary personality?

3. Do you think that the way Seema uses alcohol will inhibit, or help, in her attempt to become a more self-confident person?

4. Is there anything unethical about trying to hide a part of your personality from your friends?

CASE 7.3 *Sorry, I Was Drunk*

The first time Chris hit her, Julie was shocked speechless. They'd just come back from a keg party, where her normally considerate and faithful boyfriend had tried to pick up three different women, practically under Julie's nose. When Julie berated Chris on the walk back, he shoved her hard against a brick wall, told her to leave him the #%@!! alone, and stalked off, leaving her shaken and bruised. They'd both had quite a bit to drink that night, but at the time Julie hadn't connected Chris's outrageous flirting and violent temper to his drinking. His behavior that night was so unlike his usual charming, sober self that it was as if he turned from Dr. Jekyll into Mr. Hyde right in front of her. However, gradually Julie has learned that, as charming and considerate as Chris is when sober (which is almost always), he is violent and sexually predatory when drunk.

Now she is trying to decide whether or not to break up with him. On the plus side, she really enjoys Chris's company when he's sober; he sincerely seems to care about her; and he's very good-looking and popular. On the minus side, he's now gotten drunk four times since she started dating him, and each time it was the same. Frankly, she is scared of him when he's drunk. And when he's sober again, he never remembers anything he's done, although he's always very sorry that she's upset.

"I guess I just lose control if I get trashed," he'd say after each drunken incident. "I'm really sorry, babe. But I can't even remember what happened!

It didn't mean anything; you know I'd never hurt you on purpose, because I love you. Next time will be different. I promise. Let me make it up to you." Then he'd kiss her tenderly and buy her roses, or take her out to dinner, or give her that new CD or those earrings she'd been wanting.

"Why don't you stop drinking if it makes you act so crazy?" she once asked him.

"It's not like I get ripped very often," Chris replied, sounding a bit hurt. "And why shouldn't I be able to enjoy myself once in a while like everyone else?"

Julie thought to herself, "Chris can't seem to help what he does when he drinks. Maybe if I just stay out of his way at those times, everything will be cool."

QUESTIONS

1. Chris claims that he's not responsible for his behavior when drunk. Do you accept this?

2. Because alcohol overcomes inhibitions, does drinking reveal what Chris is really like beneath his likeable exterior?

3. Either way, should Julie stay in this relationship if she can succeed in staying out of Chris's way when he drinks?

4. Why do you think Chris abuses Julie? What can be done to stop him—either by Julie, or by others? Why do women like Julie sometimes stay with abusers like Chris?

5. By "staying out of his way" and not confronting him, is Julie enabling Chris to continue his anti-social behavior? If so, does she share any responsibility for his actions?

6. Can you think of other cases in which people deny responsibility for their conduct by claiming that they can't help themselves? Are people responsible for being unable to control their behavior if they choose to put themselves in a situation in which they lose control?

A Friend in Need CASE 7.4

Carlos, Steve, and Andy have been friends and housemates for almost a year. At first Carlos bought Steve and Andy beers and Jack Daniels with his fake ID every weekend because he looks the oldest and they are all underage, but Steve has been pressuring him to get booze more and more frequently. It's becoming a strain on their friendship. "I can't be going to the liquor store every other day, man!" he told Steve. "I'm going to get caught, and then where will we be?"

"Don't be such a dork!" Steve replied. "They don't care down at McNally's. They hardly even look at your ID. And it only takes fifteen minutes. I'd do it for you!"

Inevitably Carlos ends up going, although he's tired of being Steve's errand boy. At least they'll all be legal next year, and then Steve can buy his own alcohol.

It's not just the fear of getting caught, and the inconvenience, that makes Carlos hesitate to go to McNally's Liquor. He also worries about how much Steve drinks, although he doesn't know how to tell him this. Andy thinks it's none of their business if Steve drinks a lot. "It's a free country, and he can do what he likes. You're not his mother. Besides, he seems OK to me." Carlos isn't so sure. Steve seems increasingly depressed and edgy when he drinks. He's stopped going to his 9:00 A.M. biology lab because he's always too hung over. In fact, he seems to have stopped studying for any of his classes. He's also been having a lot of accidents lately. Two weeks ago he fell down while he was drinking and gashed his cheek, another time he smashed his hand through a window when he was drunk, and just three nights ago he fell asleep in the living room with a glass of Jack Daniels in one hand and a cigarette in the other. He woke up with a wet lap and a hole burned in his jeans, and they all laughed—but what if he'd set himself, or the whole house, on fire? "It's a good thing he doesn't have a car," Carlos thought. "He'd probably kill himself!"

QUESTIONS

1. Steve's drinking seems to be mainly hurting him. So who is right about their duty toward their friend—Carlos or Andy? Does it show respect for Steve to let him live his own life, no matter how self-destructive, or might his self-destructive acts be cries for help that a friend shouldn't ignore?

2. Because Carlos and Andy both drink regularly, are they in a poor (or good) position to convince Steve to drink less?

3. Who is most responsible for Steve's drinking problem—Steve, who seems addicted to alcohol, or Carlos, who isn't addicted but helps Steve buy alcohol?

4. Assume for the moment that Steve would find some other way to get drunk if Carlos didn't help him. What can, or should, Carlos do about Steve's drinking besides refuse to buy him booze?

5. Does Steve's drinking endanger anyone other than himself? If so, does this fact increase Carlos's duty to help him stop drinking?

CASE 7.5   *Stoned Sex*

Kathy and Matundu have been lovers for several weeks, and Matundu is starting to feel funny about the fact that Kathy always gets wasted before they have sex. She's explained that it helps her relax and feel freer, and makes the act itself more pleasurable for her. Matundu doesn't mind pot smoking in general, and in fact he's often joined her for a toke or two, but he's been wondering more and more why Kathy won't ever make love without first smoking a joint. Maybe she doesn't really like sleeping with him and has to get baked to get into it at all. Maybe she's somehow trying to hide from him at their moment of greatest intimacy and tenderness. He's lightly suggested a few times that they try making love straight, "just to check it out," but Kathy has refused, implying that he's the uptight one. "Why mess with a good thing? It's not hurting anyone."

Yet Matundu does feel hurt. Lying in bed together after sex one night, Matundu tries out the subject one more time. "Do you always smoke before we go to bed because I gross you out or something?"

"Don't be ridiculous!" Kathy reassures him, but he hears an edge of irritation in her voice. "I think you're very attractive. My smoking has nothing to do with you; I used to get wasted with my old boyfriend too. It's just that weed makes me feel sexy and makes sex so much better. It helps me get totally into it."

"But you always seem sort of far away and dreamy, or silly, when you're high. I want to know what it's like to make love to you when you're all there." Matundu hopes he doesn't sound too much like he's whining or begging.

Kathy dismisses the whole subject with a laugh. "I am definitely all here!" she giggles, and gives him a wet, smoky kiss. The conversation ends.

QUESTIONS

1. Aside from its illegality, is there anything wrong with using marijuana (or other drugs) to enhance sex?

2. Do you think using marijuana (or alcohol or other drugs) before intimacy with a partner indicates a problem in a relationship?

3. Does Kathy somehow "owe" Matundu straight sex, or is his desire for this his "hang-up" because Kathy's smoking is her business?

4. Does drug use put up communication barriers between partners (during sex or at other times), or does it remove them?

5. Where Jake in "Hate Speech" (Chapter 3) and Chris in "Sorry, I Was Drunk" (above) use drinking or drugs as an excuse for losing control, Kathy, like Seema in "Alcohol and the Real Me" (above), seems to use smoking pot as a way to access hidden parts of her personality. Marijuana seems to allow Kathy to express her sexuality in a way that she can't or won't do when she's straight. By choosing to use marijuana whenever she has sex, could Kathy make herself unable to enjoy sex without it, and limit her ability to be truly close to Matundu?

6. How might habitually choosing to use grass (or alcohol, or other drugs) change one's character and personality? How do the principles of relationships and character growth apply to this case?

CASE 7.6 *High Performance*

Rashad, like several members of his college track-and-field team, has used drugs to enhance his athletic performance ever since he was in high school. He injured his knee during his sophomore year of high school. Then he began using anabolic steroids to build up his muscles, the stimulant ephedrine to give himself more energy, and dimethyl sulfoxide to deaden his pain so that he could keep running. After he was almost caught in a random drug test during his freshman year of college, he largely stopped using steroids and ephedrine, both of which are banned and readily detectable. Now he uses mainly dimethyl sulfoxide, which he knows doesn't violate NCAA rules and isn't easily detectable anyway because it rapidly passes through the body. Dimethyl sulfoxide, or DMSO, helps reduce the pain and swelling in his knee if it starts acting up and seems to give him a more "pumped up" feeling as it improves his circulation. The only drawback is that it stinks like death and it makes his breath smell like garlic, but this seems a very small price to pay to be able to keep competing when his knee wants to give out.

Rashad's teammate Alex never used any drugs, and he was worried when he saw Rashad rubbing DMSO on his knee. "If your knee hurts that badly, maybe you should give it a rest," he told Rashad.

"Are you crazy?" Rashad responded shortly. "Thursday is our big meet, and I can't miss a practice."

Alex didn't retreat. "If Coach knew, he wouldn't let you run. He might even kick you off the team. We're supposed to be 'drug free,' and you could get us all in trouble!"

Rashad pondered this last statement. Was Alex going to rat on him? If he did, would Coach really be a hard-ass, or would he make an exception for what was, after all, an over-the-counter drug, used by some of his best runners? "What the other guys and I do as far as using drugs is really no one else's business," he decided, "and if Alex can't see that, well, I can make life unpleasant for him, too." However, out loud he just said, "Chill, Alex. DMSO helps me run better, and you want us all to perform our best Thursday, don't you?"

QUESTIONS

1. In addition to his concern about being punished for his teammates' drug use, Alex might feel annoyed with them for seeking an unfair advantage over those who don't use drugs. Is it unethical to improve athletic performance by using a nonprohibited drug such as DMSO?

2. If you said no, wouldn't it be unethical to use illegal drugs for this purpose? What is the ethical difference between the two drug categories?

3. If yes, to whom is it mainly unfair: opposing teams; other members of the same team who don't use drugs; the drug-using players themselves; the coach (who expects players to be drug-free); or parents, fans, or others less immediately involved? How?

4. If the drug actually had no physiological effects on performance but made users feel more confident, would using it still be unethical?

5. Concerning Rashad's occasional use of other performance-enhancing drugs that have potentially serious side effects (steroids and stimulants), is Rashad's drug use really no one's business but his own, or might Alex, the coach, or Rashad's friends and relatives have an interest in getting him to stop? Why or why not?

6. In addition to physical effects, what less tangible effects might using drugs to improve his performance have on Rashad's character development?

BACKGROUND READING

• "Alcohol Dependence" and "Drug Dependence," *The American Medical Association Encyclopedia of Medicine*, ed. Charles B. Clayman (New York: Random House, 1989), pp. 81–83; 278.

This source provides a medical overview of the physical and behavioral effects of alcohol and other drugs on the body, the signs and stages of addiction, and the effects of increasing blood alcohol levels, in language a layperson can understand.

• The use of performance-enhancing drugs among high school, college, and professional athletes is a hot topic. The following are a few newspaper articles about the subject: Dick Patrick, "Benefits Are Obvious, But Detractors Find Flaws," in *USA Today*, 12 October 1994, sec. C, p. 1, col. 5. Officials, from the Olympic community to the NFL and NCAA, are proclaiming victory in the drug war, but there is evidence to the contrary, frustrating some coaches and athletes. Larry Meyer, "Powerlifter Flexes Against Steroid Abuse," in *The Chicago Tribune*, 8 November 1992, sec. 18NW, p. 1, col. 4. Disturbed by the rampant and nonchalant use of steroids, Michael Collet of Park Ridge, IL, formed Strong Athletes Against Steroids, an organization dedicated to drug-free sport and to educating the public about the dangers of using steroids. Charles Seabrook, "In Haste to Win, Some Athletes Aren't Saying No," in *The Atlanta Constitution*, 23 July 1992, sec. F, p. 8, col. 5. No one knows how many athletes use performance-boosting drugs, but sports medicine experts believe the practice is so widespread that it is wrecking the health and shortening the lives of thousands of athletes.

• The Southern Illinois University's Core Institute Student Health Program publishes a semi-annual report called "Alcohol and Drugs in American College Campuses." This report describes drug, alcohol, and tobacco use patterns and attitudes among various types of higher education students by sex and by region, and is available through Southern Illinois University, Core Institute, Student Health Program, Wellness Center, Carbondale, IL 62901.

● For general, up-to-date information about alcohol and street drugs, see: *The National Clearinghouse for Alcohol and Drug Information*, www.health.org, (800) 729-6686; *The National Institute on Drug Abuse*, www.nida.nih.gov/DrugPages, (888) NIH-NIDA; *The Drug Enforcement Administration*, www.usdoj.gov/dea/pubs/intel/20005intellbrief.pdf, (202) 307-8726; and *The White House Office of National Drug Control Policy*, www.whitehousedrugpolicy.gov/prevent/parents, (800) 666-3332, which offers a fact sheet for parents called "Growing Up Drug Free Parents Guide."

ADDITIONAL MATERIALS

1. A number of recent studies suggest that while the general population is drinking less, college students are continuing to abuse alcohol with a recklessness that seems surprising in an increasingly health-conscious society. See Tom Pelton, "Even in Sober '90s, Booze Still Big Thing on Campus," in *The Chicago Tribune*, 30 March 1994, sec. 2C, p. 1, col. 5; "Editorial: Deadly Drinking," in *USA Today*, 9 June 1994, sec. A, p. 10, col. 1; and Deborah Strazheim, "College Bingeing Starts Debate over Legal Drinking Age," in Knight-Ridder Tribune News Service, December 1998, p. K09.

A study by the National Commission on Substance Abuse at Colleges and Universities, released on June 7, 1994, by Columbia University, shows that the number of college women who drink to get drunk has more than tripled in the past fifteen years, from 10 percent in 1977 to 35 percent in 1994; 55 percent of all rapes of college women occur when the victim is under the influence of alcohol; and more than one in three college students of both sexes drink excessively, with women now nearly equaling men in the percentage who drink to get drunk. See Brooke A. Masters, "Women Drinking Like Men, College Alcohol Study Finds," in *The Washington Post*, 8 June 1994, sec. A, p. 1, col. 4; "An Alcohol Alert," in *The Christian Science Monitor*, 10 June 1994, p. 18, col. 1; and Marian Sandmaier, "A Tragic Price to Pay for a Drink," in *The Chicago Tribune*, 17 June 1994, sec. 1, p. 21, col. 2.

A University of Michigan survey found that college women in general are drinking more often than previously (as well as more excessively, for some), with academic, social, and health consequences. See William Celis III, "Drinking by College Women Raises New Concern," in *The New York Times*, 16 February 1994, sec. A, p. 18, col. 3. An extensive Harvard study found that nearly half of all students on campuses nationwide are binge drinkers who cause a variety of "secondhand" problems on campus, from vandalism to rape to fatal accidents, that affect nondrinkers too. See Richard A. Knox, "Binge Drinking Linked to Campus Difficulties," in *The Boston Globe*, 7 December 1994, p. 1, col. 1; and Christopher B. Daly, "Nearly Half of U.S. College Students Are Binge Drinkers, Study Finds," in *The Washington Post*, 7 December 1994, sec. A, p. 17, col. 1.

A recent survey of Texas students showed that more than one quarter admitted to being binge drinkers, with the percentage rising to 44 percent among members of fraternities and sororities. See Pete Alfano, "Fraternities, Universities Continue to Struggle with Alcohol Issue," in *Fort Worth Star-Telegram*, Knight-Ridder/Tribune News Service, 30 March 1999, p. K2718.

And yet other studies reach different conclusions. "The percentage of college freshmen who say they drink beer frequently or occasionally is at its lowest level since record-keeping began in 1966. The record low in 1998 is 11 percent lower than in 1990 and down 39 percent since 1982, according to UCLA and the American Council on Education. The evidence shows that most college students are responsible and legal drinkers and that only a minority persistently abuses alcohol." See Edward H. Hammond, "No More Mixed Messages: Nation Needs a Consensus on Drinking Age, For Our Youth's Sake," in Knight-Ridder/Tribune News Service, 12 April 1999, p. K7613. (Hammond is President of Fort Hays State University in Kansas and chairman of the National Collegiate Alcohol Awareness Week.) However, this data may be flawed because the survey asks only about beer consumption; more popular on many campuses at present are much stronger mixed drinks, such as Southern Comfort and Coke, strawberry daiquiris, gin and tonics, and martinis, as well as exotics such as the Long Island Iced Tea, Irish Car Bomb, Sex on the Beach, Jello Shot, and Cosmopolitan.

Do you think alcohol abuse is a problem on your campus? What pressures do you think might be causing an increase in college student drinking while alcohol use in the general population goes down? Why might college women in particular be drinking more? Does the push to make college campuses "dry" (see "Examples of College and University Codes on Drinking and Drug Use" above) merely make underage students who want to drink go off campus, so that authorities now have to deal with drinking and driving? What can colleges, and individual students, do to decrease alcohol abuse on campus? See Thomas Gagliardi, "Battling Drinking," in *The Chicago Tribune*, 11 April 1994, sec. 1, p. 16, col. 4, for a summary of some programs being tried; and also Pete Alfano, "Fraternities, Universities Continue to Struggle with Alcohol Issue," in *Fort Worth Star-Telegram*, Knight-Ridder/Tribune News Service, 30 March 1999, p. K2718, for a description of the "alcohol-free fraternity" movement sponsored by the National Interfraternity Council in January 1998 and adopted by Phi Kappa Sigma, Phi Delta Theta, Sigma Nu, and Phi Gamma Delta, among others, on July 1, 2000.

2. A popular drink in the 1990s was Jaegermeister, a 70-proof German brand that has virtually no direct advertising. The hit cordial was peddled in college bars by a squad of 783 scantily clad young women called "Jaegerettes," who showered young men with trinkets when they bought shots of the drink. The Jaegermeister company also assembled a group of about 100 "Jaegerdudes," who wore tight-fitting bike shorts and catered to

the brand's gay following. See Suein L. Hwang, "Partying with the Jaegerettes," in *The Wall Street Journal*, 13 May 1994, sec. B, p. 1, col. 3; Suein L. Hwang, "Marketing: Young Drinkers Do Shots in Potent New Flavors," in *The Wall Street Journal*, 13 May 1994, sec. B, p. 1, col. 3; and Francine I. Katz, "Peer Pressure Key in Shaping Drinking Habits," in *USA Today*, 13 December 1994, sec. A, p. 14, col. 3 (this is a letter to the editor from a representative of the Anheuser-Busch Company).

Is this kind of alcohol promotion unethical? If so, why? Who is ultimately responsible for underage student drinking—the "immature" students themselves, the student peer culture, unscrupulous alcohol advertisers, parents, school authorities, or society at large? Would you answer differently regarding thirteen-year-old drinkers? If so, what is the difference ethically (there is none legally) between a thirteen-year-old drinker and an eighteen-year-old one?

3. Ecstasy may well become the drug epidemic of the first decade of the 21st century, much like cocaine was in the 1970s and '80s, say some analysts. Although teen drug use has generally fallen or stayed at the same level for the past few years, Ecstasy use is increasing "precipitously." Not much is really known about MDMA or Ecstasy among its student users or their parents; there is a "widespread but misguided belief that the drug is relatively benign." Unfortunately, increasing evidence suggests that Ecstasy can have long-term effects ranging from confusion and anxiety to paranoia and depression, and since the drug raises body temperature dramatically, users have been known to get hypothermia and go into convulsions at raves. See Peter Jensen, "Potential Agony of Ecstasy: Misinformation and the Drug, and an Increased Use of It, Worry Officials," in *The Baltimore Sun*, reprinted in *The Ithaca Journal*, 5 April 2001, p. 8A.

So why do some students find Ecstasy so appealing? The answer lies in the drug's ability to break down social barriers and dissolve the social distance that usually exists between people. Users feel a mellow glow and warmth—both literally and figuratively—that connects them to everyone around them, hence Ecstasy's nickname as "the hug drug."

Do you believe that overcoming social barriers and connecting to others is a worthy goal? If so, could the use of drugs—with known dangers, like alcohol, or with unknown dangers, like illegal Ecstasy—be a legitimate way to pursue this goal, aside from questions of legality? Why or why not? (Please note that we are not encouraging you to take drugs, but rather asking you to think about the ends for which people use them.) For more on the various reasons people have turned to drugs in different times and places, see Daniel Kunitz, "On Drugs: Gateways to Gnosis, or Bags of Glue?", a review of *Writing on Drugs* by Sadie Plant, and "Out of It: A Cultural History of Intoxication," by Stuart Walton, in *Harper's Magazine*, October 2001, vol. 3030, no. 1817, pp. 91–96.

ON GETTING A LIFE

TWO CASES: WHAT IS COLLEGE FOR?

Finding Herself

CASE 8.1

Claudia was middle aged—not a bad thing to be. She had married right out of high school, had children who were now out of school and self-supporting, been on the PTA board, gone to church, and done all the things that middle-class women of her age were supposed to do. She still lived with her husband, Ken, and she supposed that she always would. He cared for her, and she cared for him. But he had his life, and lately it only slightly intersected with hers. He was one of those men who actually enjoyed his work. He ran a small store where he sold wooden furniture, most of which he made himself. He wasn't a workaholic. He had time for her, but he thought of himself as someone who made furniture and incidentally had a family. His work made him feel engaged and fulfilled. He knew who he was.

That was the problem. Somewhere in occupying the roles of wife, mother, and community volunteer, Claudia felt as though she had lost herself. She had awakened one day to find that ever since she could remember, she had been hands and feet, cook and chauffeur, for someone else. Increasingly, she wasn't sure just who she was. She was certain that she wasn't only hands and feet. She was a whole person, but she had never had much time to figure out who this person was. She was always defined in what she now thought of as her "servant role." Perhaps that teenager who had married Ken had been on the way to becoming someone, but it was a long time ago and hard to recall.

Claudia decided to go to college to find herself. She would study literature, which seemed a good way to look for herself. She applied to the local community college. It didn't cost too much, and it was an easy commute.

She soon found out that whoever she was, she was different from the college's view of who students were supposed to be. Although the college had a significant number of older students, it was clearly designed with the assumption that "normal" students were eighteen to twenty-two. Orientation was designed to promote social experiences that only a teenager could love. She wasn't into rap music and didn't especially care to play get-acquainted games with children younger than her own daughter.

Her relations with her advisor were strained. He tried, but he was used to dealing with teenagers and had no concept of how to advise a full-fledged adult.

Classes were terrible. She soon discovered that the majority of mature students in college are there to learn something that will translate directly into more cash on the job. The mean age in the college's accounting classes was probably thirty-five. However, she must have raised the mean age of her modern English literature class by five years. She quickly discovered that maturity had something to do with making sense of literature. She found that her experience put her in a position to interact with the story in a productive way. She thoroughly enjoyed the reading. However, the rest of the students were still trying to distill the plot and the theme, and trying to get the best grade for the least work. Their questions and interpretations were, well, juvenile. By the second week of classes, she thought that she had heard the question, "Will this be on the test?" twenty times.

Worst of all was the cafeteria, where she ate between classes. Wherever the other adult students were, they weren't there. She suspected that the classes taken by most adult students were offered in the afternoon or evenings to accommodate their schedules.

"Well," Claudia mused to herself, "I really didn't expect to find myself in the cafeteria. I thought I'd find myself in fiction. Isn't it odd to look for yourself in something made up? Maybe that's not where to look. I don't know. But while I'm looking, it would be nice if I could talk to and be with a few people who understand what I'm about. Maybe I don't need a degree; maybe I need a support group. But that doesn't seem right, either. I came here to change my life. I didn't come to find people to help me endure it."

CASE 8.2 *Choosing a Career*

Toshiro had wanted to teach first grade for several years, ever since he'd volunteered at a local Head Start program. He loved little kids. He was never happier than when he was reading to them or tying their shoes or even wiping their noses. He especially liked teaching them things because it made such an obvious difference. One day they didn't know their numbers. The next day, through his efforts, a squiggle on a page had magically become the number three. Somehow teaching was what he was meant to do.

Toshiro particularly liked working on little math activities with kids. He was good at math. In fact, that seemed to be the problem: he was too good at it. He had gotten 780 on the math section of the SATs, and his father was convinced that God had made him to be an engineer. More accurately, his father was convinced that he should be a rich engineer. As always, he had done what his father wanted. He had enrolled in an engineering program, and he was doing well. He had volunteered to tutor kids at a local elementary school. The trouble was that he still liked little kids more than he liked engineering, and he still thought he wanted to teach. He looked forward to the time he spent in the elementary school. The time in his engineering classes seemed dull in comparison.

At the beginning of his junior year, he had begun to think about transferring into education and seeing whether he could get certified to teach elementary school. He thought that if he switched between semesters, he could get enough credits both to be certified and to graduate. He had written home about it. His father had provided a detailed economics lecture, beginning with comparative starting salaries for teachers and engineers and ending with some pointed reminders about the CD players and cars Toshiro was unlikely to have if he became a teacher. However, the letter had ended with, "But it's your life. Do what makes you happy."

Well, that was progress. He wasn't going to be written out of his father's will, but he had hoped for his father's approval. Moreover, in some ways, he knew his father was right. Teachers made a lot less than engineers. He didn't exactly want to spend his life scraping by, but he didn't want to spend it analyzing engineering problems, either.

QUESTIONS

1. Both Claudia and Toshiro see college as an opportunity to "get a life," but they seem to understand this differently. Claudia poses the question as one of self-identity. She wants to know who she is. Toshiro wants to know what job he should pursue. Do these questions have anything to do with each other?

2. Are there other perspectives you might use to view the point of college? Can you connect what you are doing in college with any broad view you have of your own life?

3. If your college education is successful, it may change you. You might change your mind about some important ideas, or develop new interests, tastes, or skills. You might be a different person when you leave college than you were when you entered. Is college supposed to do this?

4. If college changes who you are, how can you think about what you'll want from life after college? Do you worry you'll have to make too many choices about your career before you really know what you want?

5. How do you think about the work you want to do after college? Are you interested mainly in how much you'll earn? Are you interested mainly in whether the work will be fulfilling or enjoyable?

6. Toshiro seems concerned that he enjoys teaching more than engineering. Is that all there is to it? Perhaps Toshiro feels "called" to teach—could teaching be what he is meant to do? Do you feel this way about the work you want to do after college?

7. Could Claudia have experienced her work as wife and mother as a calling? Should she have? Could or should men experience their roles as husbands and fathers as a calling?

ISSUES

College is a place for choices. It is supposed to prepare you for life. What does that mean? What is your life? How should you see your education affecting it? Maybe you don't have a clear picture of your life. If not, how can you get one? Do you really need one? Both Claudia and Toshiro have raised questions about how their attendance at college fits into their concepts of their lives and into their pictures of who they are. However, their questions are not the same. Toshiro has begun to form a picture of who he is and what he wishes to do. His problems are, first, that his father does not support his aspirations, and second, that he will not make a good living at what he wants to do. Claudia, however, currently has no well-formed picture of herself and her life. She has decided that her old life is somehow deficient, so she is on a quest for self-discovery. She wants to find out who she is and what she is to do with the rest of her life. Although she might or might not take a job after college, she does not seem to define her life in terms of her vocation.

A view of one's life and oneself are important. They are "orienting," which means that they help us make decisions in a certain way. It's not so much that they provide information that is relevant to making decisions; it is that having a sense of who we are and a view of our lives helps us assess how relevant information is for us.

Consider something as simple as buying a car. If we wish to purchase a car, we'll probably want to know certain things, such as how much it costs and whether we can afford it. We may want to know the car's maintenance record. This information is of little use, however, if we have no sense of who we are and how the car will fit into our lives. Someone who is, for example, the chaplain of a retirement center and whose life is built around service to the elderly may not find a tiny red sports car appropriate. It would not "fit" the person. A film star might find a sedate, low-priced station wagon similarly inappropriate.

College is a place where we must make decisions that help advance us toward our vision of a good life; it is also a place where we can form, test, and appraise our picture of the life we want to lead. Toshiro, for example, has been in a process of testing a sense of himself as a teacher. He's found that he enjoys teaching and he does not enjoy engineering. But he's unsure whether that is a sufficient reason to change. His family relations are also important to him, and he is unsure whether teaching can sustain an income that will support other things he wishes to do. He needs to balance these concerns. What criteria should he use?

Claudia has no currently functional sense of who she is and what she wishes to do. Not that she is entirely directionless; she has a past. She has a network of relationships that are important to her, including her husband and children. Although her children are grown and her husband is not as central in her life as he once was, she wants to make changes in her life only if they don't disrupt these relationships. At the same time, she needs to discover some things that will allow her to get a firmer sense of direction for herself. How can she do this? Is she right about the potential of literature to help? Perhaps she, like Toshiro, should test an occupation or an avocation. How do we make decisions of this sort?

APPLYING ETHICAL PRINCIPLES TO THE CASES

The ethical principles we've been using in this book can help us figure out what a good life for us looks like. Toshiro, for example, is asking himself some questions that could be illuminated by the principle of the *greatest good*. However, he should be careful. As Toshiro tries to figure out what might be the greatest good for him and those affected by his decisions, he shouldn't just equate "the greatest good" with "the greatest income." Income may count, but so should the satisfaction he gets from teaching, and pleasing his father; these are "goods," too. Then Toshiro has to try to balance these competing goods in some way. How would you advise him? Note that the principle of the greatest good doesn't seem very helpful to Claudia right now, because she doesn't know what she wants, and so she isn't clear about what might count as a "good" for her.

Both Claudia and Toshiro also need to consider how their life choices fit into their current set of *relationships*, and into the new ones they may form. What does Toshiro owe his father? What obligations does Claudia have to her husband and grown children? How should they think about the sense of duty that may be bound up in these relationships? And will their choices now make some kinds of future relationships more likely to develop than others?

Furthermore, the concept we have of our lives and of who we are will influence, and be influenced by, our *community*. If Toshiro chooses to become a teacher, that choice will place him in a particular professional community with a particular set of beliefs and practices. If he is a member of a religious group, he might see teaching as a form of service to God. And if he prefers the company of elementary school teachers to engineers, this too might affect his decision. Thus Toshiro's choices might strengthen his membership in one community (his religion), attach him to another (the teaching profession), or move him away from a third (the engineering profession). Choosing a career or life path also means choosing communities.

The principle of *character growth* can also be valuable in reflecting on our choices about the life we want to lead. But while we can reflect on who we are and the purpose of our lives, we must also recognize that there are limits on our choices. Our character is not simply chosen. It is built, a little at a time, by what we do and the decisions we make. Moreover, every time we make one decision, we close off others—something that we Americans, constantly searching to improve ourselves, may not like to hear. Some decisions are closed to Claudia, for example, because of her previous decisions. She can wonder what her life might have been like if she had not married Ken, but she cannot go back and become that unmarried teenager. She has been formed by her life as a wife and mother, and even if she wishes to change roles, she cannot entirely escape what life has made her.

The decisions Toshiro makes may determine not only what he will do for a living, but also what kind of person he becomes. If he chooses to become an engineer, he may be taking a step toward becoming a cynical, bitter, and greedy person who acts largely for monetary gain. Not that engineering makes people this way; it is more the *reasons* Toshiro would have for becoming an engineer. For him, becoming an engineer might mean allowing his desire for a good salary and what it can buy to take precedence over his love for children. For someone else, becoming an engineer might mean expressing a love of science, order, or making things work.

So careers and the education that trains people for them can form character, but often in unpredictable ways. Getting a business degree might make some people greedy. It might give others a sense of accomplishment and public service. Almost every occupation can bring out some virtues, and some vices. If you have an idea about what occupation you'd like after college, you might ask yourself what virtues and vices it could promote. Why are you interested in this line of work? It's quite likely that your current motives will be reinforced as you continue your education and then enter your chosen profession. You should ask yourself: do I want to become the kind of person who is motivated even more by the reasons I now have for choosing this field? Think about the motives you consider worthy ones for choosing an occupation. Should people be motivated primarily by money? How important is it to enjoy what you do? Should your work help others in some significant way? Is it OK to take a job that is harmful or frivolous? (Could you be someone who advertised cigarettes, or manicured dogs' toenails?) How might the work you choose form your character?

WORKING TOWARD SOLUTIONS

The stories of Toshiro and Claudia suggest that there are five important areas to consider in choosing a life.

1. Authenticity. What kind of person are you, and what sort of a life would best suit this person? Claudia often talks as if her task is one of self-discovery. It is as though deep down there is a "real" Claudia hidden away, and now she needs to discover who this person is. She might see studying literature in college as a way to learn to talk about this vague sense of identity. Perhaps she sees studying literature as a source of models or selves that she might adopt or use to stimulate her thinking. "Maybe," she seems to think, "if I examine this character or this way of thinking, I will discover a reflection of myself that I can use to decide what I should do with my life."

Toshiro has found out something about himself—that he enjoys working with children—but he does not talk as though he has discovered some formerly hidden person he was all along. (Claudia may take the idea of "discovering who you are" too literally. Perhaps she needs to spend more time asking herself what she enjoys or thinks is important to do, and less time looking for her lost self.) Toshiro is motivated by his sense that there is a link between the kind of person he is and teaching. He has discovered this link by active explorations rather than by reading and reflection: he learned that he loves children and teaching by trying it out. Another future teacher might first determine that "I am the kind of person who loves children" and from that conclude "therefore I should teach." College can be a place for both kinds of exploration—of things you might want to do, and of the kind of person that you might be. How could you use your college experience to do this?

2. Discovering what's worthwhile. What is worthwhile? Some things are better than others, period. Some things are better than others—for us. We are not sure that we could successfully argue that Bach and Duke Ellington are better, period, than Eminem and The Dave Matthews Band (although we do believe they are). We can say that we like the artists we do because experiences and study have developed our tastes.

College is a place not only to find ways to satisfy your current tastes, but also to develop those tastes. Some things that people find worthwhile or enjoyable can only seem that way when you have the experience or training needed to appreciate them. This often tends to be true in the fine arts: good music, good literature, and good art often seem good only when we know enough to appreciate them. Perhaps you have had the experience of disliking a certain type of music until you had a chance to perform it or to dance to it. Perhaps you have been bored by a trip through an art museum until someone explained the art works to you. Perhaps you have found a book tough going until an enthusiastic friend or professor showed it to you in a new light.

Such experiences seem commonplace. They suggest that learning to enjoy new things and to appreciate new experiences is a part of personal growth. What other people have learned, with experience and training, to consider good can guide you in new directions to explore. College is an important place for such explorations and growth.

There is always something of us in what we enjoy. Often the reason we consider an occupation or a hobby worthwhile is that it takes some talent or interest that we have and extends it. Moreover, the activity provides us with new challenges and insights as we grow; if it ceases to challenge and inspire us, we tend to move on to something else that does. For example, people who enjoy solving puzzles are likely to enjoy chess more than tic-tac-toe. Tic-tac-toe cannot maintain interest, but the enjoyment of chess seems inexhaustible. As we become more sophisticated in understanding the game, it provides ever new challenges.

Worthwhile activities in general are often like chess. They extend us, and they keep our interest as we advance in them. So to discover what's worthwhile—in general, and for us personally—we must be willing to learn, to change and to grow. College offers many opportunities for this.

3. Finding a place. Where do we belong? Claudia suggests that one of her problems is that she doesn't belong. She doesn't feel as though she belongs with her family anymore, now that her children are grown and her husband doesn't seem to need her. She doesn't feel that she belongs in her literature class or in the cafeteria either, because her age and interests differ so much from the other students'. At the moment, there is no place and no community where she feels completely comfortable. So where does she belong? How might she find out?

Answering these questions is what we mean by "finding a place." It may be a matter of discovering a job that uses our talents, seems worth doing, and is enjoyable. It might mean finding a cause to work for. Perhaps it will mean finding like-minded or congenial people to spend time with. However we do it, finding a place helps give life meaning.

4. Finding a vocation. Do you feel there is some work you are meant to do? Toshiro usually looks on the choice between engineering and teaching as a choice between a job that pays well and one that he enjoys. But he has also entertained the thought that teaching is what he is meant to do, his calling or vocation.

At one point in Western history, the idea of vocation tended to be limited to religious roles—a man might be called to be a priest, but a farmer was just doing a job. After the Protestant Reformation in Europe, the idea of a "calling" was broadened to include all work that people felt called by God or conscience to do. This outlook makes a job into a vocation. That is, it gives the job a deeper purpose than something done just for money or pleasure. If you believe your intended work is so important that you feel urged to do it, then perhaps this work is your vocation. Toshiro might think this way about teaching. He might want to teach not only because he enjoys it, but also because it's vitally important work that he is particularly suited for. It's *his* work, work that he feels personally committed to—his calling. Is there some work about which you feel such a commitment? Should there be? Would your life be better if there were?

5. Money. How much money do we think we need to have, and what do we want to use it for? Toshiro's father holds a common view of the purpose of college—not to discover things, or to form a sense of self, or to find a place, or to realize a vocation—but to enable graduates to get jobs that make plenty of money.

Of course, any kind of life requires money. For those of us who were not born wealthy, this means getting a job that can provide an adequate amount of money. Usually getting a job, especially a well-paying job, requires developing some marketable skills. College can be a place where this happens. But since few students these days need to be told this, we won't discuss it further; nor will we argue that this view of the purpose of college is wrong.

We do, however, believe that it is an incomplete view. If all you ask from college is that it increase your marketability, you will miss much of what the college experience can contribute to your life. What strikes us about many students is that they, like Toshiro's father, want to use college to make money in their life after college, but they haven't thought about using college to discover what kind of a life this money will support. Few of us can ignore the economic implications of college, especially with current student loan debt loads; but it is all too easy to ignore the goals toward which we want to apply our future paychecks. We need to think about our goals and the purpose of our lives at least as much as how to support ourselves.

In our consumer culture, it is easy to assume that we know the purpose of life: to have things—late-model cars, CD players, new computers, nice clothes, big houses, sex appeal, influence, fame, power. We are told this over and over on TV and everywhere else we turn. But maybe you owe it to yourself to find out if this is true for you.

It is important not to miss the possibility that college can transform you. You may come to college expecting it to help you lead the life you have already imagined for yourself. You want this and that, and if you become an engineer or a lawyer, you know you can get them. But college is also one of the best times and places to consider some questions that are not generally asked: Why do you want these things? What kind of a person do you want to be? Do you feel called to some vocation?

The real trick to getting the most out of college is to be open to changes in yourself, about the person you want to be and what you think is worthwhile, what you want to do, and where you belong. Indeed, the trick to developing your financial potential is to apply these questions to the marketable skills you want to acquire. As well as asking, "How much does it pay?" all students should ask themselves, "How do I want to be transformed? What parts of myself do I want to bring to the fore? What kind of person will my choice of career make me?"

Questions

1. One view of higher education that emphasizes its transformative power is the liberal arts tradition. This concept of college suggests that the key to a transformative education is the study of subjects such as the arts, literature, philosophy, mathematics, and the sciences. Why should the study of philosophy be considered more liberating than the study of fashion merchandizing? What would give literature more transformative power than accounting?

2. Does the liberal arts tradition focus more on the development of rationality and taste, and less on self-discovery, than we have done? Are these goals inconsistent? Are they different? How?

3. Some people have argued that a principal goal of education is creating good citizens. Is this goal different from "getting a life"? How do you understand what it means to be a good citizen? Are there any tensions between the two goals?

4. We have suggested that part of reflecting on getting a life is authenticity, and that self-discovery is part of this, but we have cautioned against thinking of this as though there were a "real you" waiting to be discovered. We are suspicious about whether there is any "real you" at all. How does self-discovery differ from discovering a "real you"? Is a self a discovery or an invention? What else might it be?

5. Toshiro was unable to decide whether to be a teacher or an engineer. Thus he took an extra year of college in order to get a B.S. in engineering and a teaching certificate. He now has a job offer from a major corporation for $59,000 and an offer from a school district for $32,000. How would you advise him to think about his choice?

6. Yesterday you won the lottery. You have more than enough money for the rest of your life. How will this affect your view of your reasons for being in college?

7. Was Claudia a victim of sexism? How so?

ADDITIONAL CASES

CASE 8.3   *Authenticity*

The first few months of college were difficult for Stephanie in a way she'd never imagined. She'd known that going north to school would mean being far from her family and embracing new intellectual challenges, but that was exactly what she'd wanted. She had to leave home. She was tired of being treated as if her greatest glory in life would be to win a beauty contest (at age fourteen she'd placed second in the Junior Miss Southern Charm pageant, her last) and marry a millionaire. Instead, she wanted to use her mind and go where people didn't believe that girls should be beautifully helpless and graciously brainless.

However, Stephanie had never imagined that up North, people would assume she was stupid, too! At home her mane of blonde hair, polished fingernails, designer clothes, and carefully made-up face looked just like everyone else's. But in the North, hardly any of the girls ("women," they were called here) wore makeup or polish, and many seemed to have multiple body piercings and tattoos, unthinkable for "nice girls" back home. Stephanie's appearance and her slow, soft accent seemed to spell "rich dumb Southern belle" to students and teachers alike, and she felt ostracized and humiliated. Within weeks, Stephanie decided that if she wanted to fit in and be taken seriously, she would have to make herself over, lose her accent, buy "downscale" clothes, and never tell anyone about her embarrassing origins again. She'd change roommates, too, and start over with her college social life.

She worked at this personal transformation at least as hard as she worked at her classes. By the end of freshman year, Stephanie had the satisfaction of seeing that her professors now treated her with respect, and her new friends believed she'd grown up as they had, in middle-class New England.

QUESTIONS

1. Do you think Stephanie is correct in assuming that her accent and appearance are responsible for her not being taken seriously?
2. What other ways might Stephanie have responded to the prejudices she felt she encountered?
3. Is there anything ethically dubious about remaking yourself (or your self-presentation) to fit others' expectations?
4. Does Stephanie owe her new friends any true accounting of her background? Would she if she later married one of them?
5. Is she a victim of sexism or some other -ism?
6. How might Stephanie's deceit, and her perception of its necessity, affect her character growth?
7. Which other ethical principles might you use in analyzing this case, and how?

Divorce Aftermath   CASE 8.4

Jerry's parents divorced bitterly while he was in tenth grade. It was a wrenching experience, not least because his parents used him as the chief prize in their war with each other. Even after the divorce, they constantly pressured him to take sides, and they generally made him miserable without (apparently) meaning to. He survived by retreating from both of them, throwing himself into his schoolwork and his music, and longing for the day he could escape.

Jerry is finally living away from home in a freshman dorm, but his parents' battles seem to have followed him to college. Their latest fight is over who will pay for his college education. When Jerry was applying to schools, his dad promised to pay Jerry's tuition if he was accepted at State. Now that Jerry's made it, his dad is refusing to pay for another semester. The reason is that Jerry's mom is planning to remarry, and Jerry's father sarcastically insists that if she does, his "new dad" can foot the bill. Unfortunately, his future stepfather has made it clear that he will not pay for Jerry's college, and his mother certainly can't pay the tuition herself.

Jerry is not eligible for financial aid because he has never lived independently, and his parents' income bracket disqualifies him as their dependent. Thus it seems that Jerry will have to drop out of State. If he can afford college at all on what he can earn from a part-time job, he will have to settle for a community college and move back in with his mom or dad. That is, unless he can get one of his stubborn parents to change their minds.

QUESTIONS

1. Should Jerry try to influence his father to pay for college in spite of his mother's remarriage?

2. Should his mother try to get her new husband to pay? Should she postpone her wedding so that Jerry's father will keep paying?

3. Does Jerry have an equal duty to both of his parents in this situation? How can he (or anyone) respond ethically to manipulation by loved ones?

4. What would you do if you were Jerry? Why?

5. How might the principles of relationship, character growth, and the greatest good apply to this case?

CASE 8.5   *Whose Life Is It, Anyway?*

Albert is trying to imagine how to break the news to his parents. For two and a half years he has dutifully majored in computer science and done reasonably well, even though he's spent many hours practicing his violin, taking lessons, and playing in musical groups on campus. Now, before it's too late, he has decided to switch to a music performance major and make computer science his minor. For some students, it would be a straightforward choice: Albert loves music and knows that he has real talent; he is only a middling computer science student, and regards a future life as a computer programmer with bored distaste. However, Albert also knows that his parents regard his dream of being a concert violinist as crazy and undutiful. He can imagine the conversation already:

> *His mother (in tears):* "But Albert! How will you support yourself? Even if you can get into an orchestra after you graduate, you will never be able live on what they pay you!"

His father, sternly: "You've made your mother cry! Don't you realize how much she's suffered to get to this country, and to give her children a chance at a better life than we had?"

His mother: "Albert! You can still play the violin, and have a good job as a computer programmer! Your sister earns a good living as a doctor, and she plays the piano. Please, don't throw everything away! You'll regret it when you're our age, and you have children who want to go to college."

His father: "You take your privileges for granted. You would never be able even to think of such a frivolous career if we had not slaved all our lives for your sake. Have some respect for your mother and me and all that we have done for you! When I was young, none of us would have dreamed of going against our parents' wishes."

And so on. Albert knew that his parents wouldn't listen to his side, and his sister was hardly a model he wanted to follow. She never had time to play anymore, although she had wanted to be a professional musician, too, and she had even more native ability than he did. In addition, he didn't see why he should have to give up on his dreams, just because his parents had worked like dogs. They had had to leave everything and start over when they came to the United States, putting in long hours at work they did not enjoy in order to send their children to college. Making money seemed to be everything to them, but now that they had managed to send him and his sister to college and could live comfortably, why did they need his financial "success" to vindicate their struggles?

QUESTIONS

1. In Albert's parents' culture, children are expected either to follow their parents' line of work or to obey their parents' wishes in choosing a profession. Many Americans, of course, have different expectations in this regard. Albert feels trapped between the two worlds. What kind of duty does he have to consider the wishes of his parents, who have suffered so much "for his sake"? Is it disrespectful and undutiful of him to cause his parents pain, as they believe?

2. Can you think of any arguments Albert might try with his parents to convince them to let him follow his dream of being a violinist?

3. What implications does the choice before Albert (becoming a computer programmer, as his parents wish, or defying his parents by becoming a musician) have for the growth of his character?

4. How might you use other moral principles to advise Albert?

Where Do I Belong?   CASE 8.6

Bob is a scholarship student at a prestigious university. He is also the first person in his family, and his neighborhood, to go to college. When he goes home for the summer, everyone seems glad to see him and proud of his success, but he notices that a distance has grown between him and his friends, and even with his family. After the first awkward greetings, no one seems to know what to say. Then one friend comments on how different he seems, and Bob is aware of a new feeling about his friends and family: embarrassment. They all seem so small-minded, shabby, and exaggeratedly ethnic. "They talk like stereotypes!" he thinks ruefully. "Did I used to sound that way, too?"

He overhears his mother defending him to a neighbor who thinks he's putting on airs: "I don't see why Bobby wants to go to college anyway—none of us did, and we do just fine! That boy's head is getting turned at his fancy school. Now he thinks he's too good for us."

That's not it. Bob still loves his family and his old friends, but he just doesn't seem to fit in anymore. Unfortunately, he doesn't feel that he fits in at school, either. He always seems to he making faux pas or otherwise embarrassing himself there, and he doesn't have any close friends. It seems that he has to unlearn his entire past to make it in the academic world, because everything is different: he has to know one way to dress, talk, eat, relate to women and to authorities, and hang out at school, and completely different ways to do these things in the neighborhood. The guys at home even have a "tough" walk and "cool" street greetings that his fellow students would find ridiculous. It seems that he has to be two different people, and he's less and less sure which (if either) is really him.

It's too late for him to slip back into the neighborhood, even if he wants to (and who could he talk to about all the new things he's learning?). However, he worries that he will never be accepted in his new world, either, and he misses the closeness and sense of being able to count on your friends.

QUESTIONS

1. Bob is living the American dream by being the first in his family to go to college, yet he seems to be struggling with his transition from a working-class background to a middle-class future. What might be the pros and cons of getting an education that will put him into a different social class from that of his family and childhood friends?

2. Countless studies have found significant differences between the college educated and those without higher education, in everything from their political beliefs and child-rearing practices to their food preferences and taste in entertainment. How might college have this tremendous effect?

3. As Bob changes his lifestyle, he is losing the strong sense of ethnic pride and blue-collar solidarity of his early life, but he doesn't yet have any new values to replace them and make him feel that he belongs to another community. How important is a feeling of belonging or community? Why?

4. What kinds of communities might middle-class college students have?

5. What can Bob do to find a sense of community at college?

6. Can he maintain his working-class connections while entering the middle class financially and educationally?

7. How should he relate to his old community of family, friends, and neighbors in light of the principles of character growth, equal respect, and relationships?

A Good Job CASE 8.7

Kayali is very excited about her marketing internship with a major tobacco company. There's a good chance that she'll be hired when she graduates, with an excellent salary and benefits and paid business trips to the industry's annual convention in Hawaii. Kayali enjoys working with the hip, creative people in marketing who dream up new ways to "position company products" (that is, to increase the numbers of young, female, and minority cigarette buyers because the older-white-male market is shrinking). She was especially proud when one of her ideas for an ad campaign was greeted enthusiastically by the head of the department during a big brainstorming meeting. "I've got to keep doing well so they'll hire me next year," she told her roommate. She thinks she has a good chance because a coworker told her that the company wants to hire young women who can help them understand how to promote products to their peers.

Her roommate, Caitlin, who plans to be an ecologist, isn't impressed. "How can you say that's a good job? The company sounds slimy to me. Basically, they're trying to get more people, especially vulnerable people, addicted to cigarettes! How can you feel good about helping them do that?"

"No one is forcing anyone to smoke—it's the consumers' choice. You're such a tree-hugger!" Kayali responds angrily. "Just because you want to save the whales or whatever doesn't mean that's what everyone has to do. And believe me, granola types like you have trouble finding jobs at all when you get out in the real world, much less good jobs that start at sixty grand."

Caitlin realizes that she's hurt Kayali's feelings by disapproving of her future job, but she does feel that people should choose work that makes the world a better place, although she can't think how to say this without sounding smug. "I just think that a 'good job' should be interesting for you but also good for other people and the environment," she says rather lamely.

"Well, this job is good for me and for other people," replies Kayali. "This company has factories in several poor areas. The more cigarettes we sell, the more jobs we create. And jobs are more important than the environment any day."

Caitlin disagrees, but she's starting to feel that maybe she and Kayali are on such different wavelengths that they'd better drop the whole subject.

QUESTIONS

1. Caitlin seems to think that choices about employment are not purely personal because they affect society at large. She also feels that people have a duty to improve, or at least not harm, society and the environment, and that we should choose work and lifestyles accordingly. Do you agree? In other words, is working for a (potentially) unethical or socially or environmentally harmful company acceptable if it is a "good job" that is personally beneficial?

2. If you said yes, would you still agree if Kayali were planning to design atomic weapons for the military, create pesticides having highly toxic by-products for a chemical company, or work for an organized crime syndicate? If her work doesn't directly harm anyone, but the company she works for or its products might, is she still ethically responsible for this potential harm? Why or why not?

3. Would you agree with Kayali or with Caitlin about the relative merits of creating jobs versus saving the environment, or can you think of some other position?

4. Would the social value of a job help determine whether or not you would take it? Assuming that you know what kind of work you want to pursue after college, what social and environmental consequences might it have?

5. How would you define a "good job" for yourself?

CASE 8.8   *Working Woman*

Donna enjoys her rigorous prelaw program. She always assumed she'd be a high-powered lawyer someday like her father, older sister Cynthia, and brother-in-law Rafael. However, after returning from a long visit with Cynthia and Rafael, she isn't so sure. Cynthia had warned her that visiting during a work week would mean they'd have little time to hang out with her, "although it'll be great for Danielle," Donna's two-year-old niece. Still, Donna was shocked to see how little time they seemed to have for her (and each other and their daughter).

They both left the house by seven A.M. to commute to work and usually didn't get home until seven or eight at night, when Cynthia would just have time to ask the nanny how Danielle's day had been before the nanny left and they put their daughter to bed. Then they had to eat and do all the chores that had accumulated during the day before collapsing in bed.

Cynthia spent her "free" evenings running errands, walking the dog, and washing laundry and dishes, while Rafael made phone calls and watched TV. They seemed to have time for each other and little Danielle only on weekends, and even then one or both of them often had to rush out for a meeting or do some research for Monday.

They both had important positions and high salaries, but life without time for family, pleasure reading, exercising, and socializing hardly seemed like life at all to Donna. "Of course I want interesting work, respect, and good money," Donna thought, "but does that mean I'll have to be a workaholic?" She also thought about the fact that Danielle clearly seemed to prefer her Jamaican nanny to her own parents, which wasn't surprising considering the amount of time she spent with her. "I want to have kids someday," Donna reflected. "But what's the point if someone else raises them?"

Finally, she recalled that Cynthia seemed to spend her evenings and weekends doing chores while Rafael relaxed. "If I don't do this stuff, it doesn't get done," Cynthia had explained. "At least Rafa does the recycling on Thursdays." This division of labor did not seem very fair to Donna, but Cynthia seemed resigned to it.

Donna wondered, "How can I have an interesting career and still have time for my husband, my children, and myself?" When she was growing up, her father worked long hours while her mother stayed home with the children. Her mother did have time for her family and herself, but she missed the fulfillments of an outside career.

Neither her mother's life nor her sister's were models Donna wanted to follow. "It isn't fair that women have to choose between a career, a family, and personal time, and men don't!" she thought bitterly.

QUESTIONS

1. Is Donna right that women in contemporary society have to struggle to balance "a career, a family, and personal time," while men somehow do not? (See the third section of "Additional Materials" below.) If so, why does this burden fall disproportionately on women?

2. What can individual women and men, and society at large, do about it?

3. What responsibilities do you feel you and your (future) partner should each have regarding child rearing, housework, and breadwinning?

4. Do fathers and mothers have an equal duty to consider their children's needs in choosing a job, or in choosing whether or not to work outside the home? Why or why not?

5. Do you agree that jobs entailing "interesting work, respect, and good money" require "workaholic" schedules?

6. Is this a trade-off you would be willing to make, or would you have other priorities in choosing a job?

7. Do your experiences in college help prepare you to deal with the multiple demands of work, family, and personal fulfillment? If not, how might college do this?

8. How might the various ethical principles apply to these issues?

BACKGROUND READING

• Studs Terkel, *The Great Divide: Second Thoughts on the American Dream* (New York: Pantheon Books, 1988). The Pulitzer Prize–winning author interviews Americans from all walks of life about changes in American values. Pages 3–52 are particularly relevant for college students. In particular, Terkel discusses Humboldt State University's student graduation pledge "to thoroughly investigate and take into account the social and environmental consequences of any job opportunity" (p. 40 and passim); the influence of the mass media on students' education (pp. 24–27 and passim); and college students' differing views about the purposes of education (p. 44 and passim).

• Robert N. Bellah et al., *Habits of the Heart: Individualism and Commitment in American Life* (New York: Harper and Row, 1985). This eloquent bestseller describes the isolated and beleaguered selves produced by our modem culture and suggests ways to mend the private–public split in our lives. The authors asked dozens of white, middle-class Americans the big questions: How should we live? How should we think about choosing our life paths? Who are we, as Americans? How do our individual characters relate to our society? Their analysis of the interviewees' answers is helpful to anyone pondering these questions.

• Claudia Mills, "How Good a Person Do I Have to Be?" in *The Report from the Institute for Philosophy and Public Policy*, Winter 1988, vol. 8, no. 1, pp. 12–15. The *Report* is available from The Institute for Philosophy and Public Policy, School of Public Affairs, University of Maryland, College Park, MD 20742, (301) 405-4759, or at www.puaf.umd.edu.

The author humorously and philosophically discusses our "moral report cards" and what being a good person might mean in today's world.

• Clark Kerr, *The Uses of the University* (Cambridge, MA: Harvard University Press, 1995).

The author discusses the evolution of the modern university into the "multiversity" and the relationship between the university and society.

• The "simple living" movement seems to be gaining momentum currently as one description of what "getting a life" should be about, in opposition to the dominant culture's message of consumerism. Books that articulate different aspects of the simple living movement include:

Joe Dominguez and Vicki Robin, *Your Money or Your Life: Transforming Your Relationship with Money and Achieving Financial Independence* (Penguin Paperback, 1999). This bestseller explains how to "reclaim your life" through financial independence, eloquently describing the mental and emotional toll taken by a life of ceaseless getting and spending. The authors set forth a step-by-step regimen that involves accounting for every penny you spend, avoiding every expense you can, and stashing all your savings in Treasury bonds until you're able to live off the interest.

Michael Fogler, *Un-Jobbing: The Adult Liberation Handbook*, second edition (Free Choice Press, 1999). This book describes how to live a life of freedom, flexibility, and environmental lightness, in alignment with personal values and without full-time employment, while still making ends meet and doing what you love.

Jerome M. Segal, *Graceful Simplicity: Toward a Philosophy and Politics of Simple Living* (Henry Holt & Co., 2000). The author, a philosopher, political activist, and former staff member of the House Budget Committee, attempts to expand and deepen the contemporary discourse on simple living. He articulates a particular conception of simple living—one rooted in beauty, peace of mind, appreciativeness, and generosity of spirit. At the same time, he critiques much of the simple living movement for believing that we could achieve this as isolated individuals if only we freed ourselves from overconsumption. Segal argues that we have created a society in which human needs can only be met with high levels of income. Instead of individual renunciation, he calls for a politics of simplicity that would put the encouragement of simple living at the heart of our approach to social and economic policy.

ADDITIONAL MATERIALS

1. Amy Tan, *The Joy Luck Club* (New York: Putnam, 1989). This book deals with cross-generational differences in concepts of duty, appropriate sex roles, the importance of the family versus the individual, and the purpose of education (among other themes) in women from Chinese American families. Many of the best-selling novel's basic insights apply to all immigrants who suffered tremendously before coming to the United States, and then raised offspring here who enjoy privileges they never had. To what differing ethical principles do the mothers and daughters in the book seem to appeal? If your parents (or their parents) were immigrants, is there a similar generation gap of expectations in your family? What role can college play in expanding or closing that gap?

2. Benjamin Barber, *An Aristocracy of Everyone: The Politics of Education and the Future of America* (New York: Oxford University Press, 1992), pp. 253–254. Rutgers, the State University of New Jersey, recently created "an extended pilot program in which classroom civic education and practical community service were united in a number of bold new courses and a residence hall devoted to service learning." In particular, Rutgers developed a mandatory civic education course for all freshmen,

> organized around [. . .] a classroom course with an academic syllabus, but
> also including a strong and innovative experiential learning focus utilizing

group projects. [. . .] Students [are] free to choose community service or non-service projects as their experiential learning group project. (Barber, *An Aristocracy of Everyone*, pp. 256–258)

Does the idea of a required service-oriented course seem coercive, an encroachment on students' rights? Does citizenship involve duties and responsibilities as well as rights and privileges? If so, what are these duties? Is service to others in our community a private virtue, like charity, or a public duty that everyone needs to fulfill in order to maintain democracy and our sense of social connectedness? How might the various ethical principles apply to these questions?

Is the idea of "mandatory service" a self-contradiction? What are the ethical implications of making service programs voluntary, versus making them compulsory? How might participation in a service program benefit the participants? For more information, see "Chapter 7: Teaching Democracy Through Community Service," in Barber, *An Aristocracy of Everyone*, pp. 230–261; and Robert K. Fullinwider, "Mandated Service and Moral Learning," in *The Report from the Institute for Philosophy and Public Policy*, Summer/Fall 1992, vol. 12, no. 3/4, pp. 17–19. The *Report* is available from The Institute for Philosophy and Public Policy, School of Public Affairs, University of Maryland, College Park, MD 20742, (301) 405-4759; or at www.puaf.umd.edu.

3. Until about 40 years ago, it had long been assumed that raising children and making a home was full-time "women's work." Now women, especially college-educated women, have far more opportunities and pressures to work outside the home. In 1947, 12 percent of married women with children under six had paid jobs; by 1992, the number had risen almost five times to 58 percent of women with young children working. For mothers of school-aged children, the percentage working outside the home in 1992 was even higher—a full 75 percent. And these percentages may well have increased slightly since 1992. (Statistics taken from Jody Heymann, Alison Earle, and Brian Egleston, "Parental Availability for the Care of Sick Children," in *Pediatrics*, August 1996, vol. 98, no. 2, p. 226.)

Yet in families where both parents work, women still do far more child-care and housework than men. Thus women end up working "roughly 15 hours longer each week than men. Over a year, they work an *extra month of 24-hour days*" (ibid.; Arlie Hochschild with Anne Machung, *The Second Shift: Working Parents and the Revolution at Home* [New York: Viking, 1989] p. 3).

Many people see college as preparation for earning a living. Should college also help prepare students (of both sexes?) for parenting and running a home? What kinds of courses or other experiences might do this? What should a man and a woman contribute to the family? Are ethical issues involved in how wage earning, child rearing, and housework are divided by a couple? For more information see Hochschild and Machung, *The Second Shift*; Kathleen Gerson, *Hard*

Choices: How Women Decide about Work, Career, and Motherhood (Berkeley, CA: University of California Press, 1985); and Jana Singer, "Women's Work," in *The Report from The Institute for Philosophy and Public Policy*, Winter 1991, vol. 11, no. 1, pp. 1–5. The *Report* is available from The Institute for Philosophy and Public Policy, School of Public Affairs, University of Maryland, College Park, MD 20742, (301) 405-4759; or at www.puaf.umd.edu.

4. Ron Suskind, *A Hope in the Unseen: An American Odyssey from the Inner City to the Ivy League* (Broadway Books, 1999 [paperback reprint]). This touching and true story describes the hardships and moral and emotional dilemmas faced by a black youth from the ghetto as he struggles to educate himself and make it into an Ivy League college. America may be the "land of opportunity," but this story makes clear the tremendous obstacles poor youth, especially youth of color, must overcome to get into the middle class. It also reveals the poignancy of making it: for those few poor kids who do finally make it into the middle class, their moorings, even their sense of self, are disrupted. They no longer fit in back home, and they're not really accepted in their new environment either. Changing social classes seems to be a very lonely experience, even in a country that celebrates upward mobility. If moving up means losing your community and sense of place, perhaps forever, is it worth it?

5. Are today's college students more activist, or more apathetic, about political and social issues than their predecessors? Reports in the media offer conflicting evidence.

See Susan Roth, "Student Activists Focus Energy, Aptitude on Free Trade; Youthful Activism on the Rise" (Gannett News Service), in *The Ithaca Journal*, 10 May 2001, p. 2B. In addition to reporting on the student social justice movement at universities across the country, this article cites statistics showing that more students have been joining in protests since the 1980s. For example, 39.6 percent of freshman in 1990 said they had participated in organized demonstrations; by 2000, that figure had risen to 45.4 percent of freshmen.

William Damon, "The Gap Generation," in *USA Weekend*, 27–29 April 2001, pp. 6–9. This cover story disagrees with reports like Roth's (above), citing surveys that show today's students "seem to be turning inward—generally in a pro-social manner, certainly with positive benefits for intimate relationships, but too often at the expense of a connection with the present and future world beyond, including the society they will one day inherit."

In a similar vein, see Ben Gose, "More Freshmen Than Ever Appear Disengaged from Their Studies, Survey Finds," in *The Chronicle of Higher Education*, 16 January 1998, vol. 44, no. 19, p. A37. The results of the UCLA Higher Education Research Institute's 31st annual national survey of first-year college students show that fewer students seem interested in learning for its own sake, although more plan to attend graduate school. Only 23 percent considered community service important, although 73 percent had participated in such activities. Around 55 percent considered themselves political moderates.

Would you say that you and your friends fit best into the activist image described in the Roth article, the more inwardly focused picture presented by Damon's article, or the apathetic view of students described by Gose's report? Are these reports in fact contradictory, or could they—like a group of blind people feeling the ears, trunk, and legs of an elephant—all be describing different aspects of the same phenomenon? In his article Damon implies a moral critique of students for attending only to their private lives instead of caring about broader social concerns. Do you believe this is a moral issue? Why or why not? On what ethical principles are his concerns based? Do you agree with him?

6. If college is an important part of "getting a life," then what are the moral implications of the fact that rising tuition is increasingly preventing low-income students from attending or finishing college?

See Katherine Hutt Scott, "Struggling to Pay Tuition: Rising College Costs Hinder Low-Income, Minority Students" (Gannett News Service), in *The Ithaca Journal*, 26 February 2001, p. 1A. This article describes how poor families are hit the hardest by rising college costs; for them the cost of a public college is now up to a forbidding 62 percent of total family income (in 1999–2000), compared to 39 percent of family income in 1979–80. (Increases in college costs have not affected middle-income or high-income families nearly as much.) This article also contains a graph showing the widening disparity between the affluent and the poor in terms of bachelor's degrees earned, and thus their lifetime earnings. "In 1980, 24-year-old students whose families were in the top income quartile had earned about five times as many bachelor's degrees as students of the same age from the bottom income quartile. The gap now is about eight times." See also Christina Duff, "Racial College-Degree Gap Is Still Wide; Census Bureau Data Show That Income Equality Is Unlikely in Near Future," in *The Wall Street Journal*, 29 June 1998, n. 128, p. A2, col. 2. This article points out the continuing gap in the number of white and black college graduates, and in those graduates' income levels.

9

RELIGION, RELATIVISM, AND DIALOGUE

THREE CASES: "I BELIEVE . . ."

Thus Saith the Lord

"Look, I've tried to be nice about this, but I don't have time to talk to you. I am trying to study for an exam. And actually, I'm not really that interested in talking to someone I don't know about the so-called 'state of my soul.' I'm perfectly happy without your religion. So please just leave me alone."

"I'm sorry to bother you, but it is important that you listen to me. Your soul is at risk! You really need to accept the Lord, because someday He is going to return, and if you haven't accepted Him, you'll go to straight to hell."

"Yeah. Right."

"Listen, this is your chance to be saved!"

"No, *you* listen. I don't have to hear this. I don't owe you a thing! Don't you know how rude it is to bother people when you haven't been invited in? Especially when you won't leave *my room* when I you tell you to. There's a university rule against this, you know. No one is allowed to 'subject students to unwanted attempts at proselytizing.' So get out. Now."

"I'm sorry you feel that way, but I have got to get you to hear my message. Suppose the dorm was on fire and I didn't warn you? Suppose you didn't believe it was on fire—wouldn't I be justified in dragging you from the building, even against your will? And saving your immortal soul is far more important than saving your life! As for university rules, I don't care about them; I serve a higher power. God commands me to do this, and I must obey God, rather than man. Please—you must hear me out."

CASE 9.2   *After Me, Please*

"How could you do that?! While I was asleep you took my wallet out of my jeans and stole fifty dollars from me. What kind of roommate are you? I can't ever trust you again!"

"Look, I didn't steal it. I only borrowed it. I was planning to give it back. So don't get so bent out of shape! It's no big deal. Besides, I need it more than you do. I've got to get my girl a nice present for her birthday. We haven't been getting along too well, and I'm worried she's going to dump me. And your parents give you tons of money."

"You 'just borrowed' it! You were 'going to give it back'! Sure, that's why you waited until I was asleep to take it. You don't expect me to believe that crap, do you?"

"OK, so you really want the truth? The truth is, I don't give a damn how I get the money. All that matters is that I get what I want. I'm just sorry you woke up."

"You think you can do whatever you want to get your way? Don't you even care that stealing is wrong? God, are you selfish!"

"Of course I'm selfish. So are you. The difference is, I'm not afraid to admit it. I'm not trapped like you by all those stupid little rules of right and wrong, all that moral stuff. They're just cheap tricks the weak use to try to control the strong. I'm beyond them—I watch out for Number One, and let other people look after themselves. That's the way to get ahead in life! C'mon, haven't you read any Ayn Rand? And weren't you paying attention in Philosophy last week? Remember that German dude, the one who said 'God is dead, so everything is permitted'? Face it, that's reality: only cowards and wimps listen to all that 'don't do this' and 'you shouldn't do that' garbage. I do what I want."

CASE 9.3   *Let's Talk*

"'Can't we talk about this? Can't we talk about this?' If you say that one more time, I will scream. Look, I try to be a good person. So I'm not compulsively neat like you—I don't see why that's such a problem. You have your way of doing things, and I have mine. No one appointed you to be my conscience. What's there to talk about?"

"What do you mean, 'What's to talk about?' I'm always tripping over your clothes and your books and your junk. I haven't even seen the floor of our room since the first week of school—I wouldn't be surprised if the Board of Health quarantined us. And only this morning, I had to clean your toothpaste out of my hairbrush! I just can't stand having to live in all this clutter and dirt. Oh come on, don't turn away. Can't we even discuss this like reasonable people?"

"Oh no, not again. Look: we can't be 'reasonable' about this, because there's no 'reason' involved! There's just *my opinion*, and *your opinion*. I can't help it if I'm messy, and I guess you can't help it if you obsess about neatness. But there's no right or wrong to it. It's just how we are, what we like, our own personal preferences. *Nothing to discuss.* You know, maybe there's nothing you can do about being a neat freak; but if you'd just get it through your head that it's your opinion against my opinion, no point in arguing, you'd be more tolerant, and a lot easier to live with. It's because you're stuck on the idea that it's *right* to be neat that you're such a pain in the butt. Say, would you hand me that blue jacket? Yeah, the one under the book over there. Isn't that your book, by the way?"

Have you had conversations like these? Can you imagine yourself as a participant in one of them? Have you heard people say the kinds of ideas that are expressed here? We think that the reasons people give to justify their behavior in these vignettes are fairly common in our culture. One person believes God is the source of ethics and that being ethical means doing what God commands. Another believes that there are no objective ethical standards, and that therefore he can do whatever he wants. Still another thinks that many ethical dilemmas are just matters of private choice, and that no one has the right to act as anyone else's conscience. Interestingly, she also believes that if we all thought this, we would be more tolerant of each other. These kinds of claims are made all the time. Not only that, they are among the claims that are often argued about by those of us who write about ethics for a living, although we usually talk about them in ways that may be both more profound and more obscure.

We want you to notice two things about the questions these vignettes raise. First, these are not so much questions about what is right and wrong as they are questions about *how we know* what is right or wrong, or *whether we can know* what is right or wrong. For example, if we think that God is the source of ethical authority, we may spend time praying or reading scripture. And when we think that we know what God wants, we feel that we must do it. Alternatively, if we believe that there is no God, we may conclude with Ayn Rand and Nietzsche ("that German dude") that everything is permitted to those strong enough to reject conventional morality. So these questions of what is called "moral epistemology" can be important to how we live our lives.

Second, the various views expressed in these vignettes have something in common. They are all "conversation stoppers." Each view seems to lead to the conclusion that "there's nothing to talk about." If we think that there are moral absolutes and that God is their author, then once we know the will of God, there's nothing to talk about. If we believe that "everything is permitted," then there's nothing to talk about. If we believe morality is merely a matter of personal taste or cultural preference, again, there's nothing to talk about. Since we have spent an entire book trying to get you to talk about ethical issues, it follows that we are not particularly happy with these "anti-dialogical" ideas.

This chapter is not going to follow the format we've used in earlier chapters, because in this chapter we are not going to work on a particular ethical issue. Instead, we're going to discuss questions of *moral epistemology*—meaning whether we can know what's right and wrong; and, if we can, how we know it—and the implications of some of the answers to these questions. We're going to end with a problem for you to solve. We'll ask you to construct what we'll call a "dialogical forum" in answer to our questions about the problem. When you've figured out a solution, you're done with this book, and should go forth and be ethical.

QUESTIONS IN MORAL EPISTEMOLOGY

Here are some common questions about moral epistemology:

1. Doesn't ethics depend on religion? Can we know what is right apart from some revelation from God?

2. Are there any moral absolutes, things that are always good or bad? Aren't all ethical ideas relative to our culture? Aren't they just a matter of taste? How can we know that some ethical idea is true? "Your book," you might say, "has been full of options, dilemmas, and ambiguities, but there has been little talk about *knowing* something is right or wrong. Doesn't this make a good case for relativism?" Aren't we more likely to be tolerant if we believe in relativism?

3. When people disagree about ethical issues, how can they work it out? In order to agree, do they have to appeal to some moral absolute? Is there any way that they can discover what's right? Is there an ethics of solving ethical problems?

4. Must people agree about their ethical lives? Aren't ethical matters private? When we seek agreement, aren't we likely to end up imposing the ideas of a majority on a minority? Why not respect everyone's freedom and let people make up their own minds? Isn't tolerance of moral diversity the most important moral concept in a free society?

By the time we have finished with our discussion, we hope you will notice the relationships among these questions. They all have something to do with ethical dialogue. In this chapter, we suggest that dialogue is an important part of ethical decision making. We have used the word *dialogue* because we want to emphasize the importance of a certain kind of moral conversation. The basic idea is that ethical issues and disagreements should be discussed. In fact, a major aim of this book has been to teach you how to have an ethical discussion.

How do these various questions relate to the idea of dialogue? First, some answers to these questions tend to make dialogue impossible or pointless. For example, if there are moral absolutes that can be received only from God, there doesn't seem to be much to discuss. We can't discover ethical truths by reasoning about them or discussing them. When we have them, we have commands from God. How can we take divine commands and treat them as topics of open discussion? Part of the idea of an open discussion is that we enter into it entertaining the possibility that we could be wrong and that we could change our minds. Can we decide that what God has commanded is wrong? If we know what is right because God has said so, our attitude toward those who disagree will apparently have to be that they are benighted or evil. Religious certainty doesn't seem conducive to open dialogue.

Curiously, ethical relativism has a similar consequence. It might seem that if we start out believing that ethical ideas are relative or simply matters of personal choice, the possibility of useful moral conversation becomes greater. After all, people will not come to a moral conversation *knowing* they are right. They will respect other people's opinions. They won't be locked into their views. They can be flexible. Unfortunately, there is more to it than this. If ethical ideas are only matters of culture or taste or personal opinion, there doesn't seem to be much to discuss. At least there doesn't seem to be much possibility of achieving a reasoned agreement about ethical matters. It's all a matter of opinion. There isn't really any right or wrong about right or wrong; therefore dialogue doesn't get us anywhere.

Notice that the idea of meaningful dialogue makes some assumptions about ethical decision making. It assumes that we don't always know what's right and wrong with any certainty. It also assumes that it is possible to have a reasoned opinion about ethics, that some ethical beliefs are more reasonable than others, and that if we work at it, we can progress toward agreement.

So in order to have meaningful dialogues, we must look at ethical questions objectively. This means that when we try to figure out the right thing to do in a moral dilemma, we must seek a middle ground between the absolutism of "This is right, because God said so!" and the relativism of "Whatever you think is right." Absolutism is wrong in a dialogue, not because there are no answers to ethical questions, but because we don't always know what the answers are before we think through and discuss the questions. And relativism is wrong because there are answers, and if we work at ethical dialogue together, sometimes we can find them.

PLATO'S PROGRESS

We want to start our discussion of these questions with Plato, who, in a particularly interesting way, posed the question of whether right and wrong depend on God's commands or God's will. In his dialogue "Euthyphro,"

Plato lays out a dilemma that can (with a few liberties) be put this way: Does what is right depend on God's commands? Neither "yes" nor "no" seems satisfactory, even to the religious person. If the answer is yes, then right and wrong seem to depend arbitrarily on what God chooses. Thus, if God happened to decide that murder and theft were right, and kindness and honesty wrong, they would be.

In this view, knowing right from wrong would depend entirely on a revelation from God. There would be no way to figure it out independently. How could there be? God's decisions would be the only thing to know, and because God's decisions depend entirely on His choices, His will, there would be no way of knowing how God would choose. We could only know what was right or wrong if God told us.

This outcome seems highly unsatisfactory. Right and wrong don't feel arbitrary in this way. Although we may have to do some hard thinking to discover right or wrong in complicated cases, we don't usually have to think much to know that murder is wrong, nor do we need a revelation to decide this. It also seems hard to accept the idea that if God decided that murder were right and preserving life wrong, this would make it so. Something is wrong with the view that right and wrong depend only on God's choices. Strangely enough, such a view seems the ultimate in moral relativism, where right and wrong are arbitrary and depend only on what is chosen. However, in this case, the relativism is revealed only when we take a "God's-eye view" of ethics. It's all relative to God's will, not ours, but wasn't the point of making right and wrong depend on God to make moral knowledge absolute, not relative?

Plato suggests an alternative. Perhaps God commands us to do what is right because it is right, and forbids us from doing what is wrong because it is wrong. God's commands depend on His knowledge of right and wrong. If we say this, Plato points out, we also commit ourselves to the view that right and wrong do not depend on God's choices or God's will. What is right and what is wrong now seem matters independent of God—things God must discover Himself. Even if God is all knowing, His knowledge of right and wrong is like His knowledge of physics or mathematics: it is knowledge of something independent of Himself that is also independently knowable by us.

This view suggests that there is a point to moral inquiry and moral discussion. Discussion can lead us to discover something, because there may be something to discover. On the other hand, this position is equally unlikely to satisfy the religious person. Now it seems as though right and wrong have nothing to do with God.

Are there other options for the religious person? We can mention two. First, perhaps right and wrong depend not on God's will, but on His nature. Consider an analogy. Some religious philosophers believe that science is possible because the world is created by a rational and orderly God. The order of the universe reflects God's orderliness. Its intelligibility depends on God's rationality. When we come to understand the nature of space and time, we are thinking God's thoughts after him.

The same is true for ethics. The world was created by a just and good God. Justice and goodness don't depend on a capricious God's arbitrary choices. They are what they are because the created order reflects God's moral nature.

We will leave it to the reader to decide whether this is a satisfactory resolution of Plato's dilemma. What we wish to point out is that if this view is correct, right and wrong can be discovered by reflection and discussion, because what is right or wrong is, like the laws of physics, in some way part of the discoverable order of things. Moral dialogue and reflection have a point.

Another answer, possibly consistent with the first, is that understanding right and wrong depends on having a full vision of the nature of a good life, a vision that may depend on religion. We have already suggested something like this in our discussion of sex in Chapter 6. Some religions attach a spiritual meaning to sex. Those who are religious cannot fully understand the point of sex or develop an adequate belief system about sex apart from their religion's understanding of sex.

If you are attracted to such a view, we think you should also ask some additional questions. One is whether there are minimal ethical standards that seem reasonable to people independently of their religious convictions or lack of them. We may need a religious outlook to see the union of a man and a woman as sacramental. But we don't need a religious outlook to know that rape, murder, and dishonesty are wrong. Such moral concepts seem commonly accepted among human beings, regardless of their religious views or lack of them. Perhaps, then, there are basic ideas of right and wrong that can be known independently of religion. Indeed, this is just what many religions teach.

Think about your reaction to our introductory chapter. Although you may not have agreed with every detail of the ethical principles we sketched there, we are willing to bet that most of our readers accepted these principles regardless of their religious views or lack of them. There is much to debate about their interpretation or application, but ideas such as equal respect, the greatest good, community, relationship, and personal growth seem important and commonly held. They appear in most religions. Why not view them as central to all moral conversations, even between people who may disagree about religious matters?

We aren't arguing that religion is unimportant to ethics. It may inform people's ideas about what a good life is and how they should deal with others. However, we don't think religion plays this role in a way that is inconsistent with moral dialogue between people of different faiths, or no faith. People with different religious outlooks may have a great deal in common. Although religious differences may keep them from agreeing on the deeper meaning of many activities, such as sex, they probably can agree on basic standards of morality.

ABSOLUTISM AND RELATIVISM

Are moral claims absolute, that is, are they always right or wrong? Are there moral absolutes? If not, is ethics relative—a matter of personal opinion?

We are reluctant to answer these questions in this simple form, not because we wish to avoid controversy or complexity, but because we think they are bad questions. Often people ask them having only a very fuzzy sense of what they mean and what might follow if there were absolutes or if ethics were relative.

In addition, some of the answers to these questions are harmful. If people believe that they possess moral absolutes, or if they believe that all moral claims are relative, they may well refuse to engage in moral dialogue, or they may engage in it in unproductive ways. Both convictions—that we know beyond doubt what is right, and that no one can know what is right—undermine moral discussion and reflection.

Perhaps we might consider the question of whether there are absolutes by looking at one of the Ten Commandments, "Thou shalt not kill." Is this an absolute? We trust you noticed that earlier we used murder as an example of something that is clearly wrong. We have no serious doubts about this.

However, the commandment doesn't exactly say, "Don't murder." It says, "Don't kill." Never? Many people who apparently accept the Ten Commandments also seem to believe that it is acceptable to kill in self-defense, that this is not murder. Many believe that it is acceptable to kill in a just war. Some believe in capital punishment. Some believe in abortion.[1] Does this mean they don't really believe in the commandment?

Perhaps they would say that what the commandment means is "don't murder," meaning "don't kill wrongfully," but justifiable killing isn't murder. That is a perfectly sensible thing to say, but we should notice its implications.

One implication is that we can't apply the commandment until we understand the justifications for killing. Developing such an understanding may require a difficult and complicated discussion. Religious people who devoutly believe in the commandment have produced thousands of books

---

[1] Curiously, in our culture people who object to capital punishment often accept abortion, and people who object to abortion often accept capital punishment. It seems obvious that both abortion and capital punishment are cases of killing. That either or both are acts of murder or wrongful killing requires an argument, probably a very complicated and difficult one. We are puzzled at the confidence people appear to have in their convictions on these questions. Where does such confidence come from? Are people entitled to such confidence?

on topics such as the nature of a just war, or on capital punishment and abortion. Quite possibly one reason they have done so is the strength of their conviction that killing is wrong. Thus they need to be clear about the rightness of exceptions. (Probably most of us believe we should stop at red lights and that there are legitimate exceptions, but people have not filled libraries writing about what they are.)

Thus the vast majority of people who believe "Thou shalt not kill" don't see it as an absolute having no exceptions. It turns out that we can't be certain about its meaning until we have a complicated view about justifiable killing. The fact that it is a religious commandment makes no difference here. We still have to work it out, discuss it, argue about it. So the idea that religious commandments are necessarily absolutes seems untrue on closer inspection.

Many people seem to believe that religion provides us with moral absolutes, but that secular views lead to relativism. However, there are noteworthy cases of religious "relativism." St. Augustine said, "Love and do what you will." When Jesus was accused of permitting his disciples to break the Sabbath, he is credited with saying, "Man was not made for the Sabbath, but the Sabbath for man."

In Judaism, God's law in the Torah is commented on and interpreted by the Talmud, later writers of the Talmud comment on and interpret earlier ones, and scholars and Rabbis interpret both—there is an interplay between the absolute, God's commands, and the relative, the interpretations wise individuals have given these commands throughout history.

In the Qur'an, God commands all Muslims to pray five times a day at specified hours, to fast during each day of the month of Ramadan, and to make the Hadj (pilgrimage to Mecca) at least once in their lives, among other duties. However, these divine commandments admit practical exceptions: travelers can halve their prayers, and students who have an exam or class during a prayer hour may say their prayers late; the Ramadan fast is not obligatory for children under 14, pregnant and nursing women, sick people, and travelers; and the Hadj is required only of those who can afford it financially and physically.

And although compassion and respect for all life are essential values in Buddhism, some Buddhist texts justify the great evils of killing a human being, or even war, if the circumstances are dire enough and it is the only way to prevent more violence. "Desperate situations call for those who are heroically compassionate to grasp the nettle of taking the lesser evil, but only if they acknowledge that an evil is being done, and are prepared to take the karmic consequences" (Peter Harvey, *An Introduction to Buddhist Ethics: Foundations, Values and Issues* [Cambridge University Press, 2000], p. 136).

Are these really cases of religious relativism? Surely not if relativism means that moral judgments are nothing but matters of taste or opinion. Neither are they absolutes, if that means commandments that must be followed, independently of context or any understanding of the good to be achieved by following them. They all imply that the right action is relative to the good to be accomplished. In Augustine's case we should look to the good of the beloved in our actions. In Jesus' case we are to look to the needs of those for whom the Sabbath was made. For Muslims, "right action" must be considered in the context of each individual's situation. For Buddhists, the evil to be averted must be considered. Moral acts are relative to the goods to be achieved and their context. Are they still absolutes? What is gained by describing them so?

We should also note cases of what might be called secular absolutists. The philosopher Emmanuel Kant believed that moral maxims such as "Don't lie" have no exceptions, even when acting on them will have bad consequences.

Utilitarian philosophers such as John Stuart Mill believe in the greatest good for the greatest number. Is this a case of absolutism or relativism? Well, utilitarians may claim that this principle is completely general, universal, and without exceptions. It is the one moral principle from which all others follow. However, if this is true, we must judge all other moral claims by their implications for the greatest good for the greatest number. Is lying wrong? It is if its consequences are bad, but they aren't always bad. Perhaps we should lie to preserve a life or to prevent some other, greater harm.

Similarly, the way we apply the utilitarian principle of the greatest good depends on our understanding of the goods to be achieved and the bads to be minimized. We can't use utilitarianism to decide on the best course of action without knowing the consequences, because we must judge actions by their outcomes (the greatest good for the greatest number). Relativism or absolutism? It's hard to tell. Is there some sense in which utilitarians are relativists and Jesus and Augustine are not?

Let's think about relativism for a while. One thing that relativism might mean is that we need to consider moral judgments in their context. It might be right to do something in some situations but not in others. It might mean that some moral claims are relative to others, in the way that keeping the Sabbath might be relative to other, higher, human goods. However, as we have argued above, if this is all that relativism means, it is hard to see why anyone would object to it. Reasonable people, religious or not, must sometimes consider circumstances or higher principles and goods in deciding what's right. If this is what relativism means, we are all relativists. Moreover, this kind of relativism is perfectly consistent with moral objectivity.

A more interesting kind of relativism is sometimes called *cultural relativism*. In this kind of relativism, moral judgments are viewed as valid only within a particular culture. Different cultures have different values. Although it is possible to judge the rightness or wrongness of ethical questions within a culture, it is impossible to make universal judgments between cultures.

Consider a plausible example. In some cultures it is considered rude to belch at the dinner table, especially for a guest, but in other cultures, guests belch to show the host their satisfaction with the meal. In these cultures belching is actually polite. Can we decide across cultures whether belching is "really" rude?

It is also important to notice that many people are motivated to believe in cultural relativism because they believe in the importance of tolerance. A culture that tries to impose its values on another is intolerant. Anti-belching cultures, they would say, have no right to impose their views on belching cultures.

We are willing to be cultural relativists about belching. Different belching customs are no more right or wrong than are different languages. However, we do not believe that this example can be generalized to most moral issues. In fact, the example is terribly misleading.

First, notice that in both belching and anti-belching cultures, it is considered desirable to be polite. One should express appreciation to one's host at a dinner party. The difference between the belchers and the anti-belchers doesn't have to do with politeness itself. It concerns how politeness is expressed. Suppose, instead, that one culture valued politeness and another rudeness. Should we be culturally relative about this?

If you think so, consider another case. Let's imagine two cultures in two neighboring states. One group we will call the Talls; they live in Tallvania. The other group, the Shorts, live in Shortland. Now the Talls and the Shorts do not differ in their average heights. Each culture has people of various heights. However, they differ in how they regard height. The Talls consider tallness attractive and shortness ugly. The Shorts find shortness attractive and height ugly.

They also disagree about the significance of these differences. The Shorts are absolutists about their tastes. They believe that tallness is objectively bad, and therefore they actively discriminate against tall people. They prevent them from holding good jobs. They restrict them to ghettos and poor housing. They deny them proper health care and good education. No one whose height exceeds six feet is permitted to continue in school. In fact, the Shorts are so aggressive about their beliefs that, whenever they can, they insist that others practice them too. When they trade with other states, they refuse to deal with tall people. Indeed, many Shorts want to make shortness central to their foreign policy and to fight against those benighted societies that value tallness.

In contrast, the Talls regard their preference for height as a social custom. Although tall people are in fashion and on that account may have better chances for good jobs, short people do not experience active discrimination. Indeed, such discrimination is illegal. The Talls recognize that their preference for height can injure short people. They seek to prevent this as best they can. Their attitude toward tallness is a bit like ours toward what our culture considers beautiful. In fact, many Talls regard the preference of their society for height as undesirable because of the harm it can do to short people. Among them "tallism" is considered unethical.

Are the Talls relativists? And are they tolerant because they are relativists? Before you say yes, ask yourself how the Talls should feel about the beliefs of the Shorts.

Suppose the Talls are consistent and tolerant cultural relativists. In this case, they should conclude that values can be judged only within a culture, so they have a duty to respect and tolerate the values of other cultures when the values conflict with their own. Unfortunately this puts the Talls in an untenable situation with the Shorts, for they must now conclude some unpleasant things. First, the Shorts' views about tall people are "right for them." The Talls must respect the Shorts' absolutism about shortness. Indeed, the Talls must even tolerate the Shorts' aggression toward them. After all, such absolutism and aggression are right, within the context of Short culture. Ironically the Talls must accept the rightness of the Shorts' views for the Shorts, simply because the Shorts happen to hold them.

Most seriously, the consistent cultural relativist must be a relativist about tolerance. Tolerance is therefore a moral requirement only within cultures that happen to value it. It cannot be used where it seems most necessary—against the intolerant Shorts. If the Talls are consistent cultural relativists, they must not only see their preference for height as relative to their culture, but they must also see their preference for tolerance of shortness as similarly relative. Cultural relativists have to treat tolerance as only a relative good, and accept intolerant cultures without moral criticism.

Note that cultural relativists can, with equal consistency, value intolerance. Many Nazis were cultural relativists. They accepted the variableness of human cultures and their own lack of objectivity. They also asserted their right to impose their will on others. How would a cultural relativist criticize Nazis? Were they objectively wrong? Was their intolerance right for them?

These considerations suggest that the idea that tolerance rests on relativism is a deeply confused view. Tolerance itself is a moral commitment. It can be justified, perhaps, by appealing to such principles as equal respect. To root it in relativism robs tolerance of any moral force regarding the intolerant. Indeed, the main consequence of justifying tolerance in terms of relativism is to require that those who accept the value of tolerance put up with the intolerance of those who do not. What could possibly be more unacceptable? Paradoxically, we can best affirm tolerance if we regard it as an objective moral requirement.

What should we conclude about relativism and absolutism? These examples suggest several important things. First, contrary to much popular sentiment, it is not true that religion tends to support the view that there are absolutes, and nonreligion leads to relativism. The history of religious and secular moral theories offers little support for this view. Second, the terms themselves are unclear. It's not even clear what we want to say when we talk about "absolutes" or "relativism."

Third, both relativism and absolutism undercut necessary moral discussion. Absolutism does so by creating the illusion of moral certainty where there is none, and relativism by undermining the possibility of discussion and criticism, especially when it is most needed, in dealing with intolerance. In fact, no matter what view we take, we still need moral discussion. If we believe in absolutes, we still have to interpret or define them. Probably when we discuss them we'll raise the same kinds of issues, face the same kinds of problems, and appeal to the same kinds of evidence to which relativists appeal. Often we will end up talking about equal respect, the greatest good, relationships, community, and character growth. Talk about absolutism and relativism unnecessarily polarizes discussion while shedding little real light on how we should behave. We must take the stance of objectivity.

TOLERANCE AND DIALOGUE

Why should we be tolerant? What should we tolerate? A reasonable view of tolerance must answer both of these questions. Tolerance, we have argued, doesn't depend on relativism; on what does it depend, then? Can we give reasons for tolerance? Also, a sensible view will reflect tolerance of some things but not others. Any concept of tolerance requiring that we accept murder and theft, but not religious differences or differing food preferences, would be highly suspicious.

Let's consider tolerance instead as an implication of the principle of *equal respect*. What follows from this idea?

1. Because people are of equal worth, they are entitled to equal treatment and equal rights. Minimally, this requires that we treat people equally and fairly regardless of their differences. We cannot discriminate against people because of such characteristics as their race, religion, or gender. Thus we must tolerate these forms of diversity.

2. Equal respect requires that we respect people's choices and viewpoints. Respecting people partly means accepting that they are moral agents who are responsible for their own decisions and welfare. If we respect people as moral agents, we must respect their choices, convictions, and decisions.

This might mean at least two things. First, the fact that someone chooses to want something, believe something, or do something is a reason to respect that choice. If we view others as moral agents, we must see them as responsible for their decisions. We do not have the right to interfere because we disagree or would have decided otherwise. Second, we have to recognize that we hurt others in a particularly serious way when we seek to override their basic convictions. For example, to prevent people from worshiping God as they see fit, or to compel them to worship God when they are not believers, is to cause them to violate their deepest and most central obligations. Responsible moral agents will view this as an especially serious offense.

3. Respecting people's choices or convictions does not mean agreeing with them. It means that we accept an obligation not to interfere with them. Consider freedom of religion. To respect the religion of other people does not mean that we must regard one religion as equal to another, or all religions as equally true. People may continue to view their own religion as true and the religions of others as false. They may consider all religions untrue. Nevertheless, respecting the religious liberty of others requires that we not view the truth of our religion or the error of others as a reason for coercion. Here, as elsewhere, tolerance depends not on relativism, but on equal respect.

4. Respecting other people's choices does not mean that we should permit people to violate the rights of others, but if we must respect others' choices, what reasons can there be for not tolerating particular conduct? Again we can use religion to illustrate. Suppose some religion teaches that forcing others to convert to the "true faith" is permissible, good, or even obligatory. Clearly, tolerating people who act on such a belief is inconsistent with the belief that everyone has an equal right to freedom of religion. Thus the limits on tolerance are set by the conviction that whatever rights people have, they must have them equally. If we accept this, we cannot tolerate practices that permit some to act so as to deny equal rights to others. We can criticize intolerance because it is objectively wrong, and we can prevent people from acting intolerantly when their behavior interferes with the freedom of others.

Philosopher John Rawls argues that people are entitled to the greatest possible liberty consistent with an equal liberty for others. In his view, tolerance is an objective moral principle; he does not associate tolerance with relativism or moral skepticism. We ought to be tolerant because the principle of *equal respect* requires it of us. (Question: Can arguments be made for tolerance from other moral principles, such as the greatest good or community? What would such arguments look like?)

Consider how this idea might be applied to the Talls and the Shorts. Rawls' way of looking at tolerance allows the Talls to avoid the trap of cultural relativism. They do not have to accept the views of the Shorts as "right for them" simply because the Shorts have these views, nor do they need to see their tolerance as relative to their own culture. The Talls may believe that the Shorts are wrong because their views are intolerant. They may criticize the Shorts for their views and urge them to be more tolerant. They may object to the Shorts' treatment of tall people in their society and may even take action to oppose this injustice.

Of course, this doesn't mean that there aren't some hard questions to be answered about tolerance. Must the Talls tolerate the Shorts' beliefs? Quite possibly; see the discussion of hate speech in Chapter 3. However, we need to be clear that tolerating the Shorts' views does not mean that the Talls have to agree with them or to see them as true for the Shorts. It means the Talls have to believe that they have no right to try to force the Shorts to change their beliefs. The difference between ideas and actions is important here. The Talls might reasonably believe that they should tolerate the Shorts' convictions, and also resist the Shorts' attempts to act on them.

It is important also to remember that we described the Talls and the Shorts as members of different countries. Presumably, unless they resort to economic sanctions or military invasions, the Talls have little ability to coerce the Shorts. (Question: Would the Talls have a right to seek to protect tall people in Shortland?) Suppose, however, that the Talls and the Shorts were different groups in the same society. Does this change things? How?

If the two groups were in the same country, the Talls might (as we have described them doing) pass laws to protect people from discrimination on the basis of height. They might also teach their children tolerance. Notice again that these affirmative steps to secure tolerance make sense only if we believe that tolerance is an objective moral principle binding us all.

THE IMPORTANCE OF MORAL DIALOGUE

One of our objectives in this chapter is to persuade you that moral dialogue is important. It is our principal means for settling ethical disputes and for gaining moral knowledge. To demonstrate this, we've had to discuss topics such as the relationship between religion and ethics, the ideas of absolutism and relativism, and the nature of tolerance. To talk about dialogue, we've had to defend the possibility of moral inquiry against two incompatible ideas. The first view, absolutism, says that moral inquiry is unnecessary because the moral truth is known. The second, relativism, says that moral inquiry is impossible because there is nothing to find out.

Against the first view, we have argued that people of faith are not necessarily committed to moral absolutism. Against the second, we have argued that relativism does not promote tolerance. In fact tolerance seems to require a belief in moral objectivity. To believe that ethical dialogue has a point, we must believe both in the possibility of objective moral truth and in our own fallibility.

Perhaps you have noted that neither of these arguments makes a decisive case for moral objectivity or the usefulness of moral dialogue. You might, for example, accept that tolerance requires a belief in moral objectivity and conclude, "Too bad for tolerance." You might ask, "Can you prove that moral objectivity and moral dialogue are good and necessary things?"

We cannot prove this decisively. Instead we're inclined to rest our case on two kinds of experience that we believe almost everyone has had. The first is that some moral claims seem strong enough (if not certain) that we accept them without argument. For example, everyone who reads this will probably agree that it's wrong to cause pain to others for no reason, or to abuse children. Such strong moral intuitions seem to require little defense. We become skeptical about them only if we're motivated by some philosophical theory; in real life, no sane person doubts them. In addition, such moral intuitions often can be used to judge other moral claims. We can be reasonably sure, for instance, that any moral theory that says it's acceptable to inflict gratuitous pain or to abuse children is wrong for that reason.

We also believe that most people have numerous experiences with successful moral arguments. Perhaps you've had some with this book. For instance, many students believe that cheating is a victimless crime, but they usually can be persuaded that it isn't. Moral arguments often persuade us because they help us see more clearly what's involved in some conduct or belief. We are persuaded because we see that harm is done or respect denied or relationships or community broken, where we didn't see that before. Therefore, the best evidence we can give you for the value of moral dialogue is that sometimes it succeeds in changing people's minds for good reasons.

We don't mean to deny that often ethics are ambiguous and that life has tragic elements. Sometimes we must choose between conflicting goods or conflicting bads, and there is little to guide us. However, even here, when moral argument may not resolve an issue clearly, it can help us be clear about the nature of the issues. For example, moral dialogue may not (as yet) have settled the abortion debate. Perhaps it cannot. But it can help us understand more clearly the conflicting values involved. Wanting all children to be loved, respecting life, and respecting privacy all count! (We suspect that people who find the proper conclusion about abortion obvious or easy have missed something in the debate.) Even when moral discussion fails, it may help us to see our opponents in the debate as good people who are wrong about something, instead of seeing them as evil. There are evil people in the world, and there are occasions when we must oppose them, not argue with them. However, such a judgment about others usually should be earned by an attempt at conversation. It's a rare occasion when moral dialogue has no point.

Up to this point, we haven't distinguished much between moral reflection and moral dialogue. You might think, "OK, I accept that I should reflect on ethical issues, but why should I try to get others to reflect, too? Why dialogue?"

One reason is that a willingness to engage in dialogue recognizes our fallibility and our limitations. To engage in a dialogue, we must accept that we might be wrong, and also remember that we have much to learn from others. Recall the views of John Stuart Mill that we quoted and discussed in Chapter 3. Mill notes that when we refuse to dialogue and seek to enforce our views instead, we assume that we're infallible. Additionally, free and open debate is something from which we can profit. Dialogue lets us test our views by having to defend them; we grow and learn from the process. If we repress the views of others, we are presuming that we never make mistakes; if we refuse to discuss things, we are presuming that we have nothing to learn. We must engage in dialogue because we are not self-sufficient in this way.

There are other reasons to engage in dialogue. Mill's arguments bid us to view other people as sources of ideas, information, and argument. People are also objects of respect. Thus when we propose to act in a way that affects others, we should also view them as having a right to participate in decision making and to have opinions. That is one way in which respect for others is shown. Recall the opening cases in our discussion of privacy in Chapter 4. In one case, Yusif and Fred were in conflict about the use of their room. In the other, Judy and Rachel had become unhappy with each other over how Rachel's mother treated Judy. There is something to learn about dialogue from each of these cases.

Recall that we criticized Fred not only because he treated Yusif badly, but also because he refused to discuss the matter with Yusif. The basis of our criticism here isn't that Fred might learn something from Yusif. It is that Yusif has a right to a vote about the use of the room. In refusing to discuss the matter, Fred is not only saying that he doesn't care about Yusif's ideas. He is also saying that Yusif has no rights concerning the room.

Another issue is involved here. Although we think that Yusif and Fred can profitably discuss the use of their room, we don't have such a high regard for moral dialogue that we believe there is only one fair way to use the room. There may be some clearly wrong ways, in which the interests of one party dominate the other. There also may be many reasonable outcomes. Within this range of plausible outcomes, what may make one result the right one is that Yusif and Fred freely agree to it as the result of an open discussion.

The case of Judy and Rachel can help us see one further point. Judy and Rachel both believe that it is important to be polite and to avoid being rude to others. Neither wants to cause pain. However, their two families have different views about what counts as showing respect for others. Judy's family connects respect to privacy, Rachel's to openness. Is one wrong and the other right? Perhaps. That, itself, requires a discussion. We should recognize that these different views share common ground in at least two ways.

First, regardless of what might be the "right" way to show respect, both Judy and Rachel did intend to show respect; they understood the concept differently. Neither will understand this without dialogue. They need a discussion to see respect from the other's point of view.

Second, perhaps people have a right to define what counts as showing respect in their own way, consistent with their own cultural traditions or their own preferences. This right may be a consequence of the idea that equal respect requires tolerance. However, we need to be careful here. If some people tell us that they prefer to be shown respect by having us give them our paycheck every week, or wash their windows, we are quite unlikely to accept their interpretation of respect. Nevertheless, one significant way to oppress people is to insist on treating them according to our own definition of what counts as satisfactory treatment. To respect others, first of all we must understand what they mean by being respected. We should reject their understanding of respect only for good reasons; we cannot simply assume that what we mean is what they ought to mean. (Question: Can you think of some examples in which what counts as respect is understood differently by members of different cultures?)

Why dialogue? We have provided four reasons. In summary they are as follows:

1. Dialogue makes moral judgments more reasonable by bringing evidence and argument to bear on our opinions.
2. Dialogue is a way of affirming the equal right of people to participate in decisions that affect them.
3. Dialogue recognizes that sometimes what counts as the right thing to do is the product of an open and uncoerced agreement, a contract.
4. Dialogue accepts people's right to their own understanding of the meaning of respect and helps us to understand one another.

Implied in these views is an ethic of moral dialogue. Its features are as follows:

1. Dialogue involves respect for argument and evidence.
2. Dialogue respects the right of people to have a voice in matters that affect them.
3. Dialogue seeks agreements that result from the better argument rather than from superior power or social position.
4. Dialogue recognizes individuals' right to define their own understanding of the conditions of respect.

Dialogue requires and shows a certain moral stance toward the world. It expresses our rationality and our fallibility, our limitations and our willingness to recognize that others have a value equal to our own.

A final thought: dialogue can be understood as part of moral growth. At the beginning of this book, we noted that decisions not only produce actions, they also produce character. We become the kinds of people who do what we choose to do. There is an analogous point to be made about dialogue. Dialogue requires not only that we be able to argue, but also that we be willing and able to listen. Listening is a matter of both will and discernment. We must want to hear, and we must be able to hear what others want to say. When we refuse to listen, when we refuse to consider the other's position or the other's pain, we gradually make ourselves into the kinds of people who don't count others' interests and who can't hear others' pain. We make ourselves morally deaf. Fred, who will not talk with Yusif; Jake, who hates African Americans; and Peter, who seduces unwilling women, are not only selfish. They are also doing themselves moral harm from which they may have difficulty recovering. They have dulled their capacity to hear others' pain, to see the world from others' point of view, to listen, to understand, to care.

Sometimes others are hard to hear and easy to misunderstand, for example, if they come from a world quite different from our own. However, that is not true in these cases. Fred, Jake, and Peter have refused to hear. They have dulled their consciences and blunted their capacity for moral judgment. They have diminished their capacity for seeking their own good in their relationships with others. They enjoy what is base and harmful. They may be putting themselves beyond the reach of moral discourse. They are becoming lost.

Why dialogue? Because your character depends on it.

PROBLEM: UNIFIED HOUSING AT BRIGHTON COLLEGE

Brighton College is a medium-sized college on the outskirts of the town of White Oak. Originally founded by a rich abolitionist, Brighton has long prided itself on its liberal atmosphere and diverse student body. Students at Brighton can choose from a variety of housing situations to fit their needs: big, impersonal Badeker Dorm; Rosa Parks Residence Hall for students of color, built following the student protests of the 1960s and '70s; Havurah House, for students seeking a Jewish community, with a kosher kitchen and Sabbath and Holy Day celebrations; the International Student Union, a small section of Badeker Dorm reserved for foreign students attending Brighton; Mott Hall, a single-sex dorm for women, with strict visiting hours for male guests; and Mensa Club, a retreat for brainy students who have been accepted by either the international Mensa organization or by the national Phi Beta Kappa Honor Society. Many students also rent apartments in White Oak and walk or drive to campus.

For several years, Dean of Students Gail Sutton and Brighton College President Malcolm McBride have been discussing ways to make the student body feel more integrated and unified. Now they've come up with a four-part plan. Along with designing a new freshman orientation program and making changes to the curriculum, the College will forbid off-campus housing and tear down the aging and poorly built Parks Hall and replace it and the other specialty houses with renovated common dorms that will, for the first time, house all of the student body together. The renovations will eventually pay for themselves, the dean and president feel, with the long-term increase in students paying room and board at the College. Dean Sutton and President

McBride have presented their plan to the College's Board of Trustees, which gave tentative approval pending the results of a feasibility study.

While an outside firm is conducting the feasibility study, Dean Sutton and President McBride are planning how to sell the benefits of the new housing arrangements to the Brighton community. They know that the theme houses are considered "Brighton traditions" and a big part of the College experience, yet they are convinced that replacing these specialty dorms with unified housing will go a long way toward uniting the campus and giving students an important social and intellectual experience in common.

But before the unified housing public relations campaign can get under way, someone leaks the plans to the local newspaper. *The White Oak Courier* writes a scathing editorial against the proposed housing changes. The editorial argues that students, especially minority groups, benefit greatly from current housing arrangements; it also predicts that the proposal to ban off-campus housing will ruin the town economically—not only through the grave loss of rental income, but also through dramatic decreases in student spending at restaurants and other town businesses. And the town wasn't even consulted about this terrible idea!

A delegation of angry White Oak landlords and a formal protest from the mayor follow, as well as several well-attended, emotional student protests and a flood of alumni complaints. A new Students of Color Action Group is galvanized into distributing leaflets all over campus accusing Brighton of racism for wanting to tear down their hall, and theirs alone. Jewish students set up a Web site protesting the abolition of Havurah House as blatant anti-semitism and religious persecution. Others accuse the school of gross insensitivity to the concerns of minorities in general, and callous disregard for town–gown relations. The regional media pick up the story. Dean Sutton, President McBride, and the College's Board of Trustees are horrified by the storm.

What should Brighton College do now about the plans for unified housing? The College's Board of Trustees proposes that a commission be created to study the issue, hold public hearings, and make a report and recommendations. The idea is that the commission will not only come up with a plan acceptable to all concerned, but also (the Board hopes) help the College save face after this debacle.

Your task is to design this commission and the ground rules for their hearings. First, who should be on the commission, and why? Consider the following:

- What role should Dean Sutton and President McBride play?
- Should alumni be represented? How should they be selected?
- Should the company doing the feasibility study be involved, or other "outside experts," such as representatives from colleges or universities with unified student housing?

- Should there be representatives from each of the specialty houses? How should they be chosen?
- Should there be representatives of students in the campus's only non-theme housing at present, Badeker Dorm? How should they be chosen?
- What role should the White Oak business community and landlords association have?
- Should members of the media (from White Oak or the region) be included?
- Should potential Brighton College students from the various religious, racial, and other groups served by the theme houses, or other members of the general public, be included? If so, how might they be selected?
- Should anyone else be involved?
- What do you think is the largest number of participants the commission can have and still be viable?

Then you must decide the rules for the public hearing.

- Who gets to speak?
- Who gets to set the agenda?
- Can commission members ask speakers questions?
- Can speakers question commission members?
- Will there be time limits?
- Will there be any limits on what kinds of speech will be allowed?

Finally, think about how the commission will decide on what its recommendations will be.

- Will the members just vote? According to simple majority rule, or some other system?
- Should they have to reach consensus?
- Can the commission conduct its deliberations in private, or should they be public?
- And how can the Council decide if the commission's report is fair and thorough, and its recommendations likely to improve the situation?

Once you've figured out how the commission and hearings should be structured and how the recommendations will be decided on, analyze the process you've created. What features of your design might make the eventual outcome fair or unfair? Second, is it important for dialogue to occur among the different groups involved? If so, how can we distinguish real dialogue from unproductive kinds of interaction such as shouting, personal attacks, or haranguing? And last, what would you say to the idea that the

Board of Trustees should just forget the hearings and "let the experts decide" the fate of unified housing at Brighton College?

BIBLIOGRAPHY

Peter Harvey, *An Introduction to Buddhist Ethics: Foundations, Values, and Issues* (Cambridge, MA: Cambridge University Press, 2000). This is an easy-to-understand account of the ethical teachings in Buddhism as a global tradition. In addition to explaining the foundations of Buddhist ethics, Harvey gives special consideration to topics including environmentalism, feminist issues, economics, and homosexuality in a Buddhist context. This book helps explain the difference between right and wrong, and why, from a non-theistic position (based on a review by Rajith Dissanayake on Amazon.com).

James Hunter, *Culture Wars* (New York: Basic Books, 1991). Hunter argues that disputes in America are increasingly between moral absolutists and relativists who are unable to engage in dialogue or find acceptable accommodation.

John Stuart Mill, *On Liberty* (1859; edited and with an introduction by Gertrude Himmelfarb, New York: Viking Penguin, 1987). For a description of this work, see Chapters 1 and 3.

Friedrich Wilhelm Nietzsche, *The Basic Writings of Nietzsche*, translated, edited, and with commentaries by Walter Kaufmann (New York: Modern Library, 1992). Nietzsche had a powerful influence on European philosophy and literature, and thus on our culture (among other things, he invented the concept of the "superman"). His important writings span the years 1872–1887; he had a complete mental breakdown in 1889 and spent the rest of his life in an asylum.

Ayn Rand, *Atlas Shrugged* (1957; New York: Dutton, 1992).

———, *The Fountainhead*, with an afterword by Leonard Peikoff (1943; New York: Penguin Books, 1993). These two best-selling novels present Rand's philosophy of Objectivism, in which all achievement results from individual ability and effort, laissez-faire capitalism is the ideal political system, selfishness is a virtue, and altruism is a vice.

John Rawls, *Theory of Justice* (Cambridge, MA: Belknap Press of Harvard University Press, 1971). For a description of this work, see the references in Chapter 1.

FOR FURTHER REFLECTION: ADDITIONAL CASES

Out with the Old CASE 10.1

Juan and Jessica were an inseparable couple throughout their junior and senior years of high school, and they've promised each other to continue their commitment when they go to college. Freshman year finds Juan living at home with his mother and attending Stonebridge Community College, while Jessica has gone off to Rockford College, two states away. Jessica seems unable to come home for a visit, so Juan arranges to visit her school one weekend in mid-November. Jessica hasn't been very good about answering his email, and he can't afford to call her long distance as often as he'd like, so this will be their first opportunity to really talk and be together in two months. Juan is thrilled.

However, when he finally sees Jessica again, things seem all wrong between them, although Jessica won't admit it. Her obvious embarrassment over him deeply hurts Juan's feelings and offends his pride. After a particularly humiliating evening at a dance (Jessica all but ignored him and introduced him to only one of her friends, and then merely as "a friend from high school"), Juan said, "I don't think I'm so bad, but you're clearly ashamed of me. What's changed? Why'd you let me come?"

Jessica doesn't know what to say. The fact is, Juan seems hopelessly awkward, unattractive, and uncool compared to her new sophisticated college friends. In addition, she really likes one of the boys in her crowd and doesn't want him or his friends to think she already has a boyfriend, especially such a loser as Juan. She hadn't realized until she saw Juan again how little he fit into her new life. Now she doesn't want to hurt his feelings by telling him. She knows he really cares about her, and he has helped her a lot in the past when she had trouble with her family. The least she can do is be nice to him and spare him as much pain as possible, for old times' sake. But how to get him to be "just friends"?

QUESTIONS

1. There's an old saying, "It's cruel to be kind," for such a situation. What would be the ethical thing for Jessica to do regarding Juan?

2. Was it wrong or stupid of Juan and Jessica to promise each other to continue their commitment when they went off to separate colleges? Are they now morally obliged to honor such a commitment?

3. Is it reasonable or fair for Jessica to expect Juan to move from being her boyfriend to "just a friend"? What should Juan do?

4. Jessica's feelings for Juan seem to have changed at least in part because of her desire to be accepted by her new friends. Is this an ethically dubious motive for changing her feelings? Why or why not?

5. Do we owe loyalty to people who have been helpful or kind to us in the past but no longer are useful to us? Why or why not?

6. If we do owe this loyalty, how should it be expressed?

7. Do we owe something to people who care about us, even if we don't care about them? What?

8. How might the principles of relationships, personal growth, and equal respect apply to this case?

CASE 10.2 *Overloaded*

Brad, a freshman at State University, is close to panic. There is just no way he can juggle his current load of schoolwork with his part-time work-study job, his swimming team responsibilities, and his romance with his girlfriend, Lauren. A crisis is coming because he has three midterm exams the week after his six-month anniversary with Lauren (who has made reservations at a nearby ski resort for a romantic weekend, for which she has planned and saved for more than two months).

He also has newly increased responsibilities and hours at his job in the undergraduate library, and the swimming team has two away meets during the same week. He can't study for his exams and do everything else—in fact, he's not even sure how he can juggle his new work hours and his meets and practices, much less fit in the promised trip with Lauren. Something, in fact several things, have to give. But what?

Brad thinks over his choices. He can ask some friends for help with the test material. For example, maybe he can get one of them to tell him enough about the long novel he should have finished for his English class so that he can at least pass without reading the rest of it. He might try asking Abdul to cover some of his library shifts for the next week. Although Abdul seems pretty overworked as it is, Brad knows that he likes him and might do him one more favor. He can try to get Lauren to celebrate their anniversary a couple of weeks later. Of course she'd feel disappointed and probably angry about losing her deposit, and she would be hurt (understandably) that he'd waited until the last minute to upset their long-standing plans. He can pretend to be injured or sick so that he'll miss that week's swim practices and meets. None of these options really appeal to Brad—they all involve imposing on or disappointing people he cares about.

QUESTIONS

1. Brad's options all seem to involve cheating or manipulating others in order to meet his responsibilities. Which choice or choices seem the least bad ethically? Why?
2. How would you advise Brad to prioritize his commitments? Why?
3. Would different moral principles suggest different orderings of his responsibilities?
4. Do you see a moral issue in Brad's dilemma, or is it just a matter of his fitting a large number of commitments into a limited amount of time?
5. Does the university have a duty to regulate the time conflicts students might experience, for example, by forbidding away meets or games before or during midterms, or is this the individual student's responsibility?
6. What can Brad do to avoid similar crises in the future?

Performance Anxiety   CASE 10.3

Alison enjoys singing in the Heptones, the college's highly selective a capella sextet. The repertoire is enjoyable and challenging, and being in such a small group allows Alison plenty of opportunities to shine. Normally Alison doesn't mind the Heptones' busy concert schedule. She's used to performing regularly around campus and in the nearby town of Red Springs, and occasionally traveling to bigger towns upstate. In fact, Alison is looking forward to their big spring concert; it's always one of the highlights of the Heptones' semester.

Alison and her mother have been arguing a lot on the phone lately. Alison realizes that most of the trouble has been her fault, and she'd like to apologize in some way. After all, her mom has had a hard time ever since the divorce, and she sounds kind of lonely now that Alison is out of the house. Alison decides that it would do a lot to patch up their relationship and cheer up her mother if she made a surprise visit home on her mom's upcoming birthday, and it just so happens that she's noticed a sign on the Ride Board offering a cheap ride to her hometown just in time for her mom's birthday. Unfortunately it means that she will miss the spring concert.

There isn't much time before the weekend, and Alison makes a quick decision. She leaves a message with Professor Bell, the Heptones' director, that she won't be able to make the concert, and then she packs up her back-pack and catches the ride home. She realizes that her last-minute decision might leave the other Heptones in a lurch, but she feels that her relationship with her mother is more important. And at least she's giving them a couple of days' warning so they can perhaps hire someone to replace her, or give her solos to someone else.

It isn't until she returns and goes to the next Heptones rehearsal that Alison realizes how angry the director and other performers are. "Your behavior was completely irresponsible. We couldn't get a replacement for the concert; no one could learn all of the parts we've worked on for months in two days. So now we are auditioning for your permanent replacement," she is frostily informed by Professor Bell. "You are simply too unreliable."

Alison is flabbergasted—she has never even missed a rehearsal before, so this punishment seems rather extreme. She had believed that she was irreplaceable, anyway, especially this late in the year. Besides, she thought they would understand why she had to miss the concert. "You don't get replaced if you miss a concert because you're sick!" she complained. "So why am I getting booted out because I did something nice for my mom?"

QUESTIONS

1. Alison feels a conflict between her obligations to her mother and her music group duties. Where should her first responsibility lie? Why?

2. How could Alison better juggle her obligations?

3. Why might the Heptones feel more lenient toward a member who misses a concert commitment out of sickness than toward Alison's "personal" reason? Should they?

4. Professional performers, whether in the arts or sports, often feel that their first duty is to their performance. "The show must go on," and so do they, despite minor injuries, sickness, or private problems. Is this an unreasonable expectation for amateur college athletes, musicians, or actors? Do different ethical standards apply to student amateurs and professionals? Why or why not?

5. How might the five ethical principles apply to this case?

CASE 10.4 *What Was That Again?*

Wei Jie Hsu is a graduate student in chemistry and one of the section leaders for Chemistry 205. He is friendly, but unfortunately his command of spoken English seems to be minimal, and it is further hindered by a heavy accent. The students in his section often cannot make head or tail of his lab presentations or explanations of the professor's lectures, although his written comments on their lab reports and quizzes are clearer. He tries to answer their questions, but his replies usually leave them more confused than before (if not giggling at a completely incomprehensible sentence).

The students often meet after lab to compare notes and see if they can piece together something that makes sense. However, this takes extra time that many of them begrudge, and their quiz grades are suffering. After several weeks, they deputize two of their number, Mirsad and Lynn, to talk to the professor about either getting rid of Wei Jie or splitting up the members of their section among the five other section instructors.

Mirsad and Lynn are surprised to find that Professor Jarski already knows about Wei Jie's trouble in speaking English, although she doesn't seem to think the problem is as bad as they do. However, Professor Jarski explains, the students can't go into other sections, because they're already full. The chemistry department has no intention of getting rid of Wei Jie as an instructor, because all graduate students are expected to teach as part of their professional training. Furthermore, Wei Jie is a very promising chemist. His written English is fine (as proven by the fact that he passed his English as a Second Language exam in order to enter the University), and his spoken English "will no doubt improve rapidly as he teaches."

"But," protests Lynn, "we're getting graded on what he doesn't teach us, right now! We can't wait until he 'gets better.'"

Professor Jarski replies, "You can certainly come to me with any questions you have. Try to be patient with Wei Jie; it's very difficult to teach in a second language, and he's working hard."

Clearly this is supposed to end the discussion. Lynn and Mirsad, and the other students in their section, are very discouraged. It seems completely impractical to talk to the professor whenever they have "any questions," because they have questions about almost everything Wei Jie says. Furthermore, they don't see why they should feel pity for Wei Jie, when he's the one grading them!

QUESTIONS

1. After meeting with this discouragement, should the students in Wei Jie's section just forget about the class, or should they continue trying to learn the material partly on their own? What else could they do?

2. Might it be their duty to try to help Wei Jie improve his spoken English so that he can teach them better? If not, whose job is it? If so, how could they help?

3. Whose responsibility is it that the students learn the course material?

4. Should the fact that they are being graded change the students' ethical obligations toward Wei Jie? In other words, does the principle of equal respect require that they show Wei Jie as much patience or sympathy as they would a struggling peer who doesn't have power over them? Why or why not?

5. Should they try to warn future students away from Wei Jie, given that he's just beginning several years of required teaching? How?

6. Professor Jarski and the chemistry department seem to feel a greater obligation to (or perhaps interest in) graduate students such as Wei Jie than to undergraduates taking their courses. How might they better balance the needs of both Wei Jie and his undergraduate students?

CASE 10.5 *Special Treatment*

Although both of her parents were born in the United States, Juliet Fuentes's grandparents originally came from Argentina. Her family was quite cultured and well-to-do, and she grew up in a sheltered world of prep schools and country clubs. When Juliet was ready to apply to college, her parents realized that her Hispanic surname could be a valuable asset in the application process, and they encouraged her to apply for any available minority fellowships or special programs for Hispanic students.

"Colleges, especially good ones, really want to increase their student diversity," Juliet's father told her. "With your good grades and Hispanic background, you should have no trouble getting in wherever you want to go." Her father also helped her modify her applications to emphasize her ethnicity and disadvantaged status, "so you're more like what they're looking for."

Juliet was overjoyed when she got into her first choice, an Ivy League school, and received a fellowship reserved for minority students as well. She was a bit worried, however, that the college would find out that she wasn't really disadvantaged and kick her out, or at least revoke the fellowship. Her father reassured her. "Its not really a need-based fellowship. They just want to improve the diversity of their student body. You're exactly what they want: a bright, hardworking, Hispanic girl."

Juliet chuckled at this description of herself, because she didn't usually think of herself as "Hispanic" (and no one else did, either; she knew only a few phrases of Spanish and had dark-blonde hair and blue eyes). Then she realized that perhaps her getting the fellowship might mean that some poorer, really Hispanic (whatever that meant) student wouldn't be able to go to the college.

"Don't worry, honey," her father said with a hug. "Everyone pulls whatever levers they can. Just work hard and have a great time!"

QUESTIONS

1. Does Juliet "deserve" a minority fellowship or special consideration because of her Hispanic background? Why or why not?

2. Does someone like Juliet really add to the diversity of an Ivy League college's student body?

3. Many students try to modify their college applications and essays to fit the image of the person they think the college is seeking. Others mildly pad their resumes, for example, by exaggerating the importance of

an achievement, or including in their list of high school activities a club they attended briefly. Are such modifications unethical lies, or are they simply common sense in the college application competition?

4. Has Juliet's father encouraged her to do something immoral? If so, exactly what was unethical about it? If not, what kinds of modifications or padding would you consider immoral on a resume or application?

5. What's wrong with presenting a (slightly) misleading image of yourself when applying for college, a fellowship, or a job?

6. What do you think of Juliet's father's comment that "everyone pulls whatever levers they can"?

It Isn't Really Stealing   CASE 10.6

In Tom's otherwise shabby student apartment, one piece of furniture stands out: a large, glass-doored, wooden display case, which he has filled with his sizable collection of animal skulls and unusual rock samples. Tom prides himself on being a naturalist, and he has carefully labeled each item in his collection. As many of his friends have told him, the cabinet and its contents look as though they belong in a museum.

Tom is very proud of this elegant piece. He has carefully waxed and polished all of the wooden surfaces of the case, as well as re-glued some of its loose moldings. His friend Grace, who has taken a number of woodworking courses, is impressed with it. "How much do you think it's worth?" Tom asks casually.

"Wow—maybe $800, or $1000? It has that expensive nonreflecting glass, and everything's beautifully dovetailed. The wood looks like really nice cherry, too. It's beautiful! Where'd you get it?"

Tom is used to his visitors' remarking on the handsome case, and he has often told the story of how he acquired it:

"Last summer I worked as a lab assistant for Professor Costello over in the biology department. It wasn't a very exciting job, because I was mainly washing glassware, but I did get access to the entire storage area of the department. Every time I went into that basement, I saw this beautiful old case and two others just like it—covered with dust. They looked as though they hadn't been used since the building opened. It was such a waste, and I finally decided to take one home. So here it is! They've never missed it. And after a little work, it was better than new. Hey, if I slave for Costello again this summer, maybe I can fix up one of the other ones! My collection is still expanding."

QUESTIONS

1. How would you react to Tom's story if you were Grace?

2. Is anyone hurt by this kind of stealing? Tom seems to feel that he has a right to the display case for several reasons: no one seemed to be using it, or even to remember it; he needed it; he has fixed it up; and it

wasn't being appreciated or taken care of the way he appreciates it and takes care of it. Do any of these reasons lend legitimacy to his claims on the case?

3. Is it somehow less hurtful to steal something from a large organization or institution rather than from an individual?

4. How might the principles of the greatest good, character growth, relationships, and community apply to this case?

CASE 10.7 *Fender Bender*

Nguyet was preoccupied as she drove to Meadowland Community College on Thursday afternoon. She was running late for her statistics exam because she had been studying her notes and had forgotten to leave as early as she'd planned. Not only that, but she'd also quarreled with her mother that morning, and she still couldn't get some of her biting remarks out of her mind. "I have to concentrate for the test!" she told herself sternly. "And I have to hurry!"

Just then the light changed to green. Without thinking, Nguyet stepped on the gas. Unfortunately there was a Honda in front of her that was slow to accelerate. Nguyet's heavy old Ford hit the Honda with a jolt. Because she'd been going only about ten miles an hour, the damage was slight—her Ford's higher bumper missed the Honda's bumper and shattered its rear brake lights. There was no damage to Nguyet's car.

An elderly man slowly got out of the Honda, rubbing his neck. Her heart pounding, Nguyet jumped out of the car. "Are you OK?" she asked.

"I think so," the man replied. He seemed a bit dazed, but maybe he was always like that.

"I'm really sorry," Nguyet explained. "I'm late for a test at the college, and I guess I jumped the gun."

"Well, it doesn't look too bad. We'll just see what the police say when they turn up," the man said.

"Oh please!" Nguyet begged. "I'll miss my exam! Let me give you my phone number. I'll pay for the damage, but I can't wait for the police to arrive!" Then she hurriedly wrote down her name and phone number, jumped back in her car, and rushed the rest of the way to school.

The whole accident set Nguyet back only about five minutes, and she got to class just as the professor was handing out the exam. She calmed herself as well as she could and concentrated. Afterward, Nguyet reflected that it was a good thing she hadn't waited around for the police for another reason—now her insurance wouldn't go up. She'd call that old man as soon as she got home to make sure he was all right. Then, with a shock, she realized that she hadn't gotten his name or number. If he lost hers (and he did seem kind of foggy), how would she pay for the damage she'd caused? And what if he were acting dazed because he'd hurt his head? She'd never know or be able to make amends!

3. Are Diane's and Bonita's misdeeds (reading another's mail, making a profit from a roommate) equally bad ethically?

4. If Bonita refuses to split the rent more equitably, Diane has no legal way to force her to do so. What should Diane do then?

5. Should landlords, colleges, or other authorities have the power to insist that roommates split the cost of rent equally?

6. What effect do you think Bonita's arguments might have on the growth of her character?

7. Are other ethical principles involved in this case?

Suicidal? CASE 10.10

Several students are talking about whether Jeff, an apparently suicidal student, is "really serious." He certainly seems rather depressed; he doesn't seem to have any close friends, and he talks a lot about dying. However, it's hard to know what he really feels. He has a dark and sarcastic sense of humor, and all his talk about death may just be posing for effect.

"I think he's just trying to get attention, being dramatic," says Ping.

"The guy's kind of a creep," agrees Leslie. "Who cares about him?"

Fernando, who's taken some psychology courses and has read that talk of suicide should always be taken seriously, feels that he should get involved to stop Jeff from hurting himself. So Fernando decides to sound Jeff out about whether he's really suicidal. It isn't too hard to get Jeff talking about how everything is terrible and life's not worth living.

"Do you ever, you know think about ending it all?" Fernando asks him.

Jeff gives him a funny look. "All the time, man."

"I mean, have you ever tried?"

"Yeah; see these scars on my wrists? That was from one time in high school. But that's not it for me. I haven't figured out the best way yet. You got any suggestions?" Jeff adds with a half smile.

"Maybe you should go to counseling," Fernando responds nervously.

"Therapists suck. My parents made me go to some jerk after I tried to kill myself in high school. She was a real bozo. So nooo thanks."

Fernando isn't sure what to say. "Maybe you could give it another try. The people at the Health Center are supposed to be good."

"What, have you tried to talk to them about suicide? Therapists don't know crap. What's it to you, anyway?"

Jeff seems to resent Fernando's awkward interference, so Fernando backs off, defeated.

QUESTIONS

1. Fernando made an effort to advise Jeff, and Jeff seemed to resent his well-meaning efforts. Should Fernando just leave him alone? Is there something else he could or should do to help Jeff?

2. The two students hardly know each other. Do we have a duty to help people we don't really know, or people who say they don't want our help? Or are people who interfere in such situations just busybodies?

3. Is Fernando's behavior morally superior to Ping's and Leslie's, or is it just that some people are more outgoing and willing to get involved than others?

4. What ethical principles might inform Fernando's concern for Jeff and help him make a decision about what to do?

5. Because Jeff talks about suicide all the time, do you think he's actually less likely to try to kill himself than he would be if he didn't discuss it?

6. What if he does try—doesn't he have a right to die if he wants to? Why should others interfere?

CASE 10.11 *With Charity Toward All*

The Green College Student Service Organization recently conducted two different fund-raising campaigns. One was to raise money for a local homeless shelter, and the other was to contribute to the national campaign of Help the Children, a charity benefitting sick children. GCSSO's Help the Children drive was much more successful than the one for the homeless shelter, perhaps because the Help the Children organization had advertised in national magazines and television to support local fund-raising efforts during their drive. No group except the GCSSO had advertised the homeless shelter campaign.

Now the GCSSO officers are meeting to decide what to do with the money raised. The problem is that the director of the local homeless shelter recently talked to several GCSSO members, thanking them for their efforts but commenting that with recent cuts in state aid, they might well have to close. Even though the shelter operates on a shoestring, they won't be able to stay open unless they can raise almost double the amount they had originally targeted in their fund-raising drive. "So, should we divert money people donated for Help the Children to the shelter?" GCSSO Chair Kelly asks her fellow officers. A vigorous debate follows.

QUESTIONS

1. Should the final decision be made by the GCSSO officers, or by the entire membership?

2. Should they try to get opinions from the donors, perhaps through a local newspaper ad or letter to the editor? Why or why not?

3. The managers of the homeless shelter will never know that much of the donated money was originally intended for another cause if GCSSO doesn't tell them. Likewise GCSSO can easily doctor their records to show the Help the Children organization that a much

smaller amount was donated to them than was actually the case. Should these facts influence the group's decision?

4. Would such acts be unethical? Is one worse than the other?

5. Is giving extra money to the homeless shelter, which may have to close anyway, just throwing good money after bad?

6. Should the fact that Help the Children has a far bigger budget than the homeless shelter does affect the GCSSO's thinking? If so, how?

7. Which ethical principles could be involved in this case? How might the GCSSO use them to reach a decision?

Contemporary Social Problems: Who Cares?   CASE 10.12

Springview College requires that students take a one-credit interdisciplinary course, "Contemporary Social Problems," during their freshman year. The intent is to raise the mostly affluent students' consciousness about the harsh realities of hunger, poverty, and disease facing many in America and in the rest of the world, and to use these issues to introduce students to critical thinking in the social sciences and humanities. Among other topics, the course includes lectures on poverty, AIDS, and hunger, illustrated by slides of starving people, AIDS sufferers, and the desperate poor in American inner cities and in the Third World.

Hamsa Bhasin, who teaches a section of the course, is disappointed by the students' reactions to it. She's noticed that several students sleep through the lectures. The rest, while polite, seem unenthusiastic. Indeed, a number of students walked out partway through the AIDS lecture, when some rather horrific slides of lesions on AIDS sufferers were shown. There is little participation in the "dialogues" at the end of each class. The few students who do ask questions and appear engaged during discussions are treated as irritants by the others, who roll their eyes and make every sign of wanting to leave early.

Professor Bhasin would be more than disappointed to overhear the following postclass conversation. Sarah, Amy, and Liam are discussing the class in the cafeteria. "What a total waste of time it is; it's so boring," says Sarah. "Who cares about that stuff? I've slept through most of the classes, except for the time they had those gross-out AIDS pictures. We should get people to boycott the classes if they have them again next year."

Amy notes, "It's so irritating how a few people go on and on asking dumb questions at the end of class. We could be out of there a lot sooner if they would just shut up. They're so obviously trying to suck up that it's disgusting."

Liam mentions that his friends laugh about the course, calling it "sentimental liberal crap." "The worst part is," he adds, "we could have more time for other courses if we didn't have to waste time on that stuff."

"Or just spend some time relaxing!" says Amy. "It's scheduled during my favorite soap, and I hate having so many stupid requirements. I hardly have any free time."

QUESTIONS

1. Why would the college administration think this mandatory course is a good idea? Do you agree? Why or why not?

2. What does the students' apparent rejection of the course say about their values?

3. How can students become aware of the suffering of others? Should they?

4. Should such a course be mandatory for all Springview College freshmen, regardless of their interests or backgrounds? Is awareness of the plight of the poor and other social problems something colleges should try to instill in their students?

5. Might there be other more effective ways of getting students to empathize with the less fortunate?

6. Do institutions such as colleges, as well as individuals, have a responsibility to alleviate suffering in the world? If so, how might they best do this?

7. Is there something unethical about embracing ignorance about social problems and deciding not to get involved, or is this just a matter of personal preference? Why might these students seem so apathetic?

8. Which moral principles might apply here, and how?

CASE 10.13 *Freedom of Religion?*

The Coldwater College community is almost notoriously liberal, yet it seems quite intolerant toward the few obviously Muslim students on campus. There are seven Muslim foreign exchange students, two of whom are women, who stand out in their head scarves and long, baggy garments.

Many American students, particularly those who consider themselves feminists, shun the Muslim men as "sexist and intolerant" because of their supposed attitude toward women. They are no friendlier toward the Muslim women, because the Americans cannot understand "why they would put up with the way they're treated in Muslim society. Just look at the way they have to dress, even here!"

Perhaps unspoken prejudices about the Middle East's supposed fanaticism and propensity for terrorism also play a role in the Americans' hostility toward the Muslim students. Or perhaps they are simply uncomfortable with the unfamiliar.

At any rate, the American students' intolerance seems to come to a head when the college offers an assistant professorship in economics to an Arab American man who is known to be a practicing Muslim. A number of students protest his hiring even before he has taught a course, because of his supposed belief in the inferiority of women. As one of the protesters put it, "How can you expect someone whose religion says women are inferior to be fair to the women in his class?"

QUESTIONS

1. The protesting students' knowledge of the Muslim religion seems to be based on hearsay and prejudice. Do they have a moral duty to learn more about Islam before they reject it or its practitioners?

2. Do people with one world view (such as Western feminists) have a right to criticize people holding different world views (such as Muslims)?

3. If individuals find the behavior of a religious group offensive, are they ethically entitled to shun them or more actively express their distaste?

4. Are a professor's religious views any business of his students?

5. Should colleges be particularly open to religious diversity, or should they attempt to keep all religious debate off campus? Why?

6. What might Coldwater College do to smooth relations between the non-Muslim student majority and the Muslim students?

For more information about the role of women in Islam as seen by a relatively sympathetic Western feminist, see Geraldine Brooks, *Nine Parts of Desire: The Hidden World of Islamic Women* (New York: Anchor Books/Doubleday, 1995).

Yes, Master CASE 10.14

Professor Goldbaum, an instructor in Southeast University's freshman writing program, is disturbed and exasperated by what she considers her students' unhealthy deference to authority and unwillingness to engage in independent moral thinking. She devises a trick writing assignment to test their obedience to authority. First she sends Ingrid, a warm and friendly girl who seems to be the kindest student in the class, out of the room. Then she tells the rest of the class to write the nastiest character assassination of Ingrid that they can. "I want it to be really mean—critique her looks, her behavior, her morals, everything. The worse it is, the better your grades will be. When you're finished, the two best essays, that is, the two most crushing ones, will be read out loud to Ingrid. Any questions?"

Professor Goldbaum is shocked when the students have no questions about obeying this assignment and are ready to get to work. She asks them why they would be willing to do this.

Eddie says, "I want to get a good grade, and I don't have to take this class again."

Satta adds, "I don't know Ingrid, and I'll probably never see her again. So it doesn't matter what I write."

Most of the class doesn't volunteer any reasons for their willingness to do the assignment; they seem apathetic. Then the professor lambasts the class, saying, "This wasn't a real assignment, but a test of your moral fiber! I'm shocked that none of you said, 'It would make this girl feel too humiliated; my grade isn't worth that much, so go jump in a lake.' You shouldn't just do whatever you're told to by an authority figure—what if I told you to do something really evil, or stupid? You have to think for yourselves!"

The students look sullen and confused under her outburst. Bewildered, Jessica says, "But you're the teacher. If you think this is a bad idea, why did you assign it?"

Eddie asks angrily, "What do you want from us? We were just going to do what you told us. Since when is it a crime to do what the professor tells you to do?"

The professor wants to throw up her hands in despair. The class has proved her point all too well.

QUESTIONS

1. How would you respond to Professor Goldbaum's assignment?

2. Is it unethical of her to give out trick assignments in order to morally test her students? Can trick assignments be justified for some other purpose, such as to show students the impossibility of performing a seemingly simple task, or the complexity of an apparently straightforward concept?

3. Do students have a duty to consider the moral implications of their assignments, lectures, and readings, and to resist anything they find ethically suspect?

4. Whose responsibility is it to ensure that the moral dimension of a subject is not overlooked?

5. Should students be ready to question their professors' authority or integrity? Is this something you can see yourself doing?

CASE 10.15   *What's Wrong with That Girl?*

Vanessa, Mumbi, and Lisa are all transfer students, and all were assigned to the same student apartment at the beginning of their junior year. Vanessa and Mumbi have become good friends, although they both find Lisa harder to like. However, they're friendly to her because she seems otherwise friendless.

Lisa often seems strangely secretive and even dishonest about petty things, such as the number of pairs of shoes she owns (Vanessa and Mumbi are amazed that they rarely see her wear the same pair) or the grade she got on a midterm, although as Vanessa said, "It's not like I really care!" Her lies seem to be connected to her excessive concern with status: popular So-and-

So has asked her out, or her fabulously wealthy parents are buying her a sports cars. Mumbi and Vanessa have gradually realized that Lisa can be quite manipulative, telling Vanessa something bad about Mumbi, and then turning around and pretending to Mumbi that she likes her better than she likes Vanessa.

Lisa's strangest behavior involves food. Many a time Mumbi or Vanessa has left part of a carton of ice cream or some take-out Chinese food in the refrigerator, only to find it disappear in such a way that only Lisa could have taken it. She always denies stealing the food, even though Vanessa has told her, "I don't mind so much if you eat something of mine once in a while—but tell me, so I know not to count on it being there!" Her roommates have also noticed that Lisa will pig out on several gallons of ice cream and a couple of bags of cookies during the middle of the night (the telltale evidence being in the trash can the next morning), even though she's always talking about her weight and trying various diets (she doesn't look fat to them). Perhaps most troubling of all is the disgusting vomit smell that lingers after Lisa has been in the bathroom, although she never admits to being sick.

Mumbi and Vanessa describe their weird roommate to a friend, who promptly says, "That girl's got bulimia! I know because my sister was bulimic for a while, and she was just the same—stealing food, lying, trying to manipulate everyone, making herself puke to keep thin. It's an eating disorder, and it can be pretty serious, even life threatening for her, not to mention a pain for anyone living with her."

Vanessa and Mumbi confront Lisa with this diagnosis. Amazingly, Lisa confesses to years of therapy throughout high school for bulimia, but she asserts, "It's under control now; my last therapist cured me."

QUESTIONS

1. What should Vanessa and Mumbi do about Lisa's antisocial behavior? Do Vanessa and Mumbi have a duty to try to get Lisa counseling or other help with her problem, even though they don't particularly like her? Is her private eating problem really any of their business?

2. How might they use the various ethical principles in deciding what to do?

A Second Chance? CASE 10.16

It was not surprising that out of eighteen thousand applicants, Gina Grant was one of the two thousand students admitted to Harvard for the class of 1995. Gina was a bright, popular, talented, and pretty student who had been the first female student-body president of her middle school, served as co-captain of her high school tennis team, tutored underprivileged children, and graduated near the top of her class at a well-regarded high school.

Before she could attend Harvard, on April 3, 1995, the college's admissions committee held a rare emergency meeting and voted to revoke Gina Grant's acceptance. The reason was that someone had anonymously tipped them off that Gina was hiding a terrible secret—she had brutally murdered her abusive mother when she was fourteen years old. Because she was a minor at the time, Gina had served only a brief prison sentence, and her court records had been sealed.

She expected to be able to start over again, and she had tried hard to pick up the pieces of her life. Being accepted at Harvard was the high point of her amazing turnaround. However, now that her secret was out, Harvard declined to give her a second chance on the grounds that she had lied about her past. (It seemed likely that Harvard would never have admitted her if she had *not* hidden her past.)

QUESTIONS

1. We have said about the principle of character growth that you are to a large extent what your choices have made you; your ethical decisions make you into the kind of person who will continue to decide in similar ways. (See Chapters 1 and 2.) Does this view preclude the possibility of redemption and forgiveness? Specifically, has Gina's matricide made her unfit to be given a second chance, no matter how "reformed" she might appear?

2. Should we (personally, and as a society) be willing to forgive any deed, no matter how heinous, so long as the perpetrator sincerely regrets it and has "reformed"? If not, where would you draw the line, and why?

3. Should Gina's actions as a juvenile have any effect on her college career? Why or why not?

4. If it turned out that Gina had good reasons for killing her mother, should Harvard (or any other institution or person) trust her not to kill again?

5. How does forgiveness differ from trust?

6. Gina is not the only Harvard applicant to have been convicted of murder, although other murderers have been admitted to the school without incident. General Hector Gramajo, a Guatemalan officer who supervised the extermination of 100,000 Maya Indians in the 1980s, was later admitted as a Mason fellow at Harvard's Kennedy School of Government. Carlos Salinas de Gortari, the former president of Mexico who murdered a family servant as a youth, received his master's and doctorate degrees from the Kennedy School. Is it inconsistent of Harvard to forgive and forget some murders and not others in its applicants' pasts? Is there some ethical distinction between these killings that makes the two men more deserving of a second chance than Gina Grant?

7. Which ethical principles might apply to this case, and how?

For more information, see Jane Mayer, "The Justice File: Rejecting Gina," in *The New Yorker*, 5 June 1995, vol. LXXI, no. 15, pp. 43–51; Joe Mathews, "Should Harvard Accept a Student Who Killed?" in *The Los Angeles Times*, 16 April 1995, sec. M, p. 3, col. 3; Ellen Goodman, "A Promising Student, An Unclean Slate," in *The Boston Globe*, 16 April 1995, sec. A, p. 7, col. 2; Cynthia Tucker, "Saving All the Ones Who Can Be Saved," in *The Atlanta Journal and Atlanta Constitution*, 16 April 1995, sec. B, p. 7, col. 2; Alice Dembner, "Judge, Others Back Student's Right to Conceal Past," in *The Boston Globe*, 8 April 1995, p. 1, col. 3; and Alexander Cockburn, "Harvard and Murder: The Case of Carlos Salinas," in *The Nation*, 29 May 1995, vol. 260, no. 21, pp. 747–748.

The Ethics Textbook That Wasn't PC Enough (Or Was It?)   CASE 10.16

One of the early reviewers of this manuscript faulted it for being "not politically correct enough." The reviewer didn't go on to explain, but perhaps he or she meant something like the following:

"Listen, Strike and Moss, I'm responsible for the programs offered during Freshman Orientation at our college. We try to have our Freshman Orientation experience encourage tolerance and acceptance of diversity on campus. That's why we conduct anti-racism seminars and try to discourage sexism and homophobia. I thought your *Ethics and College Student Life* textbook would help, but after reading it, I doubt it.

"It's not that I disagree with your views; in fact, I usually do agree with them. The problem is that you don't make their superiority clear enough. Instead, you put your progressive views on the table for debate, right alongside reactionary and even hateful opinions. You give voice, and seemingly equal credence, to them all! When you encourage such 'open debate,' you are in fact legitimizing views that are mere smoke-screens for racial bigotry, sexism, and homophobia.

"Just look at this chapter on 'Tolerance, Diversity, and Hate Speech.' You don't tell us how to discourage hate speech; rather you treat it as an issue of free speech, to which everyone's entitled. And you don't tell us how to eliminate homophobia; instead you seem more concerned about the rights of people from narrow and intolerant religions."

After sitting up a little straighter in our chairs, we'd respond:

"Well, we do try to take a stand in this book, at least wherever we're confident about the rightness of our position. And we don't think we show sympathy toward any views that are irresponsible. In the tolerance chapter, for example, we clearly reject racism, and we don't 'give voice' to racist views. But there are many issues and cases about which reasonable people disagree. Often such cases flow from conflicts between several values that we all hold in common, but which can lead to varying conclusions when they're applied to a situation. For instance, no one approves of hate speech; but it is hard to define it precisely, and banning it can erode support for free speech. So what we've put on the table are those issues where we think reasonable people can disagree."

But perhaps this would not satisfy our reviewer. "All I can say is, this book seems to undermine everything I'm trying to accomplish in my job. What we need, especially in the kinds of Orientation seminars I organize, is some *progressive intolerance* toward views that ultimately undermine diversity and tolerance on campus. Some way to shut the haters out. We certainly don't need to give them more press than they already get, and your book does that. You don't make it clear enough which side you're on."

The reviewer might have a point there. We have to admit that we're not always enthusiastic about giving expression to views we disagree with. Probably our considered judgment on the issues raised in this book is almost as PC as our reviewer's. And it may well be true that if we made our opinions clearer, this book would better assist the work of people who want to establish diverse, tolerant campuses. We too want diverse, tolerant campuses. But we value the free marketplace of ideas even more. And that's why we've decided to try to present all sides of the controversial issues in this book, and leave judgments about them up to you.

QUESTIONS

Our defense of this book is based on the conviction that it's more important for us to promote discussion of controversial matters than it is for us to promote our own views, even though we do believe that our views form the best basis for a progressive, tolerant, and diverse campus. Does this make sense? Why might we think this? Do you agree? And do you think this is what we've actually done?